THE COMMUNIST MASK

THE COMMUNIST MASK

S.C. BHATT

GYAN PUBLISHING HOUSE
NEW DELHI-110002

THE COMMUNIST MASK

ISBN : 81-212-0735-5

Published in 2001 in India by
Gyan Publishing House
5, Ansari Road, New Delhi—110002

Phones : 3261060, 3282060, Fax : 3285914
E-Mail : gyanbook@del2.vsnl.net.in
Visit Our Web Site At http:\\www.gyanbooks.com

Leser type setting at : Apex Computer
Printed at : Mehra Offset Printers

Contents

PREFACE

The Communists were quite influential in Indian Politics once upon a time but have been losing ground gradually. They are to blame for this downward trend but they make enough noise about their strength to catch the attention of many, particularly of the media. Although the media are generally discerning and are able to see through the game sometimes, there are sections which are taken in by the deceptive game played by them.

The Communists commit grave errors and miscalculations which ultimately cost them dear an d the nation even dearer. They have abandoned all ideology and have pursued for the past few years a single point programme–to install in power a Congress government at the Centre. They, at the same time claim that they are really for the Third Front (of non-Congress non-BJP parties), much like the adherents of a particular religion draw our attention to the fine tenets of the religion ignoring how the followers today interpret them to mean aggression towards others. Simultaneously, the Communists also lay claim to opposition of the Congress's economic policies. If they are really successful in this task of installing a Congress government in power, not considered likely, would they then work to oust the Congress also from power? Then the cycle will go on merrily.

The book seeks to probe the erroneous policies of the Comrades–the CPIM, the dominant Communist party, meekly followed by the CPI, and 'the bigger than life projection of theirs in the media (or some sections) and on the political scene. The 1999 Lok Sabha elections, forced by their favoured party and themselves on the largely weary electorate, should unmask them somewhat and see their dream of domination vanish.

The book encompasses all the doings of the Communists, in the preceding few years in particular. This is not an attempt to portray the contemporary scene but inevitably some aspects had to be noticed. The faulty evaluation of the Comrades has been pinpointed while their targets and objectives have been brought out. This needed saying because, while the social justice goal cannot be overemphasised and justice to all Indians must be attained at all costs, those who masquarade as messiahs have to be exposed. It is for the first time that such a task has been sought to be accomplished.

My thanks are due to the Librarian of the Research and Reference division in Shastri Bhavan, which I have access to as an accredited correspondent, for making available a number of books relevant to my requirements. I am also grateful to the publishers for trying to locate for me a source book. I needed urgently and making available a more than useful substitute. It goes without saying that I alone am responsible for the conclusions drawn.

Delhi

S.C. Bhatt

1
ALL-INDIA DREAM

The Communists have always dreamt of capturing power in India. They, however, stood apart from the mainstream of Indian polity whether it was before independence or after it. During the years when India was fighting for her freedom from foreign (British) rule and the country was waging a life and death struggle under the aegis of the Indian National Congress (INC), led by Mahatma Gandhi, the Communists regarded the Mahatma as reactionary, feudal and, at the best of times, petit bourgeios. They were then under the sway of the Soviet Communists, who exercised their control through the Comintern, the Communist International, and the British Communist party. The latter was led by men like Rajani Palme Dutt, Harry Pollitt,Philip Spratt and Ben Bradley.

It was under the direction of the Communist International and the Britons that the Indian Communists applied the United Front approach from below and tried to penetrate the INC. This gave them legitimacy and legality. However, during the Second World War they suddenly changed front and described the war as "People's War" while, until the day before, they were calling it an "Imperialist War". Until then the British rulers of India did not allow them to function freely and effectively. The British officials cooked up one conspiracy after another against prominent Communists of which the Meerut Conspiracy Case was a notable example. But came the Second World War and the somersault of the Comrades and there was a happy marriage between the imperalists of yesterday and the frequently underground Indian Communists on the other, between the foreign rulers and people who claimed to be at the extreme end of the political spectrum.

When freedom was a reality, the Communists did not accept the fact of independence. They perceived it as phoney. Today, both the Communist parties, the main ones, the Communist Party of India Marxist (CPIM), which is a bigger formation and often leads the older party, from whose womb it sprang in 1964, by the nose, Communist Party of India (CPI), are great champions of parliamentary democracy. But for four years after freedom they considered Jawaharlal Nehru, free India's first Prime Minister, as the running dog of imperialism under the orders of the Soviet masters. It was only in the Calcutta Congress of the united CPI, held in October 1951, that it opted for participation in the first democratic elections in early 1952. The CPI adopted a statement of policy and decided to fight the elections as a means of mobilising the broad strata of people.[1]

Indian political scene was, in fact, ripe for the parliamentary onslaught of the Communists. On the one hand was the INC which had the halo of the freedom struggle and Gandhiji's martyrdom, in January 1948, and Nehru had emerged as the sole and unchallenged leader of the party after Sardar Patel's death in December 1950. During the first three years of independence Patel had unified the divided country as he merged, as free India's first Deputy Prime Minister, over 550 states ruled by the Indian princes, called the Maharajas or Nawabs, with the rest of India.

For years of India's slavery under the British, the INC, the Congress as it was popularly called, had been forged into a fighting machine, an all-India party with branches in the remotest villages. The task was accomplished by no less a person than Mahatma Gandhi. Although in the last phase of his journey on this earth he wanted the Congress dissolved and constituted into a Lok Sevak Sangh, which alas, did not happen, the organisation which Nehru had inherited from the Father of the Nation was a truly all-India party which occupied the middle ground and much of the ground to the left of the Centre as well as to the right.

On the other hand, there were several but somewhat weak political parties. Above all, the Socialists, known earlier as the CSP, Congress Socialist Party, were led by the charismatic leader, Jayaprakash Narayan, popularly known as JP. The Socialists had left the Congress soon after independence and many of them were fired by idealism, great love of the country and a strong desire to reconstruct the ancient nation as a truly democratic nation where the citizens could breathe the air of feeedom from fear and hunger and enjoy equality. The Communists, who had earlier in the days of the freedom struggle penetrated the CSP and through it the Indian National Congress, were now an organised force and were running for assemblies in several states as well as for Parliament itself. The elections to both were held simultaneously until 1967 when the Congress party lost its majority in several states and the election schedule was completely upset. The Bharatiya Jana Sangh, or Jana Sangh, JS, was then a fledgling party and was often referred to as a rightist party but posed a potential challenge to the Congress.

Madhu Limaye, who was an acute political analyst, referred to the JS (which later become the Bharatiya Janata Party, BJP) as the most stable among the post-independence political parties in India.[2] It is also least likely to be amenable to a split and has an admirable capacity to hold together. The Socialists have often split, remerged, emerged as formidable new parties and have thus undergone many transformations. The Congress itself has undergone several changes and the party split often as a dominant group left the main body or sometimes, under Mrs Indira Gandhi, the party was hijacked. The Sonia Gandhi-led party claims to be 114 year old, linking itself with the freedom fighter party under the name of the Indian National Congress and has itself given birth to the Tamil Maanila Congress (TMC) in Tamil Nadu, the Trinamul Congress of Mamta Banerjee in West Bengal, Nationalist Congress Party (NCP) of Sharad Pawar, formed in 1999, to name some of the more prominent.

The Communists, despite their close-knit nature and their reliance on the doctrine of "democratic centralism", has a splittist mentality. The first major[3] split came in 1964 when the CPIM was formed. It was carved out of the old CPI but soon grew to be the main party of the Reds and the CPI often trailed behind it. Then in 1969 the CPIM itself split when it gave birth to the Communist Party of India (Marxist-Leninist) [CPI (ML)]. This was the party of the Naxalites, or Maoists, who openly flaunted their faith in violence and practised it unabashedly, but later the party became a tame formation while the Maoists who remained outside it operate in the jungles of Bihar and Telengana, in Andhra Pradesh, and elsewhere. There are other breakaway groups of the centrist Parties, like the Lok Dal, which have a limited vision and goal, which have seen the emergence of several parties like the Bharatiya Kranti Dal (BKD), Bharatiya Lok Dal (BLD) the Indian National Lok Dal (INLD) of Haryana and so on.

In fact, there has been a great deal of party formation in the country since independence and amid all the turbulence the JS or its later incarnation, the BJP, has been left untouched more or less. When the JS was formed, soon after independence, under the late Dr Shyama Prasad Mookerjee, it spiritually assumed the mantle of the Hindu Mahasabha which was still alive but not kicking. The JS was, of course, a different party. But all through the freedom movement, the Hindu Mahasabha had failed to make any impact although it had highminded leaders like Madan Mohan Malaviya, founder of Benaras Hindu University (BHU) and Lala Lajpat Rai, both of whom also participated in the Congress movement (even Mohammad Ali Jinnah was, for a time, in the Congress although he championed as a Muslim Leaguer the partition of the country) and men like Veer Savarkar (Veer, meaning brave). Although the Muslims, by and large, opted for the separatist Muslim League, which finally achieved the partition of the country, the Hindus to whom the Hindu Mahasabha appealed generally threw in their lot with the Congress.

The BJP could not be unaffected by the splittist mood. Of course, the JS had voluntarily merged with JP's Janata Party in 1977 and the success of the party in the post-emergency elections in 1977 led to the first non-Congress government at the Centre, under Morarji Desai. The Janata Party of JP, to be distinguished from the largely paper party of Subramanian Swamy, was formed by the merger of the Congress-O, of people like Morarji who had stood apart when Mrs Gandhi first split the party in 1969, the Socialists, the JS and BLD or Charan Singh.[4] It was under the BLD symbol that the party, hastily formed after the relase of many of its leaders from Mrs Indira Gandhi's prison, had fought the 1977 elections. Prominent leaders of the JS, like Atal Bihari Vajpayee and Lal Krishna Advani, were ministers of the Desai government, from March 1977 to July 1979.

After the dismal performance of the party in the 1979 poll (often referred to as the 1980 elections), the JS members came out of the Janata Party and formed the BJP. Before that JP had died and the spirit which had brought the diverse elements together had evaportated. The real split of the BJP came in 1996 when Shankersinh Vaghela, who was an important leader of the BJP in Gujarat but was for some reason not given his due, split the party and came out of it to form the Rashtriya Janata Party which ruled the state for some time, thanks to the Communist dominated United Front government at the Centre, which encouraged the split and its leader Vaghela and outside support of the Congress. The RPI fared poorly in the 1998 elections in Gujarat and subsequently merged itself with the Congress just before the 1999 poll.

So, it cannot be said that the BJP is immune to the splittist mentality and interested media people look for potential Vaghelas at the slightest indication of dissent in one or the other state.

There has been a constant influx of MLAs MPs and just political personalities from one party to another since independence. This has happened more often as a matter of individual convenience or gain and only in a few cases for ideological reasons. Rajiv Gandhi was blessed with the largest ever Congress majority of 415 members in 1984, following his appeal for closing the ranks behind him after his mother's assassination. He promptly took steps to prevent the defection of his MPs by inacting an anti-defection law in 1985 but it had only partial success because one-third members could always form a separate party and avoid the consequences of defection.

The somewhat classic case of party hopping is that of Subramaniam Swamy. He began his political career in the Jana Sangh which had merged with JP's Janata Party. When the people had forgotten Indira Gandhi's authoritarianism and she bounced back into power he joined the Lok Dal of Charan Singh after the Janata Party broke up. After some more somersaults he revived the largely paper Janatạ Party and started working his way up from Tamil Nadu which is his home state. For a time he actively opposed Miss J. Jayalalitha and even filed corruption cases against her in courts but then cosied upto her on the eve of the 1998 election. This brought him to the Lok Sabha, as a member of the AIADMK block. When the BJP leadership, mainly Prime Minister, Atal Bihari Vajpayee, refused to give him any portfolio in his cabinet, much less the Finance portfolio on which he had set his heart and for which Jayalalitha had backed him to the hilt, he turned against Vajpayee and tried to topple him. His later convolutions have been dealt with in the following chapters, including Jayalalitha's dropping of him like a hot potato, in the list of party nominees for the 1999 poll.

The Jana Sangh was formed in the aftermath of the partition of the country and its leaders and cadres had sprung from the womb of the Rashtriya Swayamsevak Sangh (RSS) a volunteer froce which was founded or in the pre-independence era to protect Hindụ interests but with the goal of the freedom of the country in mind. But with Atal Bihari Vajpayee emerging as the leader of the BJP, both in Parliament and outside, not only a softer face was acquired by the party but Vajpayee assumed effective control of the party and its relations with the RSS. As leader and Prime Minister he got the BJP agenda changed and had it adopt the common agenda of the constituents of the BJP - led alliance. That this has not led to a parting of ways between him and the RSS would redound to Vajpayee's credit and soften the party image.

The Communist Party of India was banned by the British rulers in 1934 and the ban was not lifted until the day in 1941-42 when the Comrades suddenly had a turnaround and enthusiastically supported the British war effort. In August 1942 the people of India launched the Quit India struggle and Gandhiji and other leaders of the national movement were imprisoned and taken to undisclosed destination. This was after the failure of the Cripps negotiations with the leaders of the Congress and with Jinnah. The Communists then played a far from noble part and, as we shall see, gave every help to the British rulers during those crucial days. Today's Communists would like to forget all that and would not like others to recall it but facts of history cannot be changed.

The Communists swam against the current, not because they liked to do it, but by their nature and ideology they preferred to stand apart from the mainstream. They had infiltrated the Congress, through the Socialists, and had at one time as many as 20[5] men on the All-India Congress Committee (AICC) at a time when that body in the pre-independence days did not have more than 150 members. Even so the leading Communists were not in the AICC and they considered their association with the highest decision–making body of the Congress as secondary.

A few years before independence the Communists had chosen the path of violence which they had not abandoned as a creed. They had formed agrarian groups in the Telengana area (now part of Andhra Pradesh, then still part of Nizam's Hyderabad state). The growth and subsequent decline of the violent agrarian move has been dealt with in a later chapter but here it would suffice to say the adoption of the path of parliamentary democracy in October 1951 was preceded by large-scale adventurism on the part of the Indian Comrades. B.T. Ranadive who was the General Secretary[6] of the party then was an adventurist leader par excellence and dubbed so by many fellow Communists themselves. He expected that the urban workers, the railwaymen and others, would revolt in a big way and thus there would be a Communist revolution in India. But JP, who was the leader of the All-India Railwaymen's Federation, reached an agreement with the Railway Board on their behalf and the Ranadive-envisaged rail strike did not materialise.

In Telengana, where landowners were oppressing the tenants and which was thus helping the agrarian rebellion, the Communists did another anti-national job. They sided with the Nizam's Razakars, who fought in the name of Islam, when the Indian army moved in for the Police Action in 1948. They established thereby that they were not concerned with the larger Indian cause when they engaged in their so-called ideological pursuits. The attitude of the CPIM when the nation was engaged in a life and death struggle with Pakistan over Kargil in May-June-July 1999 is thus properly explained. One of the important CPIM leaders even said the victory was no victory because India had not captured foreign territory. In any case the Razakars of the Nizam were defeated by the Indian army in no time[7]. This proves once more that the Indian Communists have their own agenda to pursue.

The CPI had decided that the party would seek laurels via the parliamentary route. Their dream of a revolution was far from achieved and would certainly never be. But what should be galling to them is that even by the parliamentary method they are far from realising their goal of Comunist domination. They have failed to become an all-India party and one of thier complaints against the BJP, which they oppose tooth and nail, arises from pure and simple jealousy. The BJP has for several years been moving towards its goal of becoming an all-India party and has by its political moves succeeded in replacing the Congress as a national party. The Reds have been confined to just three states, West Bengal, Kerala and Tripura, and only in West Bengal they have really established a strong base from which it would be difficult to dilodge them.

The Congress party began with a bang and not only ruled at the Centre but all the states until 1967. It had virtually no competition worth the name in the first three elections—1952, 1957 and 1962, although it never secured, then or later, 50 or more per cent of the popular vote. This was in spite of the fact that under Nehru the Congress had virtually no opposition. He once called the opposition in Parliament as a "motley" crowd to which some of the opposition members took strong exception but to no avail. It was after the defeat suffered by India at China's hands late in 1962, for which he was himself, to a great extent, responsible that the people lost their faith in the Congress. The defeat shattered Nehru and his death in 1964 put paid to the Congress hopes of continued electoral victories. The country recovered from the Chinese attack later but neither Nehru was destined to see it nor his party regained its lost glory.

In the next five yearly election to the Lok Sabha the Congress was returned to power but with a much reduced majority and what is more it had to beat a hasty retreat in major states like Uttar Pradesh and Madhya Pradesh. In 1952, the party had won 364 seats in a House of a little over 500. The tally of the party went up to 371 but came down slightly to 361 in 1962 which was, of course, more than two-third[8]. In the first Lok Sabha, the Socialists had high hopes of becoming the main opposition but the Communists came second, albeit a poor second after the Congress party had secured a massive majority. The CPI had got 16 seats and the Socialists 12. The Communists did even better in some of the states.

The Reds did not, however, win a state all by themselves until the second general election in 1957 when the united CPI was able to form the first elected Communist government anywhere in the world. Kerala had been newly unified after the States Reorganisation Commission had reported and the Centre had accepted the recommendations. The Commission was headed by Justice Fazle Ali and following its report a wholesale reorganisation of India was undertaken. Nehru, of course, dismissed the Kerala Communist government in 1959 and the Communists lost also states like Andhra Pradesh and Tamil Nadu where they had a strong hold on the voters.

The Reds also lost their leading position in Parliament in 1967 as the free market Swatantra party, founded by C Rajagopalachari, a former important leader of the Congress and the first Indian and last Governor General of India, usurped that position. The ideology of the Swatantra party was appropriated by the Congress party which, under P.V. Narasimha Rao, introduced wide ranging economic reforms and virtuality ushered in a free market regime. The Swatantra party had 44 seats to the Communists[8] 42, CPI's 23 and 19 of the CPIM, since the split had taken place in 1964. This was the only time the parent body had a higher parliamentary tally than the offshoot which grew soon strong to overtake the so-called main party.

In a sweep both the Communist formations suffered in the number of Parliamentary seats. In 1977, when Mrs Indira Gandhi was defeated in the wake of her unpopular Emergency, the CPI, which had been a camp follower of the Congress, suffered a steep decline and came to the House with only seven seats. The Janata Party, of which the JS was a part, had secured 295 seats in the Lok Sabha and the Congress 154. The CPIM got 22 seats in the poll. In 1984, Rajiv Gandhi raised the bogey of Hinduism under danger, because his mother had been murdered by her Sikh security guards and the Congress party had a landslide victory with 415 seats. The CPI's tally went down still further and it obtained six seats but the CPIM held its ground and won 22 seats. Incidentally, the Communists generally have a strictly limited strength but they create much more noise.

In fact, the Communists have reached the end of their tether and have acquired an inflexible strength. They pretend that they are the Left Front, of the CPIM, CPI, RSP (Revolutionary Socialist Party) and the Netaji Subhas Bose-founded Forward Bloc (FB) but their combined strength in the Lok Sabha is never enough to be recognised as the official Opposition, not even enough for them to raise a motion in the house for which the total strength of a party or group has to be at least one-tenth of the total membership of the House. They, the CPIM and the CPI, maligned and abused Netaji when he used to thunder but they have no compounction in accepting his FB party in the Front. Recently when the FB chose to align itself with the Nationalist Congress Party of Sharad Pawar the CPIM did their best to dissuade the FB leaders not to do so but the latter were adamant. The NCP is a real threat to the CPIM's hegemony of the so-called United Front. The Left Front's strength in the 12th Lok Sabha was just 48 in a House of 545 members.

As we said the Lok Sabha rules require at least one-tenth of the total membership of the House must support a motion for its acceptance. The Communists just do not have that kind of strength, even with the Left Front and other concotions. In 1989 the Congress party, headed by the erstwhile Prime Minister, Rajiv Gandhi, had 197 members in the Lok Sabha and the Janata Dal of V. P. Singh had 142 members. As the number one party the Congress could have claimed its right to be called by the President, R.Venkataraman then, to try and form a government but he had no promise of support from any sizable group and he had to stand down in favour of Singh.

The President called in V.P. Singh because his own 142 members were joined by the BJP's 86 members on the one hand the CPIM's 33 and the CPI's 12 apart from a handful of the RSP and the FB. The JD, the BJP and the Left Front parties had campaigned on the issue of the Bofors payoff under Rajiv Gandhi's regime. In 1986 when Rajiv Gandhi was also his own Defence Minister, apart from the begin the Prime Minister, he had entered into a contract with the Bofors company of Sweden for the supply of field guns which played an important role in the Kargil operations in May-July 1999 against Pakistani infiltrators in Kashmir. The guns proved their worth and gullible mediamen gave Rajiv Gandhi the credit for acquiring them for the Indian army, no matter the corruption charges. They forget that it is not the utility and the capacity of the guns that was questioned but the payoff for the contract and the fact that Sonia Gandhi's Italian connection had come in to play in the payoff.

There is a difference between outside support from one party and outside support from another. Rajiv Gandhi first propped up the breakaway group of the Janata Dal, led by Chandrashekhar in search of power, and thus bolstred the minority government of Prime Minister Chandrashekhar. Rajiv, however, withdrew the support within four months. In 1979, his mother, Indira Gandhi, had first promised support from the outside to the Charan Singh government and pulled the rug from the unsuspecting Chaudhari's feet in just 21 days. She could sustain the government in power for as little as 21 days while the son, Rajiv Gandhi enhanced the time to four months. Indira Gandhi gave no reasons for her action. But everyone knew that she wanted the court cases against her withdrawn and Charan Singh would not do such an illegal thing. So, she needed the power of the office of Prime Minister herself and the people gave it to her in the Lok Sabha poll in December 1979.

The Constitution of India provides for so many contingencies but the makers of the Constitution did not envisage a situation when a minority government would be held in position and helped by another party without participation in the task of running the government. In 1996 the United Front formed a government with its support from the outside by the Congress party. The President could not extract any written or oral promise from the Congress party that it would sustain the UF government for a particular period. In the case of the second UF government, led by the wishywashy Prime Minister, Inder Kumar Gujral, the President, Dr. Shanker Dayal Sharma, even secured a written guarantee from Congress President Sitaram Kesri that he would support the Gujral government from outside. But that was all that he could make Kesri to pledge. He could not bind Kesri to a specific time frame. Kesri then pulled the rug from under Gujral's feet within just seven months. In the case of Gujral's predecessor, H.D. Deve Gowda, the time limit of Congress tolerance was a little longer–ten months.

And one may well ask: why should the outside support not be withdrawn at a time convenient to the party giving it ? The CPIM was the prime mover for the United Front concept because it wanted to vield influence on the Central government without being a part of it. Jyoti Basu wanted to be Prime Minister but his party was content with being the one to call the shots without holding the reins of power—having power without the responsibility. The Communists had reached the conclusion that they would never be the actual wielder of power so the next best thing was for them to have the key of influence without the responsibility of holding the office of power.

Remember what happened when despite all efforts of Messrs Harkishan Singh Surjeet and Jyoti Basu the BJP and its allies came to power in March 1998. A reluctant President, K.R. Narayanan, at heart a Congressman, who would have hated the idea of swearing in a BJP man to hold the office of Prime Minister, had to perform the task because the Surjeet-Basu duo could not instal Sonia Gandhi in the Prime Minister's Office. So, the next best thing for the duo was to topple the Vajpayee government and they were at the job for a full year and a month before they could succeed in the task.

During these thirteen months, the CPIM made one attempt after another for toppling the Vajpayee cabinet. They egged on the willing

Sonia Gandhi and exploited the AIADMK factor for which they utilised the services of Subramanian Swamy although they pretended that they would not attend his tea party when the plot for toppling was finally hatched. There were, of course, many other players, like the Congress's Arjun Singh, RLM (Rashtriya Loktantrik Morcha–national demcratic front)'s Laloo Prasad and Mulayam Singh Yadav and several others who had minor roles, but the key roles were rendered by Surjeet and company.

The CPIM had no moral or other objection in working with the BJP in 1989-90 when the BJP on the one hand was giving outside support to the V.P. Singh government and they, the so–called Leftist block, were doing the same on the other. They certainly had floor coordination with the BJP at that time because without it the Congress attempts to dislodge the V.P. Singh government would have succeeded even earlier. Earlier the Communists had worked with the BJP's predecessor, the Jana Sangh, in some SVD (Sanyukta Vidhayak Dal) non-Congress governments in States when the Congress party which was ruling these states its lost majority. The CPIM had no objection in working with Ajoy Mukherjee and making him Chief Minister when it was known that he was at heart a Congressman and his Bangla Congress was an off–shoot of the Congress.

As the times change so do the CPIM and other Communists. The BJP as a supporting party was good enough but not as a challenger and a potential threat in the quest for power in Delhi. The BJP has thus to be portrayed as a communal party and the Babri Mosque incident, which has been accepted as a grave mistake by many leaders of the party, comes handy to the CPIM in its task of portraying it with the worst colours. The CPIM's depiction of the BJP as a communal party has to be contrasted with the wider acceptance of the BJP by a number of regional formations and the failure of the UF approach of the CPIM.

Once upon a time, the CPIM rode like a colossus on the Indian political scene when it commanded the loyalty of a number of regional parties like the Telugu Desam of Andhra Pradesh, which was also the ruling patry in Andhra Pradesh, the DMK party in Tamil Nadu, the AGP, Asom Gana Parishad, the ruling party in Assam, the Samajwadi Party, mainly of Uttar Pradesh, and its dominant leader, Mulayam Singh Yadav, apart from the National Conference of Jammu and Kashmir, the ruling party of the state.

One by one, they all left the UF or Third Front of Surjeet because in his desire to crown Sonia Gandhi the Queen of India he advocated support to that party and pledged his party's support during 1998 and 1999. No doubt, the Calcutta Congress of the CPIM had said that the party should extend issue-based support to the Congress party, instead of keeping equidistant from both the BJP and the Congress, as laid down by the party's Chandigarh Congress held a few years earlier. But Surjeet who is a kind of dictator turned the authorisation given by the party as a kind of licence for toppling the BJP government and installing Sonia Gandhi in its place. In the process, he neither succeeded in his mission nor did he hold his flock together. The third front of his evaporated before his eyes as first the Telugu Desam, the AGP and the National Conference left his side, leaving him to make wild allegation against Chandrababu Naidu and calling him a traitor. Then came the turn of the DMK leader as Surjeet chose to link up with the AIADMK leader in Tamil Nadu.

Surjeet thus killed his own pet, the Third Front. One of the senior journalists, not at all friendly to the BJP once said that the Third Front would come at the end of the Third Millennium.[9] Actually, the Third Front vanished from the scene even as Surjeet succeeded in toppling the Vajpayee government but failed in putting Sonia Gandhi or his stablemate Jyoti Basu in the vacancy. The situation was, however, still favourable to the BJP because the alternative government could not fructify and the President had no choice but to allow Vajpayee to continue in office until a new Lok Sabha was elected.

The desperation of the CPIM is thus becoming evident and to some it is excusable and understandable. The influence of the party is confined to the three states, West Bengal, Kerala and Tripura, but only in of them, West Bengal the party is supreme and somewhat unchallanged although lately the Trinamul and the BJP have emerged as challengers. In Kerala, where it is customary for the Congress and even the CPIM, the two main contenders for power, to take the help of communal parties,like the Indian Union Muslim League (IUML) and some Christian bodies, the two parties oust each other from power almost in a musical chairs situation. In Tripura, the CPIM has greater dominance, but nothing compared to the happy situation in which it finds itself in West Bengal.[10]

Tripura was once a princely state but its proximity to Bangladesh (formerly East Pakistan) led to a large influx of the Bengali Hindus, many of them white collar workers, because the Hindus were always oppressed in East Pakistan. Many of them sought shelter in adjoining Indian territory of Assam, West Bengal and,of course, Tripura where they saw opportunity. If you go out for a walk in Agartala, Tripura's capital, you are in the danger of walking into Bangladesh. So close is the proximity and so close the internationmal border separating the two.

The migration of the East Pakistan Hindus (now stopped completely) led to the feeling of islolation of the tribals, the original inhabitants of

Tripura.They felt less and less important in their homeland. Violence and insurrection are no solution but to a great extent the revolts in Tripura owe the origin to this feeling. The two main parties, the Congress and the CPIM, sought to assauge the isolation of the tribals but often the leaders intentions were not translated into action. The large difference in educational attainments of the Bengali Hindus, migrants as well as original inhabitants, and of the tribals often caused a heartburn as many key and even ordinary jobs were taken by the Hindus and the crumbs left for the tribals. So, insurgency broke out in the eighties and continued in the nineties and goes on to this day as the All Tripura Tiger Force (ATTF) and the National Liberation Front of Tripura (NLFT) have been operating in the state and are the cause of widespread depredations.

"Tripura launches poster campaign against insurgency" ran a headline in an English daily in the Capital[10]. According to it, if an extremist is nabbed on the basis of information, the informer will be paid as much as Rs. two lakhs, a handsome amount in the remote Tripura in the North-East of the country, and anywhere any day in India despite the inflation.The poster adds, typically, that "the name and address of the informer will be kept secret." In the English media of Delhi, Culcutta, Mumbai and Chennai, the bearded and turbaned figure of the CPIM boss Harkishan Singh Surjeet may loom large as he vainly tries to challenge, change and chop one party after another, but the reality in remote Tripura is different. The CPIM claims to represent the tribals and the Congress has an uneasy relationship with the tribal organisation, the TUJS (Tripura Upjati Juba Sangh) which however does not carry much weight with the rebels and the reality is that despite the CPIM rule the tribals and mainline Hindus are not living in a peaceful manner.

The award or reward of Rs. two lakhs is for information leading to the arrest of Bishnupada Jamatia alias J. Bosong, president of the NLFT, and Ranjit Debarama, president of the ATT. Besides them, some other rebels are also covered by the reward scheme. Rebels of the two outfits command the loyalty of some 900 insurgents and there is a feeling of terror among all Hindus, including cadres of the CPIM. There are grave doubts if anyone will respond to this open invitation to spying.

In Kerala, although E.M.S. Namboodiripad, the late veteran of the Communist movement, formed the first government of the Communists in the state in March 1957 it was not a case of "Live happily ever after". By 1959, two years after the CPI representative were in the saddle Nehru sensed an "upsurge" in Kerala and he attributed it to actions and policies of the CPI government. The fact was that his daughter, Indira Gandhi, had recently become President of the Congress party and she wanted the Communist government out. Her word was law for Nehru who had only to invent big words to justify an unfair deed. The dynastic principle is a reality in India, whether it is the politicians, industrialists or cinema actors and actresses. (Even some journalists and mediapersons practise it).

While Indira Gandhi was anxious to sack the Communists and put in their place her partymen the then President, Dr. Rajendra Prasad, and even the Home Minister, Govind Ballabh Pant, were punctilious men who cared for the provisions of the Constitution. Both were products of the freedom movement, like Nehru himself, but Indira Gandhi was free from such encumberences having been a mere child while the war for freedom was being fought. Often the media have portrayed Nehru as liberal and Rajen Babu, as he was popularly known, as diehard obstructionist. The reality was somewhat different. Both Rajen Babu and Pant were opposed to the misuse of Article 356 of the Constitution which permits the Centre to take over the administration of a state in the event of the breakdown of the Constitution in a state.

No such thing happened in Kerala as the CPI'S majority in the Assembly was fully in tact. Even law and order were perfectly fine although the opponents of the CPI regime were frequently holding demonstrations. There was really speaking no upsurge as alleged by Nehru. It should be recalled that the first use of Article 356 by Nehru was in 1951, only a year after the Constitution was enforced, to sort out an internal problem of the Congress party in Punjab where Bhimsen Sachar, (who incidentally was the father-in-law of the noted journalist and nominated MP, Kuldip Nayar) was constantly at loggerheads with another Congress leader the late Gopichand Bhargava. This is recorded in the Sarkaria Commission's report on Centre-state relations. (Not the relationship, of course).

Nehru and Indira had their way and the CPI government was dismissed. Namboodiripad was a much respected Communist leader and again beame Chief Minister of Kerala but the misue of the article of the Constitution has continued so far as the Congress is concerned and even by the CPIM. When the UF government was in power at the Centre the CPIM was the dominant prime mover although it was not a participant in the government. The BJP government in Gujarat was dismissed even though it had obtained a vote of confidence in the Assembly and Vaghela was brought in the Chief Minister's office through the backdoor with the outside support of the Congress party. All this was done when the UF was in power in Delhi.

Then in February 1999 Sonia Gandhi, as Congress president, issued a statement denouncing the Rabri Devi government of Bihar[11] and said that "she had lost the moral right to rule the state". Rabri Devi was proxy Chief Minister in place of her domineering husband, Laloo Prasad, who could not continue to rule the state, formally at least, because he was facing a spate of corruption cases in the Rs. 1000 crore animal husbandry scam in his state. But when the BJP government imposed President's rule in Bihar and it was passed by the Lok Sabha the Congress did a turnabout and refused to support it in the Rajya Sabha, the Upper House where the BJP and allies did not have a majority.[12] The CPIM was, of course, the Congress supporter in the move and in the ensuing Lok Sabha elections in 1999 the RJD had seat sharing arrangements in Bihar with the Congress and the two Communist parties.

The strength of the Communists and their small party supporters, the RSP and the FB, had been stabilised at around 50 and is generally less than that in the Lok Shaba. The main support of the Left block and of the CPIM comes from West Bengal. In 1967 Jyoti Basu had become Deputy CM under Ajoy Mookerjee of the Bangla Congress but that government was dismissed by Indira Gandhi before it could complete its term and another election in West Bengal in 1969 produced the same result. Again the so-called UF government in West Bengal was dismissed and in the wake of India's glorious vicory in Bangladesh's liberation war the Congress party secured a massive mandate and the Communists just got ten seats in the state assembly.

But that was the last time the Congress tasted power in West Bengal and although now the CPIM is aligned with the Congress, in mind if not otherwise, the Congress has no chance of coming to power once more. Rajiv Gandhi tried hard when he was Prime Minister and the state had gone to the polls in 1987. The noted journalist, M.J. Akbar, who often became a camp follower of Rajiv, led him to believe that West Bengal would come to the fold of the Congress in that poll but that did not happen.

Actually, the CPIM was the beneficiary of the real popular upsurge against Indira Gandhi's authoritarian rule under her Emergency but typically the CPIM did not support the Central government formed under JP's auspices. Perhaps the reason was that the Communists did not like Prime Minister Morarji Desai because he was brutally frank. The CPIM had not joined the JP movement and the CPI was then hanging on to the frocktails of Indira Gandhi and had even supported her Emergency and was totally for it.

For all its love of "principles", the CPIM knows too well which side of the bread is buttered and chooses its allies carefully and likes to stand by them. Even so, its real strength is less than 50 and it does not entitle it to be called a national or All-India party although the Election Commission's rules are somewhat fancy and the CPIM's vanity is pampered by it. They have lost their base in Maharashtra, Andhra Pradesh and Tamil Nadu where they had set up a sizable strength but now they hang on to one or other regional parties to get for themselves just one or two seats.

First the CPIM, and the camp follower CPI, chose as its ally the Telugu Desam in Andhra Pradesh. That was when they were dreaming that the Congress could be replaced at the all-India level by some other party or a combination of parties. The TD had been formed by N.T.Rama Rao, NTR as he was popularly known, as a challenge to the Congress and as an assertion of Telugu self-respect because the power-drunk Indira Gandhi family used to treat the Andhra Congress leaders no better than bearers of its shoes. He was known to large sections of Telugu people as a popular cinema actor but he brought to bear on it a great flair for public speaking, leadership qualities of a high order and often travelled in a Ratham (a truck which was given the popular tittle of Chaitanya Ratham, or Consciousness Chariot) and made many popular gestures. All this enabled the party to oust the well-entrenched Congress party within just one year in 1983.

The CPIM expected that the successor, N. Chandrababu Naidu, would also follow in his father-in-law's footsteps and remain in their so-called Third Front even after the two Communist parties openly sides with the Congress party. That was not to be and Naidu extended issue-based support to the BJP-led government of Vajpayee. The CPIM could not tolerate such defiance and denounced Naidu but in the 1999 Lok Sabha poll it could not find either the Congress or any smaller party in Andhra Pradesh to align with.

In the Hindi-speaking states the CPIM and the CPI have only pockets of influence, mostly the CPI in Bihar. Nowhere else, either in Orissa or Gujarat the CPIM and the CPI have a base. The All-India Dream had evaporated before it could become a reality.

REFERENCES

1. Documents of the History of the CPI, Vol.VIII, quoted in *Birth of Non-Congressism*, Madhu Limaye, BR Publishing Corporation, Delhi, 1988.
2. *Ibid.*
3. Chapter Six–Two out of One–The Great Split.
4. The Congress For Democracy, led by Jagjivan Ram, also joined the Janata Party.

5. *Communism in India*, Gene D. Overstreet and Marshall Windmiller University of California Press, Berkley and Los Angeles, USA.
6. *Communism in India*, Gene D.Overstreet and Marshall Windmiller.
7. *Ibid.*
8. The election figures are generally taken from *India Decides* Prannoy Roy and others.
9. *Task of a Thousand Years, Inder Malhotra, Observer of Business and Politics*, Delhi, October 14, 1998.
10. *Hindustan Times*, Delhi, March 29, 1999.
11. *Hindustan Times*, Delhi, February 12, 1999.
12. *Times of India*, Delhi, March 9, 1999.

2

UNITED THEY ARE DIVIDED

'United Front' is an essential part of Communist strategy. They practised it, under foreign orders, during the freedom movement when the CPI was not a legal party. Often the Communists used to receive directives from the Soviet Communist Party, through the Communist International, Comintern, and later the Cominform, and often through the British Communist Party. The British party exercised a colonial overlordship over the Indian comrades by virtue of the fact that India was under British colonial rule and this continued for a few years even after the British left the shores of India.

Even when the Communists decided to put their faith in the parliamentary form of democracy in October 1951 they had tried to forge a united front. Before that decision was arrived at the Communists had been led by B.T. Ranadive, General Secretary[1] of united CPI, and he believed that there would be a revolution in India within six months and the party under his command, the CPI disrupted, or sought to disrupt many things. Senior leaders of the party later admitted in inner party self-criticism that "we attacked railway stations, we threw bombs on trains and buses, we tried to break up Nehru's meeting. We set fire to Congress offices. These acts, as well as the use of acid bulbs, in meetings and demonstrations were part of the old leadership's revolutionary line."[2]

Not only the Government of India, which was then led by Jawaharlal Nehru, had come out with a lot of material on the clandestine and open activities of the Comrades but earlier in 1948 different provincial governments had arrested individual Communists and banned party activities in several regions of India under the relevant laws. Some top leaders of the CPI, like S.A. Dange, Ajoy Ghosh, Jyoti Basu, S.S. Mirajkar, and Sohan Singh Josh were arrested and some went underground in the typical Communist fashion. Ranadive accused Nehru of unleashing terror against the Communists. Ranadive was opposed to the Maolist form of agrarian revolution. Which was a strong point of the Andhra Comrades, and had great faith in the capacity of industrial workers whom he expected to lead his "revolution." This failed to happen but the Andhra Communists had their revenge and one of them, C. Rajeshwar Rao, overthrew Ranadive in 1950 to become the General Secretary of the party. One of the measures the new leadership envisaged was the formation of a "united front with other leftist parties and progressive elements for contesting the elections."[3]

The united front approach is thus rooted in the thinking of the Communists, whether of the CPI or CPIM variety, in fact, all comrades. There is an Indian proverb 'as long as the fist is tight it is worth a lakh[4] (of rupees)', but when it is loosened it is worthless. Whether or not the Comrades had heard of the proverb, or for that matter of the Panchatantra story about 'united we stand' or 'in union there is real strength' they practised the UF approach to perfection. The Communist motives are, of course, different. They seek union with 'likeminded' parties because thereby they have more numbers and they seek to dominate the union at all times. They think the others are gullible and would easily swallow their prescription without question. Nor are they aware of the difficulties of working together with ill-assorted political formations as Comrade Surjeet has discovered to his cost when his Third Front lay in tatters in 1998 and 1999. There are many pitfalls in the United Front approach and the Comrades have to realise that diverse motives impel different groups to come together.

But the Communists, all the same, put their faith in united fronts. Thus they chose to infiltrate the Congress Socialist party when the British rulers denied them their basic right to form an association. They were so successful that in some areas they captured the CSP units. This happened particularly in south India. The Communists were also able to capture several all-India Front organisations of students and workers. but to be fair to them, some of the Comrades were more dedicated than the Socialists themselves as acknowledged by Madhu Limaye.[5]

Later when Subhas Bose had differences with the Congress leadership and with Gandhiji they tried to align with him and egged him on to fight the leadership, although they abused him and called him names when he became Netaji in 1943-44 and in later years. Later after independence, specially after they put their faith in the parliamentary democratic system, they even befriended the Forward Bloc, which was originally formed by Subhas Bose. This was at a time when the Left Front was formed in West Bengal, but there were again differences between the CPIM and the FB and the other constituent of the Front, the RSP (Revolutionary Socialist Party) when the RSP and the FB did not cooperate with the CPIM in their pro-Sonia policy,[6] although the CPI, another unit of the Front, meekly said yes to the big brother. Incidentally, the Left Front itself is a good example of the United Front approach of the Communists who try to entangle others also, sometimes successfully and sometimes unsuccessfully.

With their goal of capturing power at the all-India level receding further and further but never admitting defeat the Communists tried it out in May 1996 when the eleventh Lok Sabha was a hung House. The Congress which was in power at the Centre from 1991 to 1996 lost it and could secure only 140 seats in the 543 member House. The BJP had more, 162 seats and had allies like the Shiv Sena in Maharashtra, the Akali Dal in Punjab and the Samata Party in Bihar. They had other electoral allies and could muster a strength of 194, more than that of the Congress.

At this stage it may not be inadvisable to look in to the past and have a peep at the Communist attempts at infiltration of the CSP which would throw some light on their UF tactics. The CSP had been set up in 1934 as a part of the Congress and they did not hide the fact which was even written into their name. Among the founders, the most prominent of them all, was Jayaprakash Narayan who had been a kind of Marxist as a student but renounced Marxism later in the United States. He was General Secretary of the party and was glad that the Socialists and the Communists, both of whom owed allegiance to Marx, could work unitedly to strengthen socialism in India. He was to discover that the Comrades were subject to guidance, which often amounted to dictation, from abroad. The CCP, Chinese Communist Party, had written an open letter to the Indian Reds asking them to emerge from their isolation to which they had been condemned by the narrow line laid down for them by the Comintern in 1928.

The Chinese comrades told their Indian friends that they should infiltrate the other bodies which they often looked down upon as "reformist". The Chinese Communists perhaps meant only trade unions but from the front organisations the penetration of political bodies was a logical step. In the first category came the All-India Trade Union Congress, now completely under the thumb of the lesser of the two Communist parties but then a lively labour organisations in which men like N.M. Joshi and others who were not Communists held sway. The Chinese comrades wanted that the Indian counterparts should ensure cooperation between their Red Trade Union Congress and the AITUC.The word Red, be it noted, was used by the Communists themselves.

Politically the CSP was the obvious target. The Chinese seetarian leader, Wang Ming,[7] had asked them to shed their isolationist and Left sectarian policies and join the anti-imperialist struggle. One of the basic defects of the Indian Communists has been their tendency to stand apart from the main current. This has been dealt with in a separate chapter. Surprisingly, Wang Ming, in his address to the Seventh Comintern Congress, laid his finger on this very trait, although he was more concerned with the tactical approach.

The coming together of like-minded people should, under normal circumstances, be a welcome feature of any anti-colonial movement. The Indian Reds, however, did not perceive it as a logical measure but one calculated to acquire for them a foothold and responsibility which they would not get otherwise.Their British overlords, Harry Pollitt, Rajani Palme Dutt and Ben Bradley, contacted Minoo Masani, a CSP leader, who happened to be in Moscow when the Seventh Comintern Congress had held its session there. Besides being a founder of the CSP, the late Masani was also an ex-Communist himself. He welcomed the British Communists' offer of cooperation between the CSP, and the CPI, then an illegal body, but said the CPI must wind itself up and the new party would not be an affiliate of the Comintern. What eventually happened is difficult to say but nothing of the kind that Masani wanted took place.[8]

The British Comrades, however, went on to make a distinction between what they called the progressive version of the Indian National Congress and its conservative and bourgeois self. In their view the Indian Communists could form a United Front with the progressive Congress. They were so enamoured of the concept of United Front, like all Communists, that they described the Congress itself as a United Front of the Indian people. The Congress was so in reality but it had been shunned by the Reds so far but now the CPI wanted to penetrate it. Apart from the united front there is another Communist concept of progressive elements involved here. The Indian Communists formed, before and after independence, progressive bodies of writers and others. That is, people who could not join the party as such for various reasons but could associate with its activities and virtually follow the dictates of the CPI in their association and preach and practise them. Many Urdu writers fancied they were serving a good cause by being members of the body of progressive writers.The fact that the Communists supported and even advocated the partition of the country was grist to their mill. The British Communists were, however, not much of the mark in their perception that the Indian National Congress' fighting for the freedom of India, was a kind of united front of the Indian people.

The CSP, at its second conference at Meerut in 1936 adopted a secret resolution[9] requiring the Indian Comrades to apply for its membership as individuals. What JP said then is relevant from the point of the Masani-British Reds talks in Moscow. He is reported to have opined that CPI had thought of itself so far as pure and would not tolerate any pollution but some elements wanted a united front. The British Comrades wanted their Indian counterparts to work for reforming and revolutionising the Congress, the aim being to make the Congress reject Gandhi's non-violence.

The Communists wanted to cast India in their own mould but saw the wisdom of the 'British masters' thesis and P.C. Joshi, who had emerged as a leader of the Indian Communists, was an advocate of the approach. He asked the Comrades to become members of the CSP and a large number did so because thereby they could enter the Congress. Several of them joined in without disclosing their identity as Communists.This was thus the first Communist plan in action aimed at penetration of the Congress.

Important party leaders rose high in the Congress organisation, and, of course, the CSP, in this manner. Riding on the backs of the CSP as 'tailers', as admitted by a leading Communist himself people like E.M.S. Namboodiripad, P. Sundarayya, and P. Ramamurti, rose high in the Congress as well as the CSP, and even controlled the CSP units in south India. EMS, as he was popularly known, was virtually directing all "Socialist" activities in south India besides being joint secretary of the CSP at the national level. The genuine Socialists in the CSP were also getting aware of the part played by the Communists and went about issuing warnings and threats of action which the Communists ignored. The CSP finally called off the marriage of the Socialist groups in March1940 at Ramgarh in Bihar, where a INC session was being held at that time. The CSP National Executive expelled all Communists party members.

By that time the penetration plan had succeeded beyond all expectations, including the Communists. The CSP had tolerated them long enough. At times, the Communists outrivalled the Socialists declaring, tactically, of course, that Gandhi was a progressive, and declining to stand by Subhas Babu when he defied the Congress leaders and Gandhiji after supporting him when Subhas Babu stood for re-election as Congress president against Gandhiji's wishes.They dubbed the Forward Bloc founded by Subhas as counter revolutionary. To quote Netaji, the Communists had indulged in reprehensible propaganda against the Forward Bloc. "Today they have cast off all sense of shame", he said.[10]

Different games are to be played at different times and today the FB is one of the four Left Front parties of which the CPIM is the leader and boss. They would call Nehru all sorts of names when it suited them and praise him when that is more appropriate. One of the typical outbursts by the Indian Reds against Nehru was: "Nehru's role is to bark at the Communists and to hang revolutionary drapings round the Working Committee resolutions". This is part of a statement issued by the CPI in October 1940.[11]

Hegemony is a frequently occurring word in the parlance of the Comrades. They try to clothe their UF urge in soft and beguiling language but their real desire is to control all the constituents of the UF, lead them and dominate the front. They liquidated the Bangla Congress with which they had formed an alliance in West Bengal in 1967 and 1969 when they lacked the requisite majority. They achieved the happy position only in 1977 when Mrs Indira Gandhi lost in most parts of the country including West Bengal. The CPIM got a clear majority and they roped in the weak CPI and the two other smaller parties because they did not want to go astray in future. The UF is thus a double weapon in the hands of the CPIM; it helps the party to marshal the weak fellow constituents and then keep them in effective control.

It is worth recall what JP had said of the tactics of the Communists in a circular he addressed a units of the CSP at a time when the Reds had infiltrated the party. They had left "nothing undone" in destroying the unity within the CSP said JP. He said the CPI had torn off its mask completely and stood as the sworn enemy of the CSP and every other progressives with which it had worked before.[12] This circular was issued three months before the CSP formally expelled the Comrades.

The Communists openly advocated Pakistan and questioned the claim of the Congress to speak for the whole of India. They had no hesitation in putting themselves in line with the Muslim League of Mohammed Ali Jinnah who repeated again and again that he alone could speak for the Indian Muslims. In a resolution, passed at a conference in December 1940, the Communists declared that India should be a voluntary federation of regional states based on mutual confidence. India was thus not to be a single nation but a group of nations.[13] It is not without significance that the Muslim League had held its annual session at Lahore in March 1940, under Jinnah's presidentship (he was subsequently made life president) at which the Pakistan resolution was adopted after it was moved by the East Bengal leader, Fazlul Huq.[14]

As stated earlier, control of the whole of India has always been a Communist dream but the dream is far from being realised and would never be a reality. That does not prevent the CPIM and CPI comrades from trying and they took the initiative in forming the United Front in May1996 when, as saw, the country was witness to a hung house after the elections of the 11th Lok Sabha. Even before the President, Dr. Shanker Dayal Sharma, had given any thought to the formation of the government, the two CPIM bigwigs, Harikishan Singh Surject and Jyoti Basu, had met the President. They had staked their claim that the forces working with them could form a government and wanted to be invited to do so.

The UF treatment was just the kind of solution in a situation in which neither the Congress nor the BJP had secured a majority and the BJP's strength could not rise above 194. Consequently Atal Bihari Vajpayee who had been called in by the President to form a government as leader of the largest single party had to resign after 13 days in office. The CPIM had taken a lead in forming the United Front in the meantime and roped in the 55-member strong Janata Dal, its Left Front partners, the CPI, RSP and FB, the Samajwadi party of the highly ambitious Mulayam Singh Yadav, the regional outfits, like the Telugu Desam party which was in power in Andhra Pradesh, the DMK of Tamil Nadu which yet another ruling party in its own state, the Tamil Maanila Congress (TMC) a breakaway group of the Congress in Tamil Nadu, which had swept the polls in the state along with the DMK, and some really small parties.

The Congress promised outside support to the United Front. Now the problem for the Front was to find a leader and it first tried to persuade a former Prime Minister, V.P. Singh, but he proved utterly elusive and almost played truant. Then the Front turned its attention to Jyoti Basu. Barkis was willing but the CPIM central committee was not. Basu later called it a "historical blunder"and rewarded his biographer Surabhi Banerjee, by appointing her pro-vice chancellor of the prestigious Calcutta University, for putting his disappointment in the book.

Eventually H.D. Deve Gowda, who had been Chief Minister of Karnataka just before was crowned by the UF. He then belonged to the Janata Dal, which had a strength of 55 members in the Lok Sabha. Deve Gowda made almost weekly trips to his home state during the ten months he was allowed to remain in the saddle before the Congress pulled the rug under his feet, and could just mumble some words in English. He used to call himself the "humble farmer" from his Hassan in Karnataka, but this claim was not taken seriously by the media which only recalled it to make fun of the leader.

In the English media, which still dominate the press in the country despite the great leap forward by the Hindi and Indian language press, there are a number of young men and women working as reporters and deskmen. Unlike the senior men who are aware of the dubious role of the CPIM, and the Communists in general, but whose activities are confined to editorial writing and general direction, these people are impressionable and are often carried away by the CPIM's tactics. The CPIM rejected the request of the UF leaders to Joyti Basu for participation in the government. Many of these mediamen and women were impressed this act of self-renunciation on the part of the CPIM. If it was really an act of abnegation why should the CPIM be in the business of parliamentary government and why should it rule West Bengal, Kerala and Tripura?

The CPIM has its own reasons for non-participation in the UF government. The real reason why the CPIM central committee resolved not to acceed to the request of the UF was that it believes that it should not participate in a government which it cannot control; that it could not fully control the activities of the UF government was evident from its lack of numbers, just 32 seats the party held in the Lok Sabha where the majority is determined by 272 members since the total strength of the Lok Sabha is 543 members. As we have seen, the strength of the CPIM, and as a matter of fact of the entire left block, is becoming inflexible. It revolves around the figure of 50 which is not adequate for the proceedings of the House to be held up legally because the minimum strength for a motion in the Lok Sabha to be admitted is one-tenth of the total strength of the House, that is about 54 or 55. At no time, the total tally of all the Communist parties put together has risen above 50.

But non-participation in government does not hurt manipulators like Surjeet. They still acquire control over the apparatus of amorphous bodies like the United Front. Such bodies are hardly of one mind and in any given situation they display tendencies so fissiparus in nature that acquiring control over it is comparatively easy. The CPIM was not in the government, so was the RSP and so was the FB. Of the Left Front only the CPI was represented in the government by two senior ministers, Indrajit Gupta who took charge of the Home Portfolio, and Chaturanan Mishra from Bihar who made a good Agriculture Minister but failed to get reelected in the mid-term poll in 1999. Gupta, on the ther hand, got through because being from West Bengal where the CPIM has forged a unique Election strategy for itself and its fellow constituents that it generally does not fail to win specially in the rural part of the state. It fails in the metropolitan area of Calcutta and its neighbourhood.

The real influence the CPIM exercised over the UF machinery was evident when Deve Gowda was toppled by the Congress after he had been Prime Minister for ten months. At first, the UF tried the trick of threatening the Congress but the real benefacter was not to be intimidated. So the UF had to go in for a new Prime Minister, a second one for the same UF and with the same outside support of the Congress. There were several claimants for the job and usually everyone thinks he is fit to be the Prime Minister of India. There was G.K. Moopanar of the TMC from Tamil Nadu who favours monosyllables for his reaction to any situation. Surjeet never liked him and he was soon out of the race.

Deve Gowda himself tried for a second term but the man who could not last even a year because the Congress President Sitaram Kesri did not like his devious ways, some said because Kesri was devious himself and then Mulayam Singh Yadav tried his luck because he was highly ambitious and knew how to manipulate the levers of power. Surjeet liked him immensely, one of the reasons being the Mulayam was said to be in his pockets, as Surjeet believed.

The real reason, so far as Surjeet was concerned, was that Mulayam was staunchly anti-BJP and would not compromise on keeping out the BJP from power. The *Times of India*, which is a leading paper, has some of its correspondents branded as being pro-this party and an anti-that party. One of its women correspondents was strongly in favour of the CPIM and also of Mulayam because she was out and out against the BJP. She could invent or put together stories to run down the BJP from day to day and boost the image of Surjeet or Mulayam. The paper even predicted that Mulayam would be the nest Prime Minister of India. One of the strong reasons was that Mulayam himself wanted to be crowned king and the second was that Surjeet wanted him in that coveted position.

But they, Mulayam and Sujeet, and of course, the *Times* woman correspondent, had miscalculated. They had not taken note of opposition of Mulayam's name by Laloo Prasad Yadav, then President of the Janata Dal, which he was to split in another two months and the Janata Dal was to face another turbulent period two years later when it futher split. Laloo and Mulayam later come together in the RLM (Rashtriya Loktantrik Morcha) when the two announced the coming together of their parties, the Samajwadi party and the RJD (Laloo's Rashtriya Janta Dal) amid much media fanfare. They soon parted ways when Mulayam would not acknowledge Sonia Gandhi as the Supreme leader of the country and did not back her for the Prime Minister's position in April 1999. Laloo, on the contrary, was eternally grateful to Sonia for bailing out his wife in the Rajya Sabha, dominated by the Congress and the Left parties in March that year.

One was grateful to Sonia and therefore, his RJD was inclined favourably towards the Congress and the other was dead against the Congress because he could not countenance a foreigner as India's Prime Minister and, more importantly, he did not wish to lose his Muslim votebank to the Congress in Uttar Pradesh. So, without saying so, the RLM was dead and the two Yadavs lost their camaradarie and conviviality. In April 1997, the position was that Laloo Yadav wielded a clout because he had 55 Janata Dal votes in the 180 member United Front. To add to his strength the outside supporter of the UF, the Congress, was headed by Sitaram Kesri who did not like Mulayam and had already set his heart on the wishywashy Inder Kumar Gujral.

So, much to the annoyance of the *Times of India* correspondent, who had gone and predicted Mulayam as Prime Minister, Gujral was chosen by the UF to be its leader and sworn in by the President of India. Surjeet, who would have liked Mulayam to be Prime Minister, knew the art of compromise, bowed to the inevitable but retained his clout over the UF machinery.

In making the right noises, in choosing the right personnel (some say in favouring individuals placed near or far), in downing the BJP when that was required, in stalling bills that the CPIM did not like or pushing through those which it liked this clout was useful. It did not work out always and there were several occasions when what he willed was disposed of adversely, sometimes by the intervention of the head of state and sometimes by the proclivities of Gujral as Prime Minister. That does not mean that Surjeet did not try hard enough and did not wield his known authority which, however, did not yield the desired results.

Kesri toppled the Gujral government in seven months and Surjeet could do little to prevent the fall. Circumstances and political fortunes change so suddenly sometimes that individuals, however crooked they may be, have to face defeat and political forces shape the destiny of nations in their own way and leaders who think they are the colossus who wield unlimited authority on events have to eat the humble pie.

Surjeet faced a somewhat similar situation in March 1998 when the BJP-led alliance was able to forge a simple majority and the Congress party, behind which the CPIM had now put all its strength because the third front, the latest version of the UF, was in shambles, was led by a novice, Sonia Gandhi. She frankly told the President, K.R. Narayanan, who being a Congressman still invited her for consultations, that she did not have the requisite majority. So, to much of Surjeet's chagrin, the BJP-led government was formed under the same Atal Bihari Vajpayee.

It would not be Surjeet if he would admit defeat. From day one, he made it his real business to topple the Vajpayee government and egg on Sonia Gandhi to do it because the Left bloc hardly had about 50 members and the Congress had come to the house with 140 members.The media had now been bitten by the rumour and speculation bug and put out stories from time to time as to when the Vajpayee government would fall. For example, during the budget session of 1998, the fall of the year after Sonia's Congress had won two BJP ruled states, Delhi and Rajasthan, and retained Madhya Pradesh, (but lost Christian Mizoram, nobody recalled that and once *Times of India* report put Mizoram as one of the Congress-ruled States),[15] in the next session of Parliament which would be"crucial", the usual media description for all Parliament sessions, and so on.

This story needs to be told in greater detail and it would be dealt with somewhat elaborately in the next chapter. What remains to be discussed here is the role of the wishywashy Prime Minister, Inder Kumar Gujral. He started his career in politics as a Congressman and got elected to local bodies in the capital. He had come as a refugee from West Pakistan and was believed to be a card holding member of the undivided CPI before migration. In any event, he behaved as a good Congressman but had liberal, intellectual and progressive airs about him all the same. This image he kept up for a long time, as ambassador to the erstwhile Soviet Union, both under Indira Gandhi's Congress regime and under the Janata government led by Morarji Desai later.

He was virtually hounded out of his Information and Broadcasting portfolio by Indira's younger son, Sanjay Gandhi, whose star was in high ascedance as Indira's Emergency rule was about to begin.[16] I had known him fairly well during his tenure at I and B and then itself formed the impression that he was wishywashy, never firm and utterly selfish. Once he put pressure on me as the second in command to the then AIR Director of News. Late one evening he rang me up at my Bharati Nagar house (towards the end of 1974) and wanted that the AIR bulletins carry portions of a debate on a non-official resolution in the Rajya Sabha, the Upper House of Parliament, that afternoon.

Contrary to the popular belief that AIR was at the back and call of its Minister, if not any minister, we had certain norms and could, therefore justify our action whenever it was called in question in Parliament, the media and, above all, to our conscience. For a discussion on a non-official resolution we generally carried the name of the mover and a few lines of his speech, a few lines of the debate and of the Minister conerned if he spoke on that day. It should be remembered that there was very little TV in those days, no national linkup of Doordarshan's programmes, no Zee TV, no Star TV, no cable. In fact, the AIR bulletins were supreme.

What Minister Gujral wanted me to do was to carry more details of the mover's speech and of several other speeches by his partymen, Congress MPs, against our rules. I explained to him what the rules were but he pleaded that we should do what he said. Why was Gujral interested in the remarks made by his partymen covered by AIR bulletins? Because, as he explained to me then they had all made scathing attacks on Morarji Desai who was not a member of the House and could not, therefore, be present. An excellent opportunity for the Congress party of Indira Gandhi when many of its members had opened their mouths against Morarji and what if a few rules of AIR news were violated thereby.

Gujral had his way as disobedience could cause many problems and the persons who replaced you would gladly carry out the Minister's wishes. I told him that the late evening bulletins were already going on the air and few remaining would go on the air before the story desired by him could be ready. He did not mind our carrying the revised story the next morning and made arrangements with the Rajya Sabha reporters (how obliging of them considering that they were under no such ministerial dictat) so that the story could be prepared as he wished it should be.

The Minister was extremely polite and respectful but we knew that his wishes had to be carried out. By his subtlety and his extreme manoueverability he carried on the right side of the winners, joined V.P. Singh's Janata Dal, became External Affairs Minister, did nothing outstanding in that capacity, but stuck to the Janata Dal, got on the right side of the top gun of the party, Laloo Prasad Yadav, get elected from Bihar to the Rajya Sabha, by the peculiar method of some people like Manmohan Singh who got himself elected again and again from Assam to the same House (although both are from Punjab), and adorned the office of EA minister under Deve Gowda and finally stepped into the Humble Farmer's shoes in April 1997.

As EA Minister for ten months, he coined a doctrine, which he called with characteristic immodesty, the Gujral Doctrine which died with his tenure. He advocated and compelled the EA Ministry to extend visa and other benefits to the Pakistanis unilaterally under the so-called Gujral doctrine. Again, characteristically, he accepted to be nominated as a candidate for the 12th Lok Sabha from the Jalandhar constituency with the active support of the Akali Dal. The Dal President and Punjab Chief Minister, Prakash Singh Badal, was present when Gujral launched his campaign from Jalandhar. The Akali Dal was (and still is) an ally of the BJP which also tacitly supported his candidature although it was known that Gujral was a Janata Dal man.

He was naturally elected. But what did he do as a Lok Sabha member in 1998 and 1999 until Narayanan dissolved the House on April 26? He sided with Sonia Gandhi and when she brought down the Vajpayee government, in collaration with Surjeet, Gujral voted with Sonia and against Vajpayee. Remembering that the Vajpayee government was pulled down by just one vote without a substitute being provided, Gujral's error was fatal. This India International intellectual tried for another nomination for the 13th Lok Sabha but this time Badal and his BJP friends had been made wiser by Gujral's betrayal and did not accommodate him. He is believed to have tried with some other party but there was no luck there either. With people like Laloo turning their backs on him, there was no hopes for Gujral even by way of another Rajya Sabha nomination to that House. He had burnt his boats with his own party and neither Janata Dal faction knew where Gujral stood, with the Sharad Yadav group or the faction led by his predecessor in the Prime Minister's office. There could not be a greater tragedy for one who had been a Prime Minister once. But then Gujral had no base, except perhaps the IIC in New Delhi, but they could not send him to Parliament.

REFERENCES

1. Communist Party of India, and following it the CPIM, does not have a president or chairman. So the General Secretary is supreme. Surprisingly the Communist Party of China had in Mao Ze Dong, a chairman. Some of the CPI(ML) men' the original Indian Maoists, used to say that "Chairman Mao is our Chairman"
2. *Communist Violence in India*, Government of India, New Delhi, quoted by Overstreet and Windmiller.
3. *Ibid.*
4. A lakh is equal to 100,000.
5. *Birth of Non-Congressism,* Madhu Limaye.
6. *Hindustan Times,* Delhi, April 7, 1999.
7. *The Revolutionary Movement in the Colonial Countries*, quoted by Overstreet and Windmiller.
8. *Ibid.*

9. It was secret because the CPI was yet a banned organisation.
10. The Indian Struggle, Subhas Chandra Bose, quoted in Sita Ram Goel's *Netaji and the CPI.*
11. Overstreet and Windmiller.
12. *Indian Struggle*, Jayaprakash Narayan.
13. Overstreet and Windmiller.
14. See the *Great Divide:Muslim Separatism and Partition*, by the author, Gyan, Delhi.
15. *The Times of India*, Delhi, July 7, 1999. *Government to oppose call to convene Rajya Sabha Session.*
16. Recollected by the author.

3

IN THEIR UNION OUR STRENGTH

In quick succession Indian polity was terribly fractionalised in the three years 1996,1997 and 1998. After a five year term in office of the Congress government, the nation went to the polls to elect the eleventh Lok Sabha. It then appeared that the Congress was about to see the sun set on its aspirations to be able to rule the country. Prime Minister P.V. Narasimha Rao who was also Congress President, had seen his minority party acquire the status of a majority by resort to means which can only be described as less than honourable during these five years. He had, in fact, had recourse to the time honoured defection and break-up of some of the smaller and regional parties to induce the members to join the Congress party.

The electorate had other ideas and in state assembly elections in Maharashtra, Gujarat, Andhra Pradesh and Karnataka they dealt deadly blows to the Congress party over which Narsimha Rao presided. Even in the national poll to the eleventh Lok Sabha they had their revenge on the erstwhile national party and gave the pride of position to another national party, the BJP in terms of the seats secured by it in the Lok Sabha, the Congress coming only second to the BJP, 140 seats for the Congress against 162 won by the BJP. The Left bloc had by now acquired an inflexible strength of around 50, less than ten per cent of the total membership of the Lok Sabha. But as a believer in the doctrine of the United Front it saw the opportunity to dominate the diverse groups in the divided polity. As a mobiliser it could play not only a useful role in putting together a UF coalition and give the country a semblance of stability while influencing the government of West Bengal, Kerala, and Tripura.

Thus was formed the first United Front government of the "humble farmer" H.D. Deve Gowda and in, many respects the first coalition of a multitude of parties, some claiming like the Janata Dal and CPIM and the

CPI, to be national parties, although they hardly deserved that status, the Samajwadi party which was confined to Uttar Pradesh and a number of powerful regional parties. There were people like Sisram Ola and Satpal Maharaj, who were really Congressmen but for the time being were in the Tiwari Congress which eventually went back to the main party but the duo remained to hold ministerial berths in the Inder Kumar Gujral cabinet when they had no party of their own. In 1999 Ola reemerged as a Congressman and Maharaj was a forgotten figure.

There was Ramakant Khalap, the only representative of his MGP (Maharashtrawadi Gomantak Party) of Goa and he was promptly made a minister of state in charge of law. Khalap behaved with much dignity but could not hide the fact that his MGP had long been known in Goa as a party in opposition to the Congress, if party loyalties mean anything in the tiny state of Goa. As if to prove this point, Khalap himself split the four member MGP group in the Goa Assembly in 1999 and became "leader" of two MLAs including himself, and proudly announced that his group was to merge the Congress party.

Such was the loyalty of many members of the UF but that mattered little to Surjeet as long as the UF could carry on and help him in maintaining that he had formed a "secular" non-Congress front. The myth of non-Congressism was exposed twice during the career of the UF government which lasted just seventeen months, with two Prime Minister, Gowda and Gujral, to adorn its ranks. Gujral was even handpicked by the Congress boss, Sitaram Kesri, and wisely accepted by Surjeet in the week that followed the toppling of Gowda and the emergence of Gujral as a compromise candidate.

The UF found that if its mentor, Harkishan Singh Surjeet, could switch to the Congress after the Congress had brought down both the UF governments while pledging support from the outside to them, why should not lesser lights like Ola and Khalap? Ola has been named as a Congress candidate for the 13th Lok Sabha because the Jat vote, some of which Ola could garner, was seen as slipping through the fingers of the Congress. All that may be understandable for the likes of Olas but what about the UF which stood on a separate platform from the Congress, then and now, although now Surjeet's various actions have led to the demise of the Third Front, another name for the UF.

Surjeet became a fanatical Congress champion in the propagandistic belief that he was using the Congress to finish the BJP. All seventeen months of the existence of the UF when power turned the thirteen odd parties into upholders of the United Front, the Congress was good only for lending them support from the outside. It was known to the meanest intelligence in the UF that they must not do anything which would offend the Congress party. But Congressmen who always revelled in the power game and knew nothing which did not remotely smelt of power, were not the ones to keep quite when the likes of Khalap'and Ola wielded enormous clout simply because they were in the government which depended for its very existence on the 140 Congress member block.

The Congress could hardly bear the sight of much smaller parties and lesser individuals occupying chairs of power, with which went the perks, vast influence that only a government department could wield and the patronage of jobs and contracts which it held in its hands. Businessmen have the habit, one would almost say the necessity, of queueing at the doors of politicians who they know are buyable, for a price. They need their support in pursuing their business interests, which could be legitimate at times and sometimes shady. When the telecom operators realised that they had landed themselves in a real financial mess by accepting the licencing system for their extended telephone operations cellular as well as basic, they appealed to the Vajpayee government in 1999 for help and rescue.

The government was sympathetic and even transferred the BJP minister, Jagmohan, from Communication to Urban Development, his forte (Jagmohan had been Vice Chairman of the Delhi Development Authority as an IAS officer) and introduced the revenue sharing system to bail out, or just help Indian companies which would have been virtually submerged by multinationals if the revenue sharing system had not been introduced. But businessmen being businessmen they went knocking on the doors of a prominent Congressman, Pranab Mukherjee, former Finance and External Affairs Minister under different Congress governments, and now Chief Whip of the Congress party in the Rajya Sabha for help. They also sought out a CPIM party leader, Somnath Chatterjee, and both Mukherjee and Chatterjee wrote letters in support of the telecom operators, well before the transfer of Jagmohan and the government decision to allow the operators to switch from the licensing system to revenue sharing.

Like so many letters written by prominent and less prominent MPs to Ministers, on behalf of individuals and more often on behalf of businessmen and groups who can untie purse strings as the situation requires, these two would in all probability have remained on the files of the PMO (Prime Minister's Office) had it not been for the garrulousness of the CPIM and the Congress parties which thought they had caught the Vajpayee government on the wrong foot. In particular, the CPIM believed, with the supply of documents from willing officers sympathetic to the party, it had caught a tartar.

At that stage, the BJP pulled a fast one on both parties by releasing copies of the letters written by Somnath Chatterjee and Pranab Mukherjee supporting the very scheme which their partymen were going all out to attack. The point made here is Mukherjee and Chatterjee, who presumably acted in the interest of their patriotic duties and not for the obvious reasons that such support is sold, and their likes are approached by a multitude of businessmen and individuals who often are in distress. Knowing full well the implications of such actions, and having been contacted by such hordes for various reasons, Congressmen who were members of the Lok Sabha and their party bosses could not relish the presence of UF ministers like Ola and Khalap and even others, high in their ranks, but all of whom existed simply because the Congress was lending outside support to the UF government.

Such are the strings pulled in politics which makes the scene highly interesting although it also becomes somewhat smudged and detestable at times for the smell of corruption which it sends out. Politicians need money for elections so they say, but more often they need the pelf for themselves and their near and "dear" ones and they become rich without doing any big business. The businessmen requires their help in activities which are legitimate sometimes and sometimes are just money making propositions. But the Congressmen thought why should they not be on the main job instead of helping the Olas and Khalaps do their jobs when they knew that these gentlemen would sooner or later join their party.

While the average Congressmen was thinking along these lines, and the leadership was devising ways to topple the UF government they had helped to install, albeit unwillingly, there occurred an issue which convinced Kesri that he could not do business with the UF and its leaders, mainly Surjeet. The Congress and its major electoral ally in UP, the BSP had reached and alliance between the two in the UP's state's assembly elections in the latter half of 1996. They had together secured 100 seats 425. The BSP secured 67 seats and, the Congress which was reduced to severe straits in the premier state which it had ruled in the past for years, got no more than 33 seats. Kesri had promised the BSP's ambitious leader, Mayawati, that after the poll he would secure the support of the UF to make her the Chief Minister of UP.

Mayawati thought that the UF being dependent on the Congress at the Centre, where the UF government could not survive for a day without the Congress help, would surely accept whatever Kesri said. The UF meant, so far as the state of UP was concerned, the Samajwadi party and a few Janata Dal MLAs. But the Samajwadi party, led by the UF Defence Minister, Mulayam Singh Yadav, had a larger than life presence in the state from which he drew his sustenace, and only he counted in the affairs of the state so far as UF was concerned. For the reasons we have noted, Surjeet was friendly to Mulayam and always threw his weight on his side (but wisely withdrew when the occasion demanded, as we have seen).

In this action, however, he knew the entire UF, meaning the leaders of the Front like Surjeet, were united in resisting the Congress demand for the UF to support the BSP and its leader, Mayawati, in her quest for the Chief Ministership of India's biggest province. Mulayam and Mayawati had old scores to settle in UP. Both had been Chief Minister at different times and Mulayam's men had tried to rough up the BSP leader when she withdrew support of her party in June 1995 when Mulayam was dismissed by the Governor, Motilal Vora, a Congressman. Mulayam has a long memory and did not forgive Mayawati; in particular he had a grievance against Vora also. Both the Samajwadi party and the BSP had formed a coalition after the 1993 election and although the BJP had emerged as the largest single party it could not win the support of any other group. Mulayam led the coalition but the BSP thought it was getting a raw deal and the Samajwadis were eating into the BSP support. The BSP also claims to be an anarchist party and could have intended to create an anarchical situation in the state but the main reason was that there was no trust between the two and without a modicum of trust a coalition was not possible.

Mayawati became Chief Minister of the state with the outside support of the BJP. This arrangement could not last long and the government was dismissed by the Governor who had the full support of the Centre where he had been a minister in the Narasimha Rao government for some time. Well before the Assembly poll of 1996, Mulayam, using his clout at the Centre and his friendship with Surjeet, had his friend Romesh Bhandari installed as Governor in place of Vora. When the BJP-led government of Vajpayee replaced some governors the opposition parties and some media made a lot of noise but they kept quiet when Vora was replaced, although from time to time Bhandari's misdeeds as Governor were reported in the media.

Kesri's efforts to carry the UF with him were in vain because Mulayam's writ ran in the UF and so far as UP was concerned the UF only looked to Mulayam and Mulayam never looked in any other direction except that Mayawati would not become the CM of Uttar Pradesh. With friend Surjeet by his side, he would have nothing to fear from Kesri's poor onslaught. Kesri even went to the Coordination Committee of the UF, of which N. Chandra Babu Naidu of Telugu Desam, was the convener, to plead his case but the power-drunk UF, mainly at Mulayam's instigation, refused to listen to Kesri.

It was most unusual for the head of another party, however friendly it may be, to attend a meeting of the main committee of a rival political outfit. No UF leader had ever attended a meeting of the CWC (Congress Working Committee) for example, while Kesri was the chief or even while Sonia who ousted him was at the helm. There was no UF as such any longer but whatever remained of it was never invited to a CWC meeting. Even such persons as Laloo Prasad Yadav who was dined by Sonia, a rare honour and occurrence because of the special relationship between the Videshi Bahu as Sonia was known in the media and the Bihar supremo, was not invited to participate in the deliberations of the CWC.

When the BJP leaders sprang a surprise on their political rivals by announcing a six-month rotational arrangement for the BSP, that is Mayawati as Chief Minister, followed by the BJP's leader, Kalyan Singh, as CM the Congress and UF leaders were stunned. The arrangement did not last long because the BSP leader was edgy and not committed to the rotational concept. She did not reckon that the BJP, a 175 member party as compared to her 67 members, would rule almost as she had done during her tenure as Chief Minister.

Interestingly, when she withdrew support from Kalyan Singh after her six month office-turn came to an end and Singh made big inroads in the Congress party as well as her BSP and finished the small Janata Dal group in the assembly, and the very visible majority (of the BJP, the Janatantrik Congress, the BSP and the Janata Dal) voted for the Kalyan Singh government the Governor Romesh Bhandari promptly recommended his rule and dismissal of the Kalyan Singh Government taking advantage of the unruly scenes in the House. The UF, loudly proclaiming adherence to principles equally promptly accepted the recommendation. But for a peculiar provision in the Constitution and but for the fairness of President Narayanan, the UP affairs would have been topsy turvy. Despite the Congress background of Narayanan which often intrudes on his performance as a fair and neutral protector of the Constitution he sent back to the Cabinet of Gujral with Surjeet as the supremo from outside the proposal for reconsideration. The President is empowered to ask the Cabinet to reconsider any of its proposals if he so wishes and whatever the Cabinet does after reconsideration the President has jolly well got to accept. There were differences in the UF government, the Prime Minister himself being not much in favour of Romesh Bhandari's recommmnedation, his wishywashy nature coming to the fore again, and but for Mulayam Singh's enthusiastic welcome to the Bhandari recommendation the Cabinet was not much convinced but had all the same recommended President's rule. When Narayanan returned the Cabinet's proposal for reconsideration the options before Gujral were extremely limited. He had no way out except to swallow his words and let Mulayam and Surjeet stew in their own juice.

Surjeet had to tolerate humiliation after humiliation. The UF government at the Centre, his creature, fell as the rug was pulled by Kesri once again in November 1997 over another trivial issue, this time the Jain Commission's report on the conspiracy angle of the Rajiv Gandhi murder in 1991. The Milap Chand Jain Commission was at the job for years and went on seeking extensions left and right and the Congress government and thereafter the UF governments of Gowda and Gujral also extended its term as if the Jain Commission was wedded to eternity.

The Jain report blaming the DMK government for the tragedy and accusing it of a pro-LTTE bias was utterly flimsy and even its recommendations had also leaked out. The real reason for Kesri's displeasure with the UF government was, as we have seen, different. He wanted a go at the power game himself and that could only happen if the UF was out of power and the President dissolved the 11th Lok Sabha. There was no hope of the Congress gaining a majority or even a largest single party status but there was no harm in trying, the Indian electorate being forgetful could put its faith in the Congress once again, that is what, at least, Kesri thought.

The powergame played by Kesri ultimately left no option before the President but to dissolve the House and order fresh elections to the 12th Lok Sabha. As we said, the Congress had little hope of coming back and fears were widely expressed that the party was going downhill. But it now received a new shot in the arm as another member of the Indira Gandhi family, this time Rajiv Gandhi's Italian widow, came out of her self-imposed wilderness and tried to act as the saviour of a decaying party.

Sonia Gandhi had no inclination all these years to enter politics. Once Rajiv Gandhi as Prime Minister was asked in a TV interview, the kind which has now become a routine affair but with Doordarshan monopoly still prevailing at that time it became a startling media phenomenon. The question was: Why Sonia was not taking any part in politics. Commentators always believe that they have a right to attack the dynastic principle but they alone have the right to legitimise it. Anyway, Rajiv said that Sonia had no inclination and had not participated even in social service. It is fashionable for the wealthy and politically prominent to engage in a bit of "social service" to satisfy their guilty conscience and earn recognition for themselves.

There were deeper reasons for this so-called aversion. Sonia knew nothing of the rudiments of Indian politics. When I worked as a part-time correspondent of an eveninger in Mumbai, the *Afternoon Despatch and Courier*, I had reported for it a story that Sonia, when he accompanied her husband (still Prime Minister) on a visit to south India, had a stopover at Hyderabad airport. Rajiv was yet Prime Minister so Sonia could throw her weight more than she does now. Among the VIPs who met them at the airport were bigwigs of the Telugu Desam party which was in power then as now. P. Upendra, who was then emerging as an important National Front personality (soon to become V.P. Singh's I and B Minister) and was already an important leader of the TD party.

He was seated next to Sonia when she pulled him up for his alleged criticism of the Bofors scandal. Upendra, now safely ensconced in the Congress after he turned coats some years ago, was then taken aback because he had not committed any such sin. It was really K.P. Unnikrishnan, a minister in the V.P. Singh government and elected to the Lok Sabha from Kerala on a number of ocasions who had done it. Both are tall and well built. Once speaking in the House, he had attacked Rajiv and Sonia's Italian relations for their alleged part in the Bofors scandal. It so happened that Unnikrishnan was in Mumbai on the day the story appeared in the *Afternoon* and was asked by newsmen and had to admit that it could be true because Upendra had never said a word about Bofors while he had said plenty about it.

The point is that Sonia did not know chalk from cheese in Indian politics. Upendra had kept quiet about the whole affair in the typical Indian style. Sonia's aversion to politics arose from two standpoints. She did not know a damn about it and she was terribly afraid of the activities of the terrorists, the Punjab variety (now almost extinct) and the latest LTTE. She feared attacks from them on her two children. This was the primary reason for her turning down the Congress leaders' offer made on the morrow of her husband's assassination for her to take up the leadership of the party and become Congress President.

Between 1991 and 1997 more than six years had passed and she had led a sheltered existence as (life) President of the Rajiv Gandhi foundation. She knew very well that the Indian people were both generous and forgetful and had considerable regard for the Indira Gandhi family. The terrorist threat was not so severe as before and, in any case, the target could be somebody else and she was well protected by the Special Protection Group (SPG). The Congress was going to the dogs under Kesri and his ilk and without the Congress clout she would become a nobody in India. If the Congress could seize power through her efforts she could save the reputation of her family, both Rajiv Gandhi and her Italian relatives who mattered most to her. Of course, the easy way to achieve that is to shelve the whole issue. Did she not, on August 13, 1999, when she released the Congress manifesto for the 13th Lok Sabha elections, even say, not in so many words, but by implication that the Italian businessman, Ottavio Quattrocchi, was innocent whereas the Supreme Court had ruled that he could be arrested by the CBI, only, of course, if Malaysia would agree.

So in December 1997 Sonia Gandhi plunged into the electoral fray. (To be precise, December 29). The Indian media, mainly the English newspapers and some TV channels, were agog and almost went ga-ga over this foreigner- turned Indian who had taken no part in politics earlier. Now the Congress President was making welcome statements, without meaning anything good and Sonia was rushing from one city and town to another, by special plane or helicopter to address people. Many attended the rallies, some just out of curiosity, a number because the Congress organisation of the area had brought them there by free rail or bus travel, and some out of a genuine love for the party. The latter, like many in the media, thought that the days of the dynasty were back and the party had acquired a leader of real charisma. In actuality, what they received was a dull recital of written out Hindi speeches, delivered in non-Indian and really speaking European and non-English accent. The speeches would be written in Roman script and ready made speeches would be made available to the media, which was one of the reasons for their enthusiasm because they did not have to spend much effort on the copy except describe the "enthusistic" and almost wild welcome accorded by the crowds to Sonia.

Sonia's effort, however, went in vain because the old party could not win more than its 140 quota in the Lok Sabha. The figure of 140 seats had been reached by the party in 1996 when Narsimha Rao was in decline. Some friendly media said that but for Sonia's campaigning the Congress tally could have even been lower. So much was the plight of the party which claimed that it was 113 years old. In the meantime, the BJP's strength had gone up from 162 to 182. What was immensely more important it had forged alliances with a number of regional parties while its ties with the Shiv Sena in Maharashtra, the Akalis in Punjab and the Samata party in Bihar were intact. It could not, however, break the barrier of 200 seats but its alliance with the Biju Janata Dal in Orissa, the Haryana Vikas Party in Haryana, to which was added the four member strength of the INLD (Indian National Lok Dal) of the same state, the AIADMK of Tamil Nadu, the PMK in the same state, the MDMK again of Tamil Nadu as well as the Tamil Rajiv Congress. Under the banner of the AIADMK these parties, along with the BJP, had fought and won the polls in Tamil Nadu as many as 27 seats out of 39 of Tamil Nadu and one of Pondicherry.

The BJP had another uneasy alliance of importance in West Bengal with the Trinamul Congress which resulted in the seven seat victory of the Trinamul, a breakaway group for from the Congress which incidentally reduced the Congress in West Bengal to the status of a single member party and emerged as the principal opponent, along with the BJP, of the well entrenched CPIM and its Left Front partners in West Bengal. Together, the Left Block, apart from its picking in Kerala and Tripura and some crumbs in other states, was still on 48, less than 50 in the 12th Lok Sabha.

In addition to the BJP's gains in the alliances it had forged recently or those which persisted, the BJP secured powerful support of some erstwhile members of the UF which did not join its alliance formally or otherwise. Among them were the Telugu Desam of Andhra Pradesh, whose leader was N. Chandrababu Naidu, the Chief Minister of Andhra Pradesh whose support was crucial for the alliance to get a clear majority in the Lok Sabha. The Telugu Desam was driven out of the UF by Surjeet's action which wanted a Congress government installed in office at the Centre. The Congress was the Telugu Desam's main rival in Andhra Pradesh and the UF was formed on the basis that the Front would be equidistant from the BJP as well as the Congress. Now that Surjeet and other Left bloc parties had thrown in their lot with the Congress, the TD had to thwart the Congress at the Centre. It could do so only if it supported the BJP. With the TD's "issue-based" support the BJP acquired the necessary majority in the Lok Sabha and even if Mr. Narayanan was inclined to swear in Sonia Gandhi, who had by now ousted Kesri from the Congress President's office, he could not do so without being accused of partiality.

Atal Bihari Vajpayee was sworn in Prime Minister on March 19,1998. The Left Front had, as we have seen, had touched its traditional strength of under 50, to be exact 48 members. This was despite the pre-eminent position the Communists had held in the UF in the past two years. But it was the UF which was not making any progress and several of its constituents suffered badly in the elections. The Janata Dal which had 55 members in the previous House got only six seats and some parties like the Tiwari Congress which at one time had four members in the Lok Sabha had gone out of existence. The UF was in tatters so Surjeet and Basu now hitched their star to Sonia and all their efforts were directed to strengthening the Congress party which cost it the support of the TD, an important member of the UF in the previous House. That was only the beginning so far as the downfall of the UF was concerned.

The Congress party was led by Sonia Gandhi and although Jyoti Basu had referred to her as a "mere housewife" in his statements now forgot all about it and redoubled their efforts he and other CPIM leaders were making to egg on Sonia to throw out the hated BJP. This could not be accomplished unless one of the partners of the BJP alliance, principally the 18-member solid block of the AIADMK, could be persuaded to betray the alliance. Sonia needed no persuasion to oust Vajpayee. For one thing she was thirsting for power and for another Congressmen were dying to seize power by fair means or fowl. They had no need for Surjeet's egging on or persuasions because they were fully persuaded to seize power and could trot out their excuses to do so but needed the oxygen of the AIADMK to their ranks.

Vajpayee was determined not to yield to Jayalalitha's demand for dismissal of the Tamil Nadu government of the DMK party which had brought up as many as 46 corruption cases against her arising out the five year rule of hers in Tamil Nadu which had resulted in such unpopularity of her party that it failed to win a single Lok Sabha seat in the 1996 elections and just three seats in the state assembly elections held simultaneously. The Congress party which was its ally in 1996 had also drawn blank. But in 1998 the will of the voters in Tamil Nadu went in favour of Jayalalitha as we have seen.

Vajpayee having turned down her main demand Jayalalitha had several other demands like portfolios, dismissal or appointments of her favourites in ministerial offices, appointments of her favoured men as income tax officers and so on. There were, in fact, so many items in her personal agenda that it seemed inexhaustible. She seemed to have made her alliance a ground for fulfilling her personal objectives and gaining for herself what she could not win by fair methods. In Jayalalitha's pursuit of her personal targets there was more help forthcoming. She had helped Subramanian Swamy to win a seat for himself and for his largely paper party, the Janata Party, and he had somersaulted from being an enemy of Jayalalitha to becoming her close associate and adviser. In Jayalalitha's case there is only one category of people she likes—cronies—and Swamy was cut out to play that role admirably.

He had made friends with Surjeet whom he gave hopes of his "madam" living the Vajpayee ship, now, this week or today. That day, unfortunately for Surjeet and Swamy, did not arrive in 1998, and until that fateful day in April of 1999 it kept Swamy and Surjeet waiting. Jayalalitha had as many as 46 corruption cases against her in Tamil Nadu. According to an investigative report in the newspaper which circulates in many parts of the country she had total assets before she became Chief Minister of Tamil Nadu in 1991 worth only Rs. 2.01 crores (about 20 million). These went up to the staggering figure of Rs. 66.65 crores (about Rs. 666 million) after she laid down the reins of office.[2]

Swamy's tale is an unmitigated account of betrayal whether it is the BJP, his alma mater in a sense, or Jayalalitha, against whom he had sought and obtained the late Governor Channa Reddy's sanction before knocking at the doors of the High Court in Chennai and later the apex court in Delhi and finally switching sides and falling at the feet of Jayalalitha who rewarded him with a seat from Tamil Nadu and from which (Madurai) he even won, and then his bitter attacks on Jayalalitha when he was totally marginalised and ignored for nomination from Madurai for the 1999 13th Lok Sabha elections. His outbursts and making of charges, his speciality, are unlimited and in the course of the election compaign for his seat in 1999, when he contested the Madurai seat as an independent since he had nowhere to go, he even made a somersault and allegations against his old friend Surjeet's party, the CPIM[3]. By a quirk of fate, Jayalalitha had allotted the Madurai seat to the CPIM, which was her alliance partner, as Surjeet adjectly went on bended knees to the Madam and begged her for some crumbs. She threw these in the form of two seats for the CPIM to contest and one of them was Madurai.

Swamy's discomfiture and fall from the Madam's grace has been dealt with in a later chapter. Suffice it here to say that Swamy would not spare even his trusted friends like Surjeet when he is himself hurt. He told a friendly mediaperson that the CPIM should provide a 'guarantee' it would not join hands with the BJP after elections. He recalled that the Communists had joined hands with the BJP in 1989 to help set up the V.P. Singh government on the ground that fighting corruption of the Rajiv regime was a greater priority than battling communalism. But Dr Swamy told the *Hindustan Times* that "today the same party had no qualms in having a poll alliance with the AIADMK led by Ms Jayalalitha who is facing several corruption charges". According to him, the CPIM stand now was that fighting BJP's communalism was a greater priority.

What is more, Swamy went on to make charges against the CPIM government in Kerala who he said had ensured that a senior Kerala official, heading a TV manufacturing company, had withdrawn his affidavit in (a Chennai) court against Ms Jayalalitha in the colour TV scam case. He asked in his characteristics style: "Did the CPM strike a deal with the AIADMK in this regard in exchange for being allotted the Madurai seat?" Swamy there admitted that Jayalalitha had grave corruption charges against her and the CPIM was hand in glove with her.

The real fact is that in essence there is no difference between Surjeet and Swamy. When the crunch comes both can somersault and both can talk of lofty principles and values when it suits them. The CPIM is, of course, media savvy and enjoys a status among some mediamen who think that all CPIM men are epitomes of renunciation and deserve a place of honour. Most mediamen take Swamy, on the other hand, for what he is a bounder who would be inimical to Jayalalitha one day and fall at her feet the next, if it suits his purpose. Since he is always making charges against all and sundry he often gets to be reported in the media and he has, of course, his media fans who contact him as often as he contacts them to give "stories" and scoops which are generally worthless but occasionally when he is cornered may yield something.

To get back to the main narration, in 1998 Swamy was swinging from utter frustration at one end, for his failure to bring down the Vajpayee government to abundant hope when Jayalalitha changed gear and threatened to topple down the Vajpayee government on some issue affecting her personal interest. He had, in a sense, already had his revenge for denial of a valuable portfolio by running away from the confidence debate which the Vajpayee government won on March 28,1998 by 275 votes to 268. He had pretended to go away to Chennai when everyone in the BJP alliance had to be present in the Lok Sabha to cast his vote and ensure that the government was saved from the Congress and CPIM onslaught. He claimed later that he had thought that the Vajpayee government would win the vote in any case. What he meant was that by absenting he was trying to pull down the government but that was unfortunately not in his hands because one vote was not to make a difference, not yet.

The CPIM, in the meantime, was wrestling with the problem of admitting Laloo Prasad Yadav of the Rashtriya Janata Dal, RJD, into the mythical third front of which it thought it was the leader. How would otherwise the question arise? The CPIM has the habit of making a big issue of everything and Laloo being admitted to the third front was certainly a big issue. As president of the undivided Janata Dal he was even challenging the CPIM boss Surjeet, and had thwarted his attempt to crown Mulayam. Now that he had divided the JD and formed his separate RJD in Bihar he lacked the strength and the character of a national party. What is more, he was steeped in corruption cases arising out of his seven year tenure as Bihar Chief Minister and Finance Minister during which the infamous animal husbandry scam had occurred in his state. It was for that reason that he had to step down as CM but he had compounded the crime by handing over the reins of government to his illiterate wife.

As usual the CPIM leader came to the right decision. He needed the 17 member support of the RJD group in the Lok Sabha and Laloo's image as a "protector" of secularism and his capacity to make in the House were all assets of value. Laloo was kept waiting for some time. Of course, the front was non-existent as some of the key constituents had left because of the pro-Congress policy of the CPIM, the prime mover in the "front" but for Laloo being part of such a combination was important as he wanted to belong somewhere. Laloo was, therefore, made part of the mythical front and by that time Surjeet needed the company of Laloo's RJD more than Laloo needed the protection of Surjeet's third front.

While Surjeet and Basu were busily engaged in egging on Sonia Gandhi to topple the Vajpayee government, Swamy was doing the same job in his own way but Jayalalitha was not yet ready to walk out of the alliance and disrupt the whole government and be responsible for uprooting what Vajpayee and his colleagues had done. Of course, what takes months and perhaps years to build can be destroyed in a matter of days and the final blow can be delivered in an hour. But to arrive at that stage takes time and Swamy was aware of the difficulty as much as Surjeet and company.

In September 1998, the Congress held a convention at Pachmarhi in Congress ruled Madhya Pradesh and held there what the media loved to call "brain storming" session. In a way the term was a misnomer because before you could storm a brain there must be one. The Congress President had around her a bunch of courtiers like R.D.Pradhan, who had served Rajiv loyally as Home Secretary and Sonia liked him for that reason, Vincent George, who had served Rajiv for years in the Congress and the government as a steno and personal assistant and after Rajiv's death Sonia had his services, and the usual crowd of politicians.

Sonia ruled with an iron hand and the Pachmarhi conclave was soon forgotten in the pursuit of power, which as we have seen is the loadster for all Congressmen who sense it from miles like Arjun Singh. They obeyed her because they were convinced that their power dream would be fulfilled through her. They knew that she, was a foreigner, was above the powergame the Congressmen loved to play at all times and as the 'bahu' of Indira Gandhi who had stood by her loyally, as they thought, the family charisma was inherited by it her.

People like P. A. Sangma, whom she consulted in the beginning, had a reputation for integrity which very few politicians enjoyed. The only other person in the Congress ranks one could think of was A.K. Antony who was a politician about whom you could say 'here is a person of absolute integrity.' Sangma felt that the party needed at least two years for rebuilding itself but people like Arjun Singh wanted power here and now and they were the ones close to Sonia, however misleading their advice may be.

Sonia's self-esteem and image in the obliging media got a big boost by the success of the Congress party in the Assembly elections in November 1998 in Delhi and Rajasthan, which the party captured from the BJP, and held its fort in Madhya Pradesh, which the BJP, despite favourable poll opinion surveys, failed to regain. The ignoble defeat suffered by the party in Mizoram in the same assembly elections, when the incumbent Congress regime suffered a crushing defeat, despite the head of the Congress party, herself being a Catholic which almost all Mizos were was forgotten. Nobody in the media paid the slightest attention to this failure and, as we have seen, a leading paper even said that Mizoram was a Congress-ruled state (as late as July 1999).

This victory in the Hindi areas gave an unprecedented fillip to the Congress and people like Swamy and Surjeet were filled with hope that now Sonia would play the toppling game with gusto and the result which they desired but which was beyond their reach because their own parties were too weak to play that game. In Swamy's case, his party was, of course, the AIADMK whose leader Jayalalitha could be a gambler but one who relied on her own judgement rather than the advice of others.

Vajpayee made calculated moves to frustrate the toppling game. He had the bomb to which he now added two more bus, the bus to Lahore and the Budget for 1999-2000 which had a magical effect on the sentiment of the stock exchanges. Between February 1999 and July that year, despite a virtual war in Kargil, the sensex of the Mumbai stock exchange, the barometer of the investor's world, went up by 1,500 points, from 3,000 to 4,500 and even beyond. The bus journey to Lahore followed the interview granted by Nawaz Sharif, the Pakistan Prime Minister, to the *Indian Express* newspaper group editor Shekhar Gupta, in Islamabad in which the Pakistan head of government told Gupta that he would welcome Vajpayee if he were to visit Pakistan and the two countries could come together otherwise too. He mentioned a Delhi to Lahore bus too.

This was vigorously pursued by Vajpayee and the Indian Foreign Office and within just 17 days the Delhi-Lahore bus was on its way and Vajpayee travelled on it for a short distance to Wagha Border from a point within Indian territory near Amritsar. Later, when the Kargil war was fought and won by the brave Indian forces and the world intervened on India's side, and the whole thing ended as a military and diplomatic victory for Vajpayee's "caretaker government", the Congress and the CPIM taunted Vajpayee for ignoring the Pakistani threat to Kargil which, according to them, was planned by Pakistan even as Nawaz Sharif was welcoming Vajpayee with open arms and nobody recalled the role of Shekhar Gupta. If Nawaz Sharif was intent on mischief, as would be apparent to most observers, then Gupta was as much to blame for being beguided by Sharif first and then Vajpayee falling a prey to the Pakistan Prime Minister's protestations of friendship for India. It is typical of the society in which we live that a journalist would walk away with credit when it is due but would hide when the blame is to be shared by him for the same "scoop".

Whatever Vajpayee did for the alliance did not satisfy the madam from Poes Garden in Chennai. She was, of course, being constantly instigated by Swamy who in turn was being kept continuously provoked by Surjeet. It is part of the manouvering instinct in oneself that one accepts all human beings provided they are useful. Surjeet had no compunction in embracing Sonia despite her Italian birth, although his colleague, Jyoti Basu, had once called her a mere housewife. Jayalalitha had gone further and dubbed her a foreigner but now neither Basu nor Jayalalitha cared to remember their slighting words. The CPIM, at the Calcutta session of the party Congress in October 1998, had obtained the CPIM's carte blanche for issue-based support to the Congress which Surjeet and Jyoti Basu interpreted as all-out support to Sonia in ousting Vajpayee.

The Budget for 1999-2000 had produced a favourable image for Vajpayee to which was added his recent triumph in Lahore. But there was no peace for the Prime Minister yet. To add to his woes, Jayalalitha was due to arrive for an extended stay in the capital and Swamy was to throw a tea party in her honour to which all his friends and Jaya's friends were invited. For the first time the two important ladies of the political scenario met at the tea party in the capital in early in April 1999 and this was more than a meeting of hearts. It was a union of two minds who had the common objective of ousting a Prime Minister from office without providing for a replacement government. They failed to realise that the government of India was not a child's play. Their failure to place in position a substitute government after ousting Vajpayee was to prove fatal for the Congress, the CPIM and Jaya's own AIADMK.

The CPIM leaders pretended to be not interested in the Swamy tea party. They were invited to it by Swamy who wanted to make a jamboori show at the Ashok Hotel where the party was hosted by him but behaved as though they were least interested in the entire entertainment drama although their hearts and minds were in it all the time. They made the world feel that they were not bothered by the eatables and the other nourishment served by Swamy. In this respect, they emulated the Chinese Reds who would entertain all the drinking guests as though it was their life's mission to please them but would not partake of the drinks themselves. Perhaps they did it after the last guest was out which, of course, means that they have to wait for a pretty long time. Some of the guests may not leave at all.

Some foolishly raised the question of resources for such a big party as Swamy was considered unable to meet the heavy expenses. They should remember that it is our custom for the chief guest to foot the bill in such cases it being presumed that she or he is more interested than the host in making a success of the occasion. At least, both were equally interested but Jaya having a lot of dough could have relieved Swamy of the cares of financing such a big party with his limited resources. After all, Jaya paid as much as Rs. 40,000 per day for at least ten days for a whole floor of a five star hotel in the capital when she camped in Delhi to oust Vajpayee after withdrawing her support a week earlier. Sketchy reports of her royal living appeared but no investigative journalist dared to probe either the fact of luxurious living of Jaya and her formidable entourage nor the source for so much money. Is not there and Indian proverb that the source of a river and the family tree of a seer (rishi) should never be probed. Jaya is no rishi but no journalist, nor his proprietor, would dare to investigate the matter. So much for investigative journalism.

On April 17, Vajpayee government fell by just one vote, 270 against the government's 269, in the Lok Sabha. The vote surprised many knowledgeable people who were led to believe by the turn of events that the Government would go through. First the DMK, a loyal supporter of the CIPM-led "Third" front, which had its ministers in the UF government of Gowda and Gujral, had turned a staunch supporter of the Vajpayee government for the simple reason that its arch rival in Tamil Nadu, the AIADMK of Jaya, had now withdraw from the Vajpayee-led alliance. But the DMK had only six members in the House against the AIADMK 18 (the reason in the main, why Surjeet had opted for her and deserted the time-tested DMK) and so the BJP's party managers had the job of covering the gap of 12 members.

Surjeet and company had left nothing to chance in organizing the downfall of the Vajpayee government and, of course, Sonia who had visions of ruling a foreign country by the democratic process had thrown in everything in the ring to topple Vajpayee. Apart from lining up the entire opposition, mainly the organized parties and groups, there was the question of very small parties or individual members. Several of these had been won over by the BJP which had also a notable success in getting the INLD, Indian National Lok Dal, a four member Haryana group of the former (and as it turned out, the future) Chief Minister of the state Om Prakash Chautala, to support it.

On the eve of the voting day, on April 16, the five member BSP group, led by the formidable Mayawati, announced that it would abstain. This eased the situation further for the BJP and its allies and they looked forward to a favourable verdict as the house met for the crucial vote after Prime Minister's spirited reply to the debate on the vote of confidence. It must be recalled that President Narayanan had displayed his anti-Vajpayee attitude once again when he asked Vajpayee, as demanded by the Congress and the CPIM-led Left Front, to seek a vote of confidence in the Lok Sabha after Jaya had withdrawn her group's support.

The question was whether the Prime Minister should go out to seek a vote of confidence or the opposition should move a vote of no-confidence or have recourse to a cut in the budget demands for grants which, if adopted, would instantly require the government to resign, or do anything which would compel the opposition to move in the matter. The BJP and its allies had opposed it in so many words. Yet the President chose to ask Vajpayee to seek a vote of confidence and thereby display his partisan attitude.

Secondly, the President, being an active participant in political affairs and generally an active head of state instead of being a shrewd observer of the scene as the Constitution requires him to be, often issues, or causes to be issued denials and refutation of some stories involving the President or his Rashtrapati Bhavan. But when Mamata Banerjee, leader of the seven member Trinamul party in the Lok Sabha, accused him of seeing off Sonia Gandhi to the door of his study in Rashtrapati Bhavan, Sonia being singled out for the honour, Narayanan did not contradict Mamata.[4]

Narayanan had worked for years as a foreign service official and had been promoted to the position of Ambassador in the course of his career.

He had been Ambassador to China at a critical time in the now-friendly no-hostile relations between the two countries, under the Congress governments for many years. He had been a minister of state under Rajiv and then Narasimha Rao and was chosen by the Congress party, making it clear that he was a member of the Sheduled Castes, for the office of the Vice President of India and then sponsored him for the office of President. In both capacities he has acquitted himself with honour and earned a reputation for fairness.

He did not rise in the IFS hierarchy to be Foreign Secretary, the highest office open to an Indian Foreign Service officer, but that does not take away from his success as a diplomat. I had met him in Bangkok when he was Ambassador of India and I was touring South East Asia as AIR's correspondent in the region. Then as Director of DAVP (Directorate of Advertising and Visual Publicity) I had the honour to invite him in 1979 to head the jury for the selection of our annual awards for excellence in printing and designing. He was then Vice Chancellor of JNU (Jawaharlal Nehru University, one of the many Centrally-financed universities in the capital) and he readily accepted and I had to inaugurate the work of the jury. On both occasions, I had found Narayanan a self-effacing and unassuming person but I could see that a fire was burning inside.

In other respects too, Narayanan has proved that he is not merely a figurehead, as the Constitution would require him to be, but an active head of state. He himself said that he is not a rubber stamp President and had made the government arrange for his interview by a left-wing journalist on the eve of independence day 1998. It is curious that he did not opt for it in 1997 nor in 1999. Perhaps he wanted to take full advantage of the uneasy ties of Jayalalitha with Vajpayee and tell the Prime Minister indirectly that he was a super boss. No doubt, he saved the BJP's Kalyan Singh government in UP in the October 1997 by asking the unsteady government of Gujral to reconsider its recommendation for imposition of President rule in UP, as recommended by the partisan Governor Romesh Bhandari. But Sonia Gandhi entering the scenario of Indian polity in March 1998 made all the difference to the perspective of the man.

That was to become evident in a few days when the Vajpayee government was pulled down without the Congress, the CPIM and others in the opposition making sure they would be able to replace it. In particular, Laloo Prasad Yadav, RJD leader and hero of the Congress and the CPIM, had boasted in the Lok Sabha, on April 15 that they (meaning the opposition parties) would be able to offer an alternative in 'five minutes'.The five minutes of Laloo extended to five hours and even five days and more without the opposition being able to make the President invite Sonia or Basu (who was now willing like Barkis) to form the government.

It is easier to destroy something and difficult to build something anew. Mulayam Singh Yadav, leader of the 20 member block in the 12th Lok Sabha, who had predicted the fall of the Vajpayee government times without number, was the one now to refuse Sonia the support of his party in forming the government. Sonia had claimed the support of 279 members, beyond the simple majority figure of 273 (actually 271 would have done), but this figure included Mulayam's men. Besides Mulayam, two of Surjeet's Left front partners, the RSP and the FB, had said it on many occasions that while they were all for the fall of the Vajpayee government (and had actually voted for it on April 17) they were opposed to the Congress being installed in its place. The reason was that they believed in the theory of equidistance from the two national parties, the BJP and the Congress, while the CPIM, meekly followed by the CPI, wanted somehow to see Sonia crowned.

Sonia was destined to fail. She took and was given an abnormally long time by President Narayanan to put together her supporters and had to finally admit on April 25 the utter failure of hers, saying she had less members than she had originally claimed the support of. Mulayam's reason for denial of support to Sonia had a lot to do with his support base in his native UP where the Muslim votebank was being perceived to be hijacked by Sonia Gandhi.

As we have seen the two smaller members of the Left Front themselves went against the CPIM and the total effect of it all was to defeat Sonia Gandhi's move to become the Prime Minister of India.

Now the question arose should Basu not try and become head of the Indian government while the going was good? The CPIM Politburo met on April 25 and Sonia had promised to let Basu know of her CWC decision on the issue of Basu forming a government. The Politburo had retired for lunch and perhaps for the afternoon siesta (which old people like Basu (86) and Surjeet do need) when Sonia rang him up to say that the CWC had "unanimously" decided not to back a "third front" government, in other words,not to back Basu for the Prime Ministership. That the decision was unanimous would naturally include the negative vote of Sonia herself and she could have strongly conveyed her support to the CWC if she felt it that way, even if she did not exercise her vote.[6]

The CPIM Politburo which met on April 25 went against its own party Congress in October1998 in Calcutta where the party's plenary session had decided against participation in a minority government. But in the face of the decision, taken in a different context, of course, the Politburo had decided in favour of Basu leading a government, if only Sonia Gandhi had succeeded in pleadging the party's support to a CPIM-led cabinet *a la* the 1996 and 1997 experiment. How foolish of the CPIM even to expect that the Congress could commit the same mistake again and what guarantee was that Sonia would not pull the rug from under Basu's feet in the same manner in which Kesri had done it to Gowda first and then to Gujral?

Whether it is the CPIM or any other party there is no difference in grabbing power if it is to be had just for fun. But power seldom is available for nothing; a lot of effort has to be made and, as Chandrashekhar would tell you, many principles have to be sacrificed and you have to go on bended knees for your minority regime to be backed from the outside. Basu's CPIM, even with the loyal CPI and the two small Left Front partners, was less than Chandrashekhar's 65 members when he got Rajiv Gandhi's Congress party of 192 members to back him.

Basu had called the CPIM's decision not to allow him to head the UF government in May 1996 as a "historical blunder" and had even rewarded his biographer for including his quotes in the Bengali book on him. In his "Memoirs" he himself had said: "Surjeet and I favoured participation in the government. But we were in (a) minority..."[7] But Basu contradicts himself in the same Memoirs when he says:'... but we in the CPIM do not act like the bourgeois parties; the policy and party directives are always more important than the individual..." How much more important? When the CPIM supported Sonia had failed to form a government, as she admitted to the media on April 24, and Mulayam had proposed his name as a future Prime Minister duly backed by that epitome of honesty-the AIADMK supremo J.Jayalalitha, the only thing necessary for Basu was to approach Sonia Gandhi and how she flatly denied the support we have seen.

Basu has even now expressed himself in favour of making another try at the job after the 13th Lok Sabha elections if only there is a situation similar to 1996,[8] the Congress not able to form a government but willing to support from the outside a Third Front goverhment and the BJP and its allies scoring so low that they cannot even dream of forming a government and the President being ever ready to swear in Basu. So many ifs and buts. That is no reason for Basu not to offer his services and like Barkis to be willing.

The recriminations and bitter exchanges that followed the failure of the Congress to install Sonia Gandhi and of Surjeet to do that as well as fix up Basu for the Prime Minister's job were to be seen to be believed. Friends fell out and called each others the choicest names. Sonia Gandhi's principal adviser in the toppling exercise and later also, Arjun Singh' called

Mulayam Singh an imposter of secularism. Mulayam had committed an unforgivable sin by not backing Sonia in the eyes of Congressmen and the CPIM and Mulayam returned the compliment when he called the Congress a communal party. Surjeet vent his spleen on both Mulayam and the Congress, but not on Sonia almost saying "plague on both your houses". That was only a momentary reaction because he was soon going to Jayalalitha seeking support in the 13th Lok Sabha elections and it was too precious for him to waste words in anger.

Narayanan dissolved the Lok Sabha on April 26 and before the parties could engage themselves in the bitter election compaign two important events occurred which had a great impact on the electoral prospects of the Congress, the CPIM and other parties including the BJP. Sharad Pawar. P.A. Sangma and Tariq Anwar were expelled from the Congress party after Sonia staged a week-long drama of resignation because the expelled tall leaders had called for an Indian born leader to be elected for the office of Prime Minister, which ruled out Sonia, and secondly Pakistan infiltrated Kargil which made Vajpayee an instant hero as he won the war in military terms as well as diplomatic.

Why did Mayawati change her stand of declared neutrality to one of active participation in favour of Sonia Gandhi which converted Vajpayee's majority in to a minority? Was it her inherent urge to plunge the scene into one of chaos and anarchy or was it a case of machinations of Sonia and her advisers who persuaded Kanshiram, boss to Mayawati, to intervene and save the situation ? We shall never know the truth but the fact remains that Mayawati and her faithful four members, making five in all, voted for ushering in chaos which hopefully was soon cleared up.

Surjeet would not be his own meddling self if he did not try his hand at the toppling game, persuading a Sonia Gandhi who really speaking needed no persuasion at all, only support for her effort in return for nothing, and thinking that Mulayam would do his bidding. Surjeet behaved throughout 1998 and 1999 as though the Vajpayee government was so fragile that he had only to blow a whistle and the government would come crashing down. Sonia acted, more out of her inexperience in the art of politics and always ready to carry out the prompting of her close advisers, like Arjun Singh, who always think that politics is all about a toppling exercise. Narayanan was anxious to swear in Sonia Gandhi but did not want his reputation for fairness to be sullied.

In the entire exercise of the CPIM tinkering at the BJP-led alliance Surjeet relied on two figures—Swamy to make the madam of Poes Garden to switch her loyalty from Vajpayee to another madam, Sonia Gandhi. The utter lack of principles on the part of the CPIM as a party and Surjeet as a leader resulted in the erosion of the Third Front or, as Sonia sarcastically referred to the fourth front, (the first time she showed herself capable of such sophistication). In fact the third front evaporated before Surjeet's very eyes–first the Telugu Desam, a staunch supporter of the UF and its leader, Chandrababu Naidu who acted as the convener of the UF Coordination Committee, then the National Conference and the AGP and finally the DMK of Tamil Nadu. Karunanidhi, Tamil Nadu Chief Minister and president of the DMK, had to say that communalism was preferrable to the corruption of Jayalalitha whom Surjeet was openly courting for the AIADMK's support in his destructive plans.

The CPIM's dream of installing Sonia on the throne of India lay shattered as also its urge to bring the Congress round to destroy the BJP. From a position of strength he had reduced himself and the CPIM to one running around to save themselves.

REFERENCES

1. Sonia Fires Bofors salvo at BJP Government, *Hindustan Times*, Delhi, August 14, 1999.
2. *The Jayalatitha beggage*, *Indian Express*, April 28,1999.
3. *Swamy taunts CPM for its 'somersaults'*, *Hindustan Times,* Delhi' August 17, 1999.
4. *Indian Express,* Delhi, April 28,1999- "President biasw: Mamata".
5. It is not for nothing that the CPI is often dubbed as a proto type of the much bigger CPIM. See the Delhi *Indian Express*, of August 18,1999 which has a headline "CPI manifesto a clone to CPM's". Small parties like the CPI (total Lok Sabha strength in the best of times 12 and the worst seven) are in the habit of issuing their manifesto and you produly hold it up before TV cameras only to satisfy your conscience that they are also there. But the essence of CPI's manifesto has been summed up here and it only says that it will support a Congress government after the polls, like the CPIM.
6. "Now comrades fight over Basu, " *Indian Express*, Delhi, April 27,1999.
7. "Comrade Basu on himself", *Indian Express,* Delhi, May 2, 1999.
8. "Basu shies from 'historic blunder", *Pioneer*, Delhi, August 18, 1999.

4
IN THE BACKYARD

In the exultation of the fine victory in December 1971 when India humbled the might of the Pakistan army in the plains of what was then East Pakistan, and a sovereign Bangladesh was born, the people of West Bengal voted the Congress to power. The voter attributed the success to Indira Gandhi, who was an effective Prime Minister and successfully guided the nation during the critical days of the Bangladesh liberation war. She was also the leader of the Congress party which was now voted to power in the state which, alas for the Congress, was the last time it enjoyed power in the state.

The CPIM-led Left Front was in a coalition with Ajoy Mukerjee's Bangla Congress in 1967 and 1969. It was seeking power for itself in the 1972 poll to the state assembly but secured only seven seats. It accused the Congress of rigging thc polls and was thus administered the dose of its own medicine. It has become customary for the CPIM to rig the polls after it came to power in West Bengal in 1977 and mastered the art of poll management soon thereafter. This has been the charge of the opposition.

In reality it was the success of the Indian armed forces and Mukti Bahini (Liberation Army) of Bangladesh and of the will of the people of that country who wanted to drive away forever the tyrant from West Pakistan which now became Pakistan.[1] It is a different story that many in Bangladesh have forgotten (and forgiven) the atrocities of the Pakistanis and even the blood shed by the jawans of India in their cause. It is also a different story that the Indian Communists who played no significant part in the liberation have tried to exploit the Bengali-Bengali bhaiship on many occasions and have openly or clandestinely welcomed the illegal Bangladeshi immigrants because they thereby become CPIM's voters in elections. But if the CPIM and the weak CPI try their utmost to install Sonia Gandhi in the office of the Prime Minister, after what the Congress had done to them in rejecting Jyoti Basu's candidature in April this year, anything could happen.

But if we recall the abuses they showered on Sonia's mother-in-law after the 1972 debacle they experienced the changing face of the Comrades could be seen. Then they had called Indira Gandhi a semi-Fascist, the usual Communist expression for any party and individual they do not like, and the Congress party of unleashing semi-fascist terror[2] in West Bengal. They also accused the Congress party of practising rigging in the elections. But when their turn came in the next assembly poll, the CPIM, which dominated the Left Front, emerged victorious and for the past 22 years the Congress party had the misfortune of crying fowl.

The Congress tried every trick in the trade but has not been able to turn Jyoti Basu and his comrades out. Rajiv Gandhi was still at the peak of his form, or very nearly so, when the state elected its assembly again in 1987. Rajiv personally campaigned hard for his Congress party then, aligned with the elusive Subhash Ghising, leader of the Gorkha National Liberation Front (GNLF) in Darjeeling, believed M.J. Akbar, who was then well on the way to becoming a camp follower of Rajiv, when the journalist-turned-politician-turned-journalist told him that he would win. If one were to say that the CPIM tries to scare away the Congress from West Bengal when it tries to fire its anti-BJP gun from the shoulders of Sonia Gandhi now we could not be much in the wrong.

Miss Mamata Banerjee, founder and all in all of the Trinamul Congress, now the CPIM's worry no. 1, is a by-product of the constant infighting in the West Bengal Congress in which many leaders appear and disappear. Pranab Mukherjee looks larger than life in Delhi, where he is counted by the media as a top leader of the Congress party, but he is a virtual nobody in his home state. He is not even the leader of a faction. In 1986, when Rajiv Gandhi had ousted him from power and every position of vantage, he had formed a separate Congress (S) but in the assembly poll in West Bengal in 1987 his newly formed party performed miserably. He had no option but to return to the parent body like a wet cat holding his tail between his legs. But the case with Mamata is different. She could even challenge the might of Sonia and of CPIM which specialises in holding rallies and public meetings in Calcutta and disrupt the traffic and drive away the industrialists. What the CPIM could do, Mamata could do even better. She taunted the Congress party as the CPIM's B team, following the sport language which could be well understood in sports-loving West Bengal. The Congress leaders envied her for her crowd-pulling power because she could outdo even the Communists but could not bring themselves to accept her as a leader. Sonia supported them and finally she broke away from the parent body.

She defied Sonia and the then Congress President, Sitaram Kesri, who specialised in talking glibly, without meaning anything, and formed the Trinamul (literally grassroots') Congress on the eve of the 1998 Lok Sabha poll. Her party had seat adjustments with the BJP trying to open its account in the new region, which had virtually become a preserve of the Communists. As we have seen, the Communists lost their influence all over India save the states of West Bangal, and by rotation with the local Congress in Tripura and Kerala.

In the February 1998 elections to the 12th Lok Sabha, Mamata's new party, making a debut virtually ousted the Congress from Calcutta city and its suburbs, she also helped the BJP to secure a seat from the state. She became a thorn in the side of the Communists in the house because she could expose their tall talk and their claim to wisdom. She had an uneasy relationship with the BJP all through 1998 and part of 1999 but the media which naturally played up some of her tantrums overlooked the fact that she was a staunch Vajpayee loyalist. In that she reflected the popular mood in India which gave increasing evaluation to the Prime Minister. If in May 1999 the people gave him 48 per cent approval, in the favourable trend which followed his Kargil victory the people rated hm even higher. His standing had gone upto 57 per cent as against Sonia's 27 per cent in August 1999[3]. That was when the 8,000 voters in the Timespoll were asked who was the best leader and they replied Vajpayee "57 per cent" but the *Times of India* had to admit that a big majority, 64 per cent of the respondents "say that they are satisfied with the performance of the Government; this is a much improved rating compared to the level of around 40 per cent estimated in early 1999. Mr Vajpayee's rating as Prime Minister, at 74 per cent, is even higher than that of his government."

In April 1999, when the CPIM was helping the Congress in the ousting the Vajpayee government, the Calcutta high court disqualified a leftist MLA of the West Bengal assembly. He was Makhanlal Bangal, belonging to one of the smaller parties in the CPIM-led Left alliance, the Biplabi Bangla Congress.[5] Allegation against the CPIM and its allies have always been made about its rigging of the elections, both for the state assembly and the Lok Sabha, but this was the first time in the 22-year history of the Left Front's rule in the state that a legislator of the ruling party was unseated by the high court for corrupt practices during his "election".

The verdict came at a time when the chairman of one of the few remaining big industries, Satyabrata[6] Ganguly of the Exide Industries, had been abducted by professional kidnappers from his morning jog and a few days later returned unharmed to his posh Calcutta residence without Basu's police lifting their little finger on his behalf. A hefty amount was naturally paid to the abductors but there was complete hushhush on the part of the Exide industries and the Ganguly family. The kidnappers were, in fact, so kind to the Exide chairman that they gave him some money to enable his to buy air-conditioned rail coach ticket and pay for his taxi in Calcutta city. As usual, Basu's deputy, Home (Police) Minister Buddhadeb Bhattacharya, generally touted as Basu's successor whenever he retires (Basu is fond of making statements of his impending retirement) had meanwhile goofed up when he announced that Ganguly was back home when he was nowhere to be found in Calcutta.

The important thing was that Basu's police had no role to play in the whole episode. No doubt, there are instances of moneyed men, and sometimes even far from wealthy men, being kidnapped for ransom in Delhi and elsewhere, and even in West Bengal, but at a time when industry is on the run from West Bengal a top industrialist being abducted from near his residence was cruelty indeed on the part of the Comrades.

Incidentally, the Communists pride themselves on the fact that they are secular and attack the BJP as communal. Basu, in particular, has made it a habit to call the BJP both communal and barbarous. Undoubtedly, the demolition of the Babari mosque in Ayodhya was a reprehensible act but so far it has not been established that the BJP was responsible as an organisation for the act, which is why Basu is fond of calling the BJP barbarous. On the contrary, no less a person than the Home Minister in the Narasimha Rao government, Shankerrao Chavan, accused his own Prime Minister (much after the ghastly incident, of course) that Rao had not allowed him to use the Central paramilitary forces against the alleged *Kar Sevaks* who demolished the mosque. The Muslim masses, acting as voters in several elections in the nineties, punished Rao's Congress party.

Was the laziness of Basu's police and their total failure to get Ganguly back an act of civilised behaviour? What happened in the February 1999 ugly incident in Calcutta's famous Eden Garden stadium was even worse. India then had played Pakistan whose tour was specially sponsored by Vajpayee, even after the Shiv Sena, an ally of the BJP, had stoutly opposed it, in the first of three preliminary matches of the Asian three-nation test series, the third nation being Sri Lanka. On the final day of the match the Calcuttans in the stadium threw bottles and stones in the Eden Garden ground. The police thereupon emptied the entire stadium, presumably under Basu's orders, and the formalities of the match were gone through like a funeral.

Vajpayee had taken personal interest in the matter and, as we have noted, had gone against the wishes of the BJP's oldest ally, the Shiv Sena, whose followers had gone to the mad extent of digging up the Delhi pitch where one of the matches in the series between India and Pakistan was to be played. Vajpayee had sent down his Home Minister., L.K.Advani, to Mumbai to persuade the Sena supremo, Bal Thackeray, and he was sufficiently mollified to call off his agitation against the Pakistan team's visit of India. The Delhi pitch was also repaired and one of the tests was played there which India won.

If, as alleged by Basu, the BJP was barbarous and communal, what to talk of the behaviour of Basu's own Calcuttans who prevented all play in the test at the Eden Garden and the action of Basu's police which emptied the entire stadium ? True, there was enough provocation from a Pakistani fielder, the world's fastest bowler, Shoaib Akhtar, who stopped the world's best batsman and a national hero in India, Sachin Tendulkar, when Sachin was taking a run and Akhtar's action resulted in his being run out. There was insufficient evidence that Akhtar's act was entirely intentional but what mattered was that the crowd at the stadium believed so and it appeared to be so to many TV viewers. The technicalities of the cricket rules notwithstanding, the relevant question in the present context of the CPIM's role in national politics is: if the Calcutta crowd was so secular, as Basu would have us believe, why did it obstruct the test match and if Vajpayee's BJP was so communal and barbarous, as alleged by Basu, why did Vajpayee intervene to allow the Pakistan tour to go ahead.

Indeed the question can be asked also about the behaviour of another crowd, that of Bangalore, later in the year when it interrupted the proceedings of a one-day match between India and Pakistan when the then Karnataka government was supposedly secular and Vajpayee and his BJP communal and barbarous as alleged by Basu. Vajpayee allowed the Indo-Pakistan matches to go on uninterrupted even when the situation in Kargil developed and India was playing in the World Cup in Britain and also met and defeated Pakistan in a Super Six match and the Kargil threat had clearly surfaced.

Going back to the disqualification of a Left Front MLA by the Calcutta High Court, it is common knowledge that both the CPIM and the Congress are guilty of rigging the polls in areas they can influence. Yet they accuse each other of doing it, particularly in West Bengal which has been under

Communist rule for 22 years and the Congress has little hope of re-entering the scene now that Sonia wants to ride piggybank on the shoulders of the CPIM to the office of Prime Minister, a false hope but seriously entertained by both sides. So far as the charges of rigging the polls is concerned, the difference between the two organisations is that the CPIM does a thorough job of it while the Congress does a half-hearted job. The CPIM never gets caught, except in the case alluded to, and the law is that only those are guilty who are caught in the act and against whom evidence can be adduced.

In the West Bengal countryside the rule of the thana-in-charge and of the revenue patwari prevails as much as in other parts of the country. The vital difference is that the CPIM has mastered the art and technique of keeping the people under the party's thumb and has also enlisted the services of the relevant bureaucrats in the task. They ensure that the entries in the electoral rolls are properly made, the right people are posted as the presiding and polling officers in the polling booths, and every other factor goes in favour of the ruling party.

Apart from preaching the "welfare measures" adopted by the CPIM in power for the last 22 years, the Comrades also ensure that the non-official agencies and individuals, under their control, are manned by the party nominees and one of the tasks they perform is to keep a watchful eye on the parliamentary and assembly elections whenever they are held. All this mechanism can be more successfully operated in the rural areas of West Bengal because in Calcutta city the people are trained, by the CPIM itself, to protest against such interference and they would approach the media. Not that the media are not vigilant about the affairs in the rural areas but everything in West Bengal is concentrated in Calcutta and the countryside is rather quiet and docile. In much of Calcutta, therefore, the CPIM is not so successful in elections as it concentrates in the rural backyard.

India is no doubt, a democratic country and the people choose their representatives by the exercise of their adult franchise. But there are a number of processes before you enter the polling booth on the fateful day. The Comrades take charge of the problems and relieve you of the worries on that account. For instance, if your name is not in the electoral rolls, the Comrades would help you to get yourself registered or solve all those numerous problems which you have to face. Naturally, you feel grateful to the Comrades for their help and they, in turn would inform you of the CPIM candidates in the next assembly or Lok Sabha poll. You would naturally arrive at the booth to cast your "valuable" vote in favour of the CPIM candidates but if you have changed your mind, for some reason, in the meantime the Comrades are there at the booth remind you of your sacred duty. If in spite of your obligation being doubly reinforced you are going to exercise your free will the presiding and polling officers are there to help you make up your mind.

Of course, all this depends on the vagaries of the election process which might result on your vote being cast by a CPIM enthusiast before you enter the polling booth. This Red supporter has impersonated you with the connivance of the officials and the agents of the other parties, if they have not been purchased already, can make some noise. If they make more than "some" noise they are liable to be arrested by the state police many of whom consider it a sacred duty to act in the interest of the CPIM.

With this kind of elaborate skullduggery the CPIM is able to retain control of West Bengal having lost all its influence in other parts of India except Kerala and Tripura where, as we have seen, they have to alternate with the Congress. In West Bengal, the CPIM has so emasculated the Congress, by promising its Central leadership, meaning Sonia, support in the ambition of become Prime Minister, that is has abandoned the fight long ago. The Trinamul and to an extent the BJP, in West Bengal, have taken on themselves the responsibility to fight the CPIM. The state Congress, as we have noted, is otherwise also weak and fractionalised and some like Pranab appear big in Delhi but count for nothing in the affairs of their own state.

The CPIM cannot 'however, be denied its due in such matters as land reforms, incomplete and unsatisfactory as they are. In West Bengal, as in the rest of the country, this is extremely important because the cultivator must be the owner of the land, the title deed must be in his own name and justice must be done to the farmer. This is crucial to the success of agriculture and the satisfaction of the farmer on which depends the prosperity of the entire rural sector. Harekrishna Konar, president of the West Bengal unit of the All India Kisan Sabha, an organisation of farmers now largely defunct, and first CPIM minister for Land and Land Revenue,[7] did much work for distributing land among the farmers and drew up a broad framework of the CPIM's land policy. "The primary task was abolition of large-scale holdings and distribution of land to the landless," he said.

According to Suryakant Mishra, West Bengal's present Land and Panchayat Minister,[8] land reform is a major success of the Left Front government since 1967. He claimed a membership of the 10 million for the Kisan Sabha, which would seen to make every farmer in the state a member of a largely inactive organisation. It of course, suits the CPIM to inflate the membership of its front organisations to make itself look so popular. If

Mishra is to be believed the CPIM has distributed 10 lakh (one million) acres of land to the farmers. It must be remembered that in 1967 and later in 1969, after the first government was dismissed by Indira Gandhi, the CPIM was one of the 13 parties in the coalition government of Ajoy Mukherjee, and in 1972, after the second government of Ajoy Babu was also dismissed, the Congress had emerged in the assembly election as a majority party and the CPIM was routed. From 1977 onwards, of course, the CPIM had a straight run. It is possible as Mishra says, the distribution had taken place in the years in which the CPIM was one of the partners in a coalition, albeit a dominant element.

The newspaper, the *Telegraph* of Calcutta, which interviewed Mishra said 2,38,000 acres of land was distributed in the rule of the first of the United Front government. (Possibly part of it in 1968 also). In the reign of the second UF government, another eight lakh acres (800,000) acres was distributed to the same categories of farmers, namely the landless and the marginal farmers. If these figures are correct the Left Front did pretty little by way of distribution in the 22 years of its unalloyed rule since 1977. Possibly, it was busy in ensuring that the land distributed would not be grabbed back by the landowners and attend to related problems and court cases.

But, according to Mishra, the land was acquired in the years 1967 and 1969 and "the primary task was to acquire the land and distribution was completed mainly in the LF regime. "In a way he has confirmed the newspaper's assumptions and also tried to dispel the impression that nothing of substance was done either in the two UF governments or in the long reign of the LF. Mishra claims that even now, on an average 2,000 acres are being distributed every month. He admits that land reform is a continuous process (there must be some finality about it brother). The original plan of Konar, according to the highly sympathetic book of Sen Gupta, the CPIM was to encourage farmers' cooperatives which remains a day dream. Nehru tried it out, without any success, on an all India scale and the CPIM would only burn its fingers if it tried it out in their limited field. The Chinese tried and failed and the CPIM lays great store by what the Chinese do.

Contrary to the tenet that the boss lays down the law, which would require Mishra to toe the line of Surjeet who tries very hard to see that Sonia and her Congress party are gifted the reign of India, Mishra assails the Congress in these words: "What the Congress claims is not a fact but announced data. The job has been done in the Left Front regime only. This is an established fact."[9] Mishra was replying to the *Telegraph* correspondent, Sujit Roy's question about the Congress claim that during its five year rule from 1972-77 (not 1971 to 1977, as the paper would have it) the West Bengal government had acquired 632,000 acres of land and even distributed it among 2.5 million farmers. "Mishra did not directly reply to the question and merely said that the claim was not a "fact."

But surprisingly Mishra himself volunteered the information that feudalism, which he said in one breath, no longer existed in the state, "has come back in a new form. The *zamindars* (landowners) today, on the one hand, are socially and economically powerful, and are, on the other, ploughing their own lands. They are basically rich and own different businesses. They are not *mahajan* (money-lenders) but they provide loans and get interest."[10]

In other words, the landowning class is well entrenched and the CPIM is able to do pretty little about it. Mishra also went on to admit that the government was facing hundreds of litigations from the owners over acquiring excess and 'benami' (land or property held in others' names) lands, "More than 190,000 acres of land is left untouched due to these legal proceedings."[11]

Thus despite Mishra's variety of claims he had to admit that the legal and other difficulties and the appearance of the landlords in other garb including that of providers of the much needed credit.

Land reform is a difficult task and despite the tall claims, as in the Mishra interview, the Communist regime in West Bengal has to be given the credit that it has attempted to solve the problem. In most of the states, where also this problem exists the governments have sought to solve it in largely successful or partly successful measure. In Bihar, no real attempt has been made and all the Laloo rhetoric is intended to throw dust into the eyes of the farmers as evidenced by repeated massacres by the landowners illgeal army 'the Ranbir Sena' or by the CPIM's violent Naxalites masquerading as upholders of the rights of the landless. The media, as usual, show little understanding of the problem 'for example, when they refer to the Ranbir Sena as an "army of the landlords". These are only small farmers and when they are attacked by the Communist armed gangs they also have to protect themselves as the administration does not raise its little finger.

Several Congress leaders are themselves owners of large holdings held under relatives names often called as 'benami'. This is done to evade the clutches of the Land Ceiling Acts of different states. The former Prime Minister and Congress President, P.V.Narasimha Rao, is among the big names of large owners of land and even a former Congress leader G.K.

Moopanar whose TMC was an offshoot of the Congress, is another. In his case, one can say that once a Congressman always a Congressman. The efforts of the state governments to increase the productivity of the land and give gainful employment to the rural people have not been rewarded always as evidenced by the existence of vast slums where people live under sub-human conditions. Among the dwellers of the JJ (*jhuggi-jhonpdi*) makeshift complexes live rural (some urban) people from different states and, of course, the illegal migrants from Bangladesh. And the CPIM hugs the latter because they constitute the CPIM's votebank.

The land reforms must be reckoned as one of the CPIM's notable achievements although the process has hardly been completed and the large hordes of lawyers many of them CPIM supporters, thrive on the miseries of the landless and on the landowners. But apart from that what are the other "achievements"? Are there any, in fact, for the 22 year rule by a single party, of course in association with a host of small parties which are all obliged to the big brother for their existence? What about higher education which was once the pride of West Bengal? We cannot do better than quote Santosh Bhattacharya, a former Vice Chancellor of the famed Calcutta University.

He said in an article: "Except one or two instances, the top positions in universities have always been filled by persons loyal to the ruling party.[12] "Bhattacharya was commenting on the appointment of Surabhi Banerjee as Pro Vice-Chancellor of Calcutta University. She had written a biography of the Chief Minister, Jyoti Basu. Santosh Bhattacharya spoke from the high pedestal of his experience and according to him this was coming. The CPIM have "never given a damn" for such "bourgeios" norms as "excellence, seniority, rank etc. for nominating candidates for top positions in universities. They started by pushing a junior professor of the university with no experience in university administration as Pro Vice-Chancellor and then as Vice-Chanceller."'Santosh Bhattacharya then went on to say a college principal was straightaway made Vice Chancellor of a university. "In another instance, a junior professor of Calcutta University was voted as Vice-Chancellor of another university 'excluding a candidate of international academic records."[13]

Such rank favouritism in the name of rewarding fellow travellers and CPIM sympathisers, if not regular members of the party, is practised by the Leftists, according to Bhattacharya, in order to establish party hegemony over teachers at all levels. The teachers then play a vital role in spreading the CPIM ideology in society. They are also useful in spreading the party's influence in rural areas as opinion leaders, in particular the rigging aspect which we have examined earlier. The teachers are also expected to help change the emphasis in syllabus in consonance with its orientation, a part from recruiting party activists to similar key posts.

Bhattacharya said that the BJP, often accused by the CPIM (and the media) is not fit to hold a candle to the CPIM in the matter of subversion of academic bodies and institutions.[14] No wonder many bright academicians no longar try to find a place in prestigious institutions in West Bengal like—the Presidency College in Calcutta, the Calcutta Medical College or the Bengal Engineering College—and seek a place for themselves in all-India institutions or go abroad. The CPIM thus indirectly contributes to the brain drain because its party activists and fellow travellers are placed in positions of vantage and other deserving persons have to seek their laurels elsewhere.

The Communists control the educational field in this manner as they keep a close and tight rein on other key areas which explains their continuous reign over West Bengal for the past 23 years. The Bengalis often boast of their intellectual prowers and there is an element of truth in it. But of the two regions the Communists have infiltrated Kerala holds a preeminent position in literacy while West Bengal has been marked out as a problem area in this regard in the country. The Keralites avidly read different newspapers and the Congress party there gives the Reds a good battle than does the faction-ridden Congress party in West Bengal. The proud Bengali has thus allowed himself to be overawed by the Comrades.

The CPIM has also given up its strict adherence to honesty and begun to compromise on corruption. In 1989 the V.P. Singh government was formed and sustained in office by the BJP on the one hand, with its 86 members and by the Left group on the other with just a little more than half the BJP's strength. We have often pointed out in this book that the Leftist strength in the Lok Sabha has become inflexible. In the 1989 elections the CPIM had 34 members and the CPI 12, thanks mainly to their anti-Bofors campaign. The Janata Dal, which had 142 members, the BJP as well as the Leftists had all gone to town on the Bofors payoff issue. Singh has now lost all his Bofors ardour, not due to his poor health, and even the BJP tried to marginalise the issue during its rule at the Centre, but the Communists have just forgotten the issue.

That should not surprise us. The Comrades have made so many compromises on the issue of corruption and they go all out to back up Sonia for the office of Prime Minister naturally they keep silent on Bofors (would that not annoy the Italian Lady?) and one ceases to wonder. They put out stories in the favourable and gullible media that Laloo Prasad

Yadav was not acceptable to them for admission to Third Front, a largely mythical front. He was deeply involved in the Rs. 1,000 crore scam of animal feed during his seven year tenure as Chief Minister and Finance Minister of India's second largest state Bihar. But they went all out to embrace Laloo much before the 13th Lok Sabha poll in September-October 1999. When the CPI fell out with Laloo the CPIM still stuck to the one-sided Laloo dominated alliance as did the Congress of Sonia, out of necessity.

What were the deeper motives in befriending Laloo despite his alleged corruption and his failing charisma? The CPIM would go to any limit to keep the BJP out of power and install Sonia as India's Prime Minister so that she would be eternally grateful to them and would look kindly on their regime in West Bengal and in the other two states and Comrade Surjeet would be able to whisper words of "advice" into Sonia's ears. Yet some of motives would need time to uncover. Similarly when the Comrades made bedfellows with the AIADMK supremo, Jayalalitha, they closed their eyes to 46 corruption cases against her in Tamil Nadu arising from her five year rule in the state, during 1991-96, after which the Congress party entered into an electoral alliance with her and suffered the worst defeat of its career. As usual, the Comrades behaved as though they were keeping their distance from the tainted Dravidian leader but as soon as she threatened to withdraw support from the Vajpayee government they showed keen interest in her because they needed her support for placing Sonia at the helm.

During the crucial days of the failed negotiations of installing Sonia in April 1999 Jyoti Basu was seen seated with Jayalalitha. After the failure of the Sonia gambit Surjeet was seen calling on the madam of Poes Garden at the five star hotel in Delhi and beseeching her to keep his CPIM in view in the electoral alliance for the 13th Lok Sabha along with Sonia. This prompted Rudrangshu Mukherjee to say in his article in the *Telegraph* of Calcutta: "A frail old Communist talking to a plump lady from Chennai was not a sight that many Communists wanted to behold. In his eagerness to form an alternative to the BJP government Surjeet threw to the winds whatever political and ideological scruples he had."[15]

During those crucial days when both Sonia and Surjeet failed to provide an alternative government after ousting Vajpayee he shone as the "ideal fixer".... there was a time when many people believed that (the) Communists in India were above wheeling (and) dealing, that they stood for scruples, principles and ideology in politics. Surjeet has put paid to this myth. He has proved himself to be the fixer to end all fixers."[16]

With this flexible attitude to corruption it is no wonder that the CPIM-ruled West Bengal is more than tolerant towards corruption, especially in the ranks of its own cadres and higher ups with the media in Delhi and elsewhere outside Calcutta are hardly aware of it. Thanks to the vigilant media in Calcutta, however things sometimes come to light when shocking incidents take place. Commenting on the West Bengal government's move for having a Lok Ayukta (a kind of Ombudsman) a leading paper said: "Whether Jyoti Basu will allow ministers to be accountable for misdemeanours, the objective of the proposed bill, is a moot question. He has already earned the dubious distinction of never calling corrupt ministers or bureaucrats to account. On the contrary, he has shielded and rewarded them and frowned upon those who dared to expose them... Corruption is rampant and institutionalised under Left Front rule more than any previous government... Even Jyoti Basu has been accused of promoting his son's business interests..."[17]

"CPM leader caught taking bribe of Rs.1 lakh from businessman" screamed a headline in a prominent daily.[18] According to the story, a senior party member was charged with taking a bribe of Rs. one lakh (100,000) from a businessman. The accused was named as L.K. Chatterjee, a member of the North 24 Parganas District CPIM Committee. He was caught in the act by the detective department (the city CID) of the Calcutta police when be tried to hoodwink the owner of an engineering unit in Kamarhati, himself a CPIM activists (In the prevailing climate many find it convenient to be in the good books of the CPIM party). The comments of the correspondent reporting the event are interesting: "There was surprise and anger in Mr. Chatterjee's reaction in the police closing in on him as the police are not known to lay their hands on high profile CPIM leaders under normal circumstance".[19] It is customary for reporters to interpret the event and offer comments, although in the present case they were justified.

So the arrests are not normal in West Bengal although corruption is. The story also recalls the case of Rashid Khan a CPIM activist involved in bomb explosions in Calcutta. A Calcutta newspaper had more interesting details to add in an editorial: "The apparatchik in question who also happens to be a trade unionist was said to have taken a "huge bribe" from the owner of a closed engineering unit in Barrackpore for disposing of his "excess" land. This is not the first time that local party men are involved in "shady deals" in the area. They have been used to exploiting their links to government to render a variety of services to owners of closed units against illegal gratification."[20]

There was the curious case of a veteran CPI leader who had to quit his party when he found himself helpless against the corruption charges against his party's Minister of Water Investigation and Development, Nandgopal Bhattacharya. The CPI activist who left the party is Manoranjan Sur who joind the party way back in 1940 and is now 76 years of age. He accused the party of being in the doldrums[21] but the party spokesman, Himansu Das, said that Sur was served with a suspension notice apparently for having the audacity of making corruption charges against a partyman in the state government. The CPI, as a second fiddler of the boss, the CPIM, shouts a lot about corruption while in Delhi but cannot tolerate even a veteran partyman making them against so precious a person as a minister.

When big bosses like Surjeet and Basu pursue headlong policies of encouraging corruption and give a go-by to scruple what to talk of partymen in Calcutta who accept" huge" bribes? The CPIM's pursuit of policy without any regard to principles provoked party bigwig gifted with the capacity to wield words like a sword, Ashok Mitra, a former Finance Minister of West Bangal and one of the party members in the Rajya Sabha, to flay party leaders for their utter lack of scruples. In an article in the *Telegraph* of Calcutta[22] he said:... "there is a growing impression that among large sections of ordinary men and women that it (the left) has slipped from the high moral ground, the ground which had been till now its natural inheritance." It was but natural for an ardent Communist, but one with a conscience, Ashok Mitra, that he should hold the "high moral ground" to be the natural inheritance of his party. The CPIM had to eat the humble pie from Mitra's scathing attack but, perhaps in recognition of his valuable services to the party or because he paid left-handed tribute to it in such terms, as quoted here, that the CPIM ignored the article. Others, lesser folks in the party, would have been at once called to account. Anyway, Mitra is in good company because a number of mediamen are subject to the same illusion that the CPIM is a wonderful party.

Mitra quotes examples to prove his point of view. He refered to the notable example of the DMK which, according to Mitra, had been a staunch supporter of pro-Left policies from the days of the National Front (1989 onwards) and which was driven by Surjeet and Basu's manipulative policies to join the BJP. "It was decided to ditch the DMK because it had only five (really six) members in the Lok Sabha while J. Jayalalitha's All India Anna Dravid Munnetra Kazhagam had as many as eighteen. The Left (read Surjeet and Basu) took the lead in the finalisation of the decision".[23]

Surjeet showed cynical disregard of principles when he befriended Jayalalitha during the futile efforts to dislodge the Vajpayee government and replace it with Sonia rule. In the Communist thinking such adherence to principles is a bourgeois virtue not for the Comrades to practice. Mitra refers to this phenomenon as... "it became necessary to cut a few ethical corners: the nation had to be saved from the clutches of the BJP and a lapse from the code of moral conduct here and there was rendered inevitable."[24]

A fellow Communist, much valued by the party for his intellectual attainments which are on the discount in the party although it boasts off and on of its intellectual prowess, had hard words to say in a published article about his own party and its two leaders. Mitra went on to call for "some introspection" and exposed the claims of Surjeet and others that the Congress was secular. "On several relevant issues the record of the Congress had hardly been any more glorious than that of the BJP."[25] Mitra proceeded to refer to the action of the Congress in defeating the Supreme Court verdict in the Shah Bano case, the revival of the Ramjanmabhoomi issue by Rajiv Gandhi, as Prime Minister, whose inexperience he cited as the reason. Mitra also quotes the failure of the Congress government at the centre to raise its little finger to prevent the demolition of the Babari mosque to prove that the Congress was also far from secular.

In controlling the educational system at all levels in West Bengal, as evidenced by no less than a former Vice Chancellor of Caluctta University, and by the systematic rigging of the polls the CPIM has tried hard to remain in power. In addition to all other tricks of the trade, it has held the West Bengal Congress party enthralled by promises of putting its Sonia madam on the throne of Delhi and thus neutralised the only opposition in the state. But wishes cannot always be horses and the Trinamul, in collaboration with the BJP, is posing a serious challenge to the CPIM in the 13th Lok Sabha poll after ousting the Congress in the 12th Lok Sabha election.

The CPIM cadres and activists browbeats the administration specially at the middle and lower levels. "The Calcutta High Court's order in respect of the non-monk teachers at Baranagar should induce the Left Front to finally abandon its ambition to fashion education in its image. It was nothing short of a political conspiracy on the part of the Northern 24 Parganas District Primary School Council to use its puppet organisation to paralyse the administation of the Baranagar R. K. Mission School," said the *Statesman* in an editorial which was titled "Slap in the Face".[26] The second heading was even more telling: "Will the CPIM leave the R. K. Mission schools alone?" For those who might not know, the R. K. Mission is none other than Ramakrishna Mission which has a proud record in spreading education in Ramakrishna Paramahansa's native Bengal as in several other states and countries.

The paper accused the CPIM of furthering its party objectives when it said: "To the CPIM state support to education sanctioned by the Constitution is an opportunity to advance party interests. To seek to improve party support on pain of withholding grants is illegal and morally indefensible."[27] Illegal, my foot, the Comrades would say in private, of course, and morality has been completely abandoned by the party as can be seen from the article of Ashok Mitra quoted already.

Sunanda Sanyal, a former member of the West Bengal Education Commission, attacked the CPIM rulers of the state, in an article, for allocating Rs. 100 crores (1,000 million) for opening 3,000 new education centres in the state as part of the "literacy" campaign.[28] He cited the report of the CAG (Comptroller and Auditor General of India) and spoke of the government plan to recruit women of about 40 years of age as "Educational assistants" on a fixed honorarium of Rs. 1,000 per month and concluded: "Understandingly, the CPIM sets itself this impossible task (of spreading universal primary education) through so little an amount (Rs.100 crores as against Rs. 3,000 crores really needed for the task) not because it aims to dazzle the electorate with spectacular results, but because it needs personnel for what it calls its "election machinery". In the villages 35/40 year-old women will mostly be housewives with easy access to their neighbours... they can make sure that votes are either cast for the party or not at all. Since they are going to be put on contract, these women will not lack drive. They will be aware that they must deliver the ballots, or back they go to the kitchen... In the terrorised countryside today, the schools will vie with one another to bestow that qualification (class seven pass) on the right women, never mind if the right women are actually illiterate."

Needless to add that neither the comments nor the other reports quoted in this chapter were answered by the ruling party. The party organ, the *Janashakti*, regularly attacks the unbound press. In fact, from Jyoti Basu downwards it is customary for the Comrades to attack the "bourgeios" press for what they call maligning them, their party and the state government, at party rallies. Basu, of course, does not acknowledge his debt to the same press when, out of its love for Bengal and its culture, they project him as the "tallest" Indian now and again.

While West Bengal is saturated with the CPIM propaganda and its entire ethos is determined by the CPIM, or was until the Trinamul successfully challenged it, the case with Kerala is different. Although it is also under CPIM rule, the Congress is organisationally sound and has not been overawed by the fact that the CPIM (and the CPI) would always stand by the Congress leader Sonia in Delhi. The Left Front in the state, now in power, is both more fractionalised and often independent of the Surjeet-Basu duo in its anti-Congress formulation. In West Bengal the Comrades look down upon the Congress as a poor relative in Kerala they have to fight the Congress all the way. The Bengal unit of the CPIM has been in power right from 1977; in Kerala the Comrades have to virtually alternate with the Congress.

That the writ of Surjeet does not run in Kerala, not to the full extent, is also shown by the curious existence of the Left Front in the state including even the Congress (S) which has since merged with the Nationalist Congress Party (NCP) of Sharad Pawar. This heterogenous composition of the Left Front has been maintained in the face of Surjeet opposing the NCP, firstly because it is anti-Sonia and secondly because Pawar wants to take over the leadership of the so-called Third Front.

The Trinamul leader, Mamata Banerjee, who has been making a big impact on the 1999 elections, was asked in an interview; "do you think Jyoti Basu will make a good Prime Minister?". She replied:

"Look at West Bengal and draw your own conclusion. They (the CPIM) have made made the state a pauper in real terms. Unemplyment is now close to six million. Industries are stagnating and the promised investment has remained elusive. Just look at our potholed roads and you know the kind of administration Basu has provided. He is more interested in his foreign trips, his personal comforts, welfare of his cadres than the welfare of the state and its people."[29]

REFERENCES

1. See author's book: "*The Great Divide*: Muslim separatism and Partition:", Gyan, Delhi, 1998.
2. *A brand new line, poineer,* Delhi, 1999.
3. *Times of India,* Delhi, May 2, 1999.
4. And 6. *The Statesman,* Calcutta and Delhi, "A deal was struck" April 10, 1999.
5. "*Unseated*", the *Telegraph*, Calcutta, April 9, 1999.

6. *Communism in Indian Politics*, Bhabani Sen Gupta, Columbia University.
7. *Left Worked, not Congress,* the *Telegraph*, Calcutta, April 15, 1999.
8. *Ibid.*
9. *Ibid.*
10. *Ibid.*
11. *Ibid.*
12. *Mediocrity matters, not merit, Hindustan Times*, Delhi, March 21, 1999.
12. *Ibid.*
13. *Ibid.*
14. *Ibid.*
15. *Singh will fix it,* Rudrangshu Mukherjee The *Telegraph* April 20, 1999.
16. *Ibid.*
17. *Jyoti's Lok Ayukt, the Statesman,* Calcutta, April 16, 1999.
18. *Hindustan Times*, Delhi, April 22, 1999.
19. *Ibid.*
20. *Living dangerously, the Statesman*, Calcutta, April 17, 1999
21. *CPI leader accuses minister of corruption, Indian Express*, Delhi, April 29, 1999.
22. *Policy of the principle*, Ashok Mitra, the *Telegraph*, Calcutta, May 29, 1999.
23. *Ibid.*
24. *Ibid.*
25. *Ibid.*
26. *Slap in the face, the Statesman*, Calcutta, May 3, 1999.
27. *Ibid.*
28. *Left Literacy*, Sunanda Sanyal, the *Statesman*, Calcutta, May 27, 1999.
29. *Hindustan Times* Delhi, September 19, 1999, "Jyoti Basu is more interested...."

5
AGAINST THE MAINSTREAM

The Communists have always been out of and even against the mainstream, whether it is because of their underground status for a long time, which developed into a kind of fancy, or for some other reason. The British rulers of India, who showed the same paranoia about the Communists as their masters at home or in the wider western world, did not lift the ban on the Reds until they embraced foreign rule because their fatherland in Russia had overnight turned into a victim of Hitler from being its ally in the middle of the Second World War. They stayed away for a long time from the freedom movement, called Gandhiji and other leaders agents of the British rulers and dubbed the freedom movement as bourgeois. Later they entered the Congress, through the Congress Socialist Party (CSP) in order to sabotage the Congress from within.

It would be a task for the psychoanalyst rather than a student of contemporary history to fathom the reason for this trait of being an outcast, always against the mainstream. Only a few suggestions, based on an analysis of events, are made here. The Comrades have always found themselves ranged against the nation on major issues, whether it is the struggle against the foreign rulers, the proposal and the movement for the partition of the country and the eventual division, the support extended by them to the divisive Muslim League, their opposition to the Quit India movement, their fanatical opposition to Subhas Bose's armed struggle for the freedom of India from outside its shores, calling him all kinds of unbecoming names, their aloofness from the Total Revolution of Jayaprakash Narayan (popularly called JP), their habit to make compromises with principles and finally their tooth-and-nail opposition to Atal Bihari Vajpayee and their subservience to Sonia Gandhi and all-out effort to make her ruler of India.

Before independence, the Indian Communists were under the thumb of the British Reds and the Comintern (later it became the Cominform).

They did resent at times being dictated to by the Communist International (Comintern) and the British Comrades but in the end had to swallow the dictation, because, apart from other reasons, they got monetary and other support from outside the country. After independence, they were obeying the dictates of the Soviet Communist Party and did not consider for a few years that India was as independent as they willed. Then came in 1962 the Chinese attack on India and the Comrades were in difficulty. Within two years, CPI split and the CPIM (Communist Party of India Marxist) became a separate party and even overshadowed the rump original CPI. The CPI generally toed its line and today in the midst of 1999 elections the CPI General Secretary, A.B. Bardhan, says equidistance between the Congress and the BJP is not sustainable and surely after the national election it would go along with the CPIM and give its wholehearted support to Sonia Gandhi's dynasty-ridden Congress. The role of a section of the CPIM, which tried to believe that "China's Chairman is our Chairman" has been examined in a separate chapter later.

The Communist's love for things foreign, often called 'phoren' is thus deep rooted and it is no wonder that they plump for a foreigner, Sonia Gandhi, in political affiliation too. Many in other political parties cried fowl when Sonia Gandhi and the Congress projected this Italian as the future Prime Minister of India. There top leaders of the Congress itself, Sharad Pawar, P.A. Sangma and Tariq Anwar, were expelled from the party for questioning a foreign born person like Sonia to aspire to be Prime Minister. Sharad Pawar was the topmost leader of the party and had been Defence Minister and Chief Minister of Maharashtra twice. Sangma had been Speaker of the Lok Sabha and Anwar had been a General Secretary of the Congress for several years. Pawar and his colleagues also formed soon after their expulsion a separate party, the Nationalist Congress Party, NCP,[1] but Surjeet and his CPIM as well as the obedient CPI remained steadfast in their loyalty to Sonia.

This is typical of the Communists to remain immersed in their pursuit something they have inherited from the days when India was engaged in fighting the foreign rulers. Of course, even at a time when the masters of the Communists from abroad were telling them to launch a full-scale attack on Gandhi, Nehru and the Indian National Congress, the British rulers had a special fear about their capacity to upset the imperial applecart. They entertained the same apprehension that their counterparts in Britain had for the Soviets. Partly this is explained by the Communist fascination for going underground. You always fear a person who is in hiding because you never can be sure what he would do to you.

In any case, the British did not trust the Reds even more than they thought the Congress, not the Sonia-led party but the original INC, could not be trusted. They launched several cases against the Comrades of which the Meerut Conspiracy case was the most elaborate and ramified in time also. It was launched by the British rulers on March 20,1929. A day before a meeting was held in Mumbai and 31 of the Reds were arrested, along with some British Comrades like Philip Spralt, and charged with waging war against the British king-emperor. The Communists were accused of seeking to deprive him of his sovereignty over India.[2]

The Meerut trial went on for three years and a half in which 320 witnesses were examined. Spratt said in a book, entitled *Blowing up India* that the Communists charged in the case were not treated badly. One of the accused, P.C. Joshi, who later was to become the General Secretary of the CPI, was even permitted by the British rulers to take law examination while being tried, the Reds could read favourite books and newspapers and could play games for recreation and "lived well."

Finally, when the trial ended and verdict was pronounced one leader was given life sentence and some other leaders received twelve years. This was in January 1933. Some others received lesser sentences which were reduced on appeal and the British were so liberal with the Comrades that they were all out of jail by the end of 1933.[3] The trial, however, generated sympathy for the Communists and a defence committee was set up by the INC. The long trial also helped the Comrades to establish themselves in the eyes of the people of India as men who meant business. The British treated them, in this case at least, with kidgloves. The Communists also tried to get near the people of the country by identifying themselves with the national hero, Bhagat Singh.[4] They even proclaimed him a Communist although he was not one. Possibly, the fact that Ajay Ghosh was one of the defendants at the Bhagat Singh trial accounts for this description. Bhagat Singh was, however, sentenced to death and hanged by the British while Ghosh lived to be a balanced and respected General Secretary of the CPI after independence.

These incidents apart, the Communists kept away from the mainstream of Indian life and the political movement. When Gandhiji launched his famous Dandi March from his ashram in Ahmedabad in 1930 and some 60,000 persons all over India defied British laws at his call the Reds had no part to play in that landmark struggle. Nor again when the "Do or Die" struggle was launched at his bidding and the Quit India movement started in 1942, engulfed the whole of India the Comrades stayed away from it. At that time, the Communists were actually collaborating with the British rulers of India. They also acted as informers on the freedom fighters because in the pursuit of their goal, which was victory for the Soviet Union in the Second World War, they considered anything which came in the way as obstruction which must be put down at all costs.

Nehru had, among others, set up a committee for the defence of the Communists when the British prosecuted them in the Meerut Conspiracy Case and Gandhiji himself had gone to the jail where they were lodged to meet them. This, however, did not change their evaluation of him as a reactionary person to be shunned and opposed by the Reds. They always tried to project him in a negative vein although they never succeeded in the task. They knew in the heart of their hearts that the people of India worshipped him, even more than many comrades, like their supreme boss, worship Sonia Gandhi.

They tried hard to take control of the freedom movement but failed because they were outside the main current of India and the movement was firmly under the control of the Congress and its leader, Mahatma Gandhi. The Communists abused him as a bourgeios leader, as a reactionary, an upholder of the traditional Indian system, a defender of the propertied classes and generally one whom the Comrades should not fraternise with. They were in this matter, as in other respects, under the dictates of the Comintern, through the intermediary role of the British Reds and otherwise. Even after independence, this domination continued until after the Communists system collapsed in the world. In 1955, the two great leaders of the Soviet Union, Nikita Kruschev, who was the General Secretary of the Soviet Communist party, and the President of the USSR, N.A. Bulganin, visited India and enduring friendly ties were forged between India and the Soviet Union, which have continued even after the Soviet Union evaporated and Russia was re-born. They made laudatory references to Gandhiji. These fell below expectations but the Indian Communists never changed their attitude. Some people like E.M.S. Namboodiripad were less hostile than the others and some of them were greatly influenced by his supreme sacrifice and the work done by him in putting out the communal fires. But that is about all.

If a digression could be permitted about the psychological make-up of the Indian Reds, quite apart from their underground tendency and such other factors, one has to understand their dependence on the money sent out to them from abroad. For years, M.N.Roy, held a position of vantage in the international Communist movement and was considered an important part of the Comintern until he was sacked. Roy was a brilliant writer and expounder of the Communist cause and all the Comrades in this country looked upto him for the key position he held and for the dough. The British manning the Intelligence Bureau in India and the British intelligence at home knew this well. In 1928 Roy was expelled from the Comintern but until then he was looked upon by other Comrades abroad as an authority on India, although he had left India long ago and had not returned until much later. He often misled fellow world Communists about conditions in India but the Comrades at home depended on him for money for their party activities, illegal as it was, and even sometimes for their very existence.

Roy later returned to India and was shunned by the Comrades and he shunned them. The lack of fascination was mutual. His philosophy now was radical humanism and the Comrades who were always imbued with loyalty to the Fatherland, the Soviet Union, could hardly swallow it. But as long as he controlled the funds needed by the Comrades, specially in the twenties, they pampered him although many threw scorn on him also. He was often termed the 'Boss' and many Comrades said he lived a life of luxury. They used to abuse him in words which signified utter contempt. "The boss and family are living as princes... and the boys here, real, sincere workers, are starving. You hypocrites mean no business, you are simply exploiters" which was, of course, a cry in the wilderness.[5]

To come back to the main narrative, the lack of adulation for the Father of the Nation was in sharp contrast to the open support the Comrades gave to Mohammed Ali Jinnah, the founder of Pakistan. When he unleashed the evil theory of two nations, the Hindus and Muslims, and advocated the partition of the country the Communists reacted to him with enthusiasm. They approved of his logic (rather the lack of it) that the Hindus were to blame for the estrangement of the Muslims, and they openly preached their theory of many nationalities in India, which, of course came down from the Soviet Union. Jinnah talked of only two nations, that too on the basis of religion, but the Reds said there were many nations in India. This diversion in views did not bother the Comrades in becoming the flag bearers of Jinnah's pernicious philosophy.

The Union of Soviet Socialist Republics, the official name by which the Soviet Union was known, comprised a cluster of nationalities which differed from one another as chalk from cheese. This was finally proved in the eighties and nineties when the Soviet Union broke up. The federating republics had then cut off their ties with the Russians who had dominated the Union much before the Czar was overthrown in the October Revolution. The Comrades of Lenin had then taken over the Czar's vast empire stretching from Europe to Asia bordering on Iran and Afghanistan. To a significant extent, the Soviet sympathy for India was based on considerations of geopolitics which made them realise that India must be wooed.[6] This was apart from Nehru's pre-independence and post-independence love for the Soviet Union. The country was regarded in the Czarist days as a desirable object and the British rulers who had a pathological fear of communism wanted to defend their Indian empire against the "Russian threat."

The promise of freedom did not materialise for the federating republics until the USSR broke up. The Union was held together by old ties and the concept of nationalities. During Stalin's days the emphasis was on unity and a tight control on the federating republics. The remarkable resistance put up by the Soviet Union against the onslaught of Hitler's armies was largely due to the appeal to Russian nationalism as much as it was due to the Stalian's amazing organizing capacity. The Indian Communists held to their belief in the Soviet theory of nationalities, although it was known to those who know that the Russian Communists had no use for it in their own country. The supremacy of the proletariat was upheld in practice as well as theory but the leaders of the various nationalities continued to face the dilemma of dual loyalty.

Many western educated Indians also question the unity of the country in the mistaken belief that other nations were just born as such. The fact is that nationality is a highly complicated issue and most nations have been held together by a hard core. For India there was a concept of Indianness from the early times and even the Communists subscribed to it before Jinnah sprang a surprise on all Indians. They, of course, slavishly followed the nationality theory of the Fatherland but knew that it could not be practised in India.

Under Gandhiji's leadership, the Indian freedom movement had recognized the importance of the linguistic principle which was basically different from the Communist nationality. There was some superficial resemblance to it. Under his guidance, the Congress had, while upholding national unity, organized such linguistic committees like the Andhra provincial committee and the Gujarat provincial committee although these states came much later after independence. Andhra Pradesh was formed as a state after seven years of independence and Gujarat came even four years later. Even then, the states were only integral parts of India. These have been cited as only examples because there were similar Congress committees in other provinces, now called states.

Acceptance of the linguistic principle did not contradict national unity and even today, when the principle governs the formation of most of the states, the nation is united. The barricades of a myriad states and so many boundaries were broken when Sardar Patel united India within three years of freedom. (Patel died in December 1950.) Under his persuasion, most of the rulers of more than 550 states agreed to integrate their states with the rest of India. The pull of language is, no doubt, great but that does not stand in the way of national unity and after the Communists accepted late in 1951 that they would go along with the parliamentary democratic system they have also not raised the question of unity. Whether they would do so in future is something difficult to say. But generally Indians, including the Communists, have accepted that there is no conflict between the linguistic principle and national unity. But, as we said, the pull is great. For example, the Bengali speaking people of West Bengal state of India feel drawn towards the people of Bangladesh, although it is much less than the pull of Islam. The Tamil people of Tamil Nadu state of India have an affinity towards the Tamil people of Sri Lanka.

What Jinnah expounded went against the linguistic principle. He was, in fact, opposed to the linguistic idea because he knew that his philosophy did not recognize Sindhis, Punjabis, Bengalis and Maharashtrians. He only targeted the Muslims among them and regarded them as a nation[7] and all Hindus among them as a separate nation. For Jinnah, one can say, the Sindhis and Christians just did not exist. The Communists took to his philosophy as fish takes to water and as Muslims, first in the minority provinces and later even in Punjab and Bengal, embraced the Pakistan idea the Reds also did so.

Soon after the Muslim League, at its Lahore session in March 1940, passed the Pakistan Resolution, a leading Communist[8] Dr. K.M. Ashraf, wrote in June that year that "the fascination of the Pakistan slogan grows and develops among the Muslim masses". (Words like masses come easily to the Communists). Incidentally, Ashraf was also a member of the AICC. The CPI was still illegal.

Ashraf also gave credence to Jinnah's theory that the Indian National Congress had failed to unite the Hindus and Muslims and thus there was indirect endorsement of Jinnah's arguments. There was, of course, more internal democracy in the Congress party before independence, under Gandhiji's leadership, than now in the shadow Congress led by Sonia Gandhi. Holders of such views would be summarily expelled without the courtesy of a show-cause notice. Ashraf said : "I have no hesitation in repeating that responsibility lies almost wholly with the leaders of the National Congress."[10] He went on to denounce the Congress leaders, calling them in the typical Red language, as "bourgeios", for conceiving

Indian self-rule in terms of reactionary Hindu Principles rather than those of "Progressive" social ideals.

In denouncing Hindu principles and Hinduism Ashraf was only voicing his party's line of appeasement of the Muslims. To this day, this has been a cardinal principle of the Communists: appease the Muslim votebank as much as possible and forget about fine Communist principles and values. They were, of course, mistaken, then as now, that the Muslim masses would be appeased by such sleight of hand. They were then solidly behind Jinnah, except a notable few who defied him and his hooligan supporters.

Ashraf, it has to be admitted, was not a staunch votary of Pakistan but the CPI was sold on it and the allied principle of two nations of Hindus and Muslims in India. An important party leader, P.C. Joshi, called the Muslims a nation. How this fitted in with their nationality theory is not explained. There were at least sixteen nationalities in India the "Pathans, Western Punjabis, (meaning, of course, the Muslims,) the Sikhs, Sindhis, Hindustanis, Rajasthanis, Gujarathis (spelt wrongly following the prevailing Maharashtrian style, the correct rendering being Gujaratis), Bengalis, Assamese, Beharis (correct Biharis), Oriyas, Andhras, Tamils, Karnatikis (should be Karnatakis), Maharashtrians, Keralas (should be Keralites, better still Malayalees) etc." This was in a resolution of the CPI Central Committee.

There was no place in the long list for Punjabi Hindus, the Haryanvis, the Madhya Pradeshis, and surely none for the smaller North-Eastern groups like the Garos and Khasis, who inhabit the Meghalaya state, the Mizos of Mizoram, the Nagas, who live in India's state of Nagaland, and many of whom are still unreconciled citizens of India, the Arunachalis and others. Surely the "etc." in the CPI resolution cannot take care of so many groups. True, those listed in the resolution are now residents of Indian states, not separate nations, and that is no tribute to the foresight of the CPI resolution and both the Communist parties now seek the vote of these people and others in elections and that is no tribute to its political acumen.

The Communists had now a problem on their hands. On the one hand, they wanted to appease the Muslims whom they wrongly thought of as their supporters. In reality, except for a small section which remained loyal to the Congress and some to the Reds the bulk had gone over to Jinnah. On the other hand, the Comrades wanted to uphold their pet doctrine of nationalities, having imbibed that from the Soviets. This dilemma led them into all sorts of conclusions. P.C. Joshi now advocated three separate states of India, Pakistan and Bengal.[11] This was not a case of historical foresight (because Pakistan broke up in 1971 into Pakistan and

Bangladesh), but a horrible miscalculation on the part of the Communists because Joshi really envisaged a Muslim majority state of Bengal. The Reds wanted to gift the whole of Bengal to the Muslims instead of West Bengal becoming an Indian state where they are in power for the last 22 years.

Finally partitioned 'the country was divided into India and Pakistan and what Jinnah got was, in his own words' a moth-eaten and truncated Pakistan. The Indian Communists did not have even a bit role to play in the whole denoument. Some of them strutted about the place as though the destiny of India was in their hands. They, however, could not erase the impression that they stood by Jinnah in his campaign to partition the country. Similar miscalculation on the part of the Communists has cost them their once strong influence over the regions of Andhara Pradesh, Tamil Nadu and Maharashtra, which are now ruled by anti-Congress regimes and the Communists have to tag themselves to other regional parties or the Congress for crumbs from the table.

During the People's War phase of their existence in the course of the Second World War, they had close links with the British rulers. But the latter did not trust them even then although they kept up the liaison with the Reds for a long time. Just before the Second World War began, Germany under Hitler and the USSR under Stalin had entered into a pact, the famous Ribentroph-Litvinov pact, which divided up virtually the whole of Eastern Europe between the two giants. Then in the midst of the war, Hitler took it into his head that Stalin could not be trusted and attacked the Soviet Union. The Indian Communists also changed their front and the "Imperalist War" in Europe became overnight for them a "People's War". One of the consequences was that the British rulers of the country became their friends and Gandhiji and the Congress leaders, fighting for the freedom of India, remained enemies. P.C. Joshi, who was then General Secretary of the overground CPI, had more than one meeting with the Home Member of the Viceroy's Executive Council, equivalent to the Home Minister of today, Sir Reginald Maxwell. He also had a meeting with a senior Indian officer of the Intelligence Bureau, Ghulam Ahmed.[12]

During the war, the Comrades had three main issues on which to pronounce themselves, besides offering their cooperation to the British rulers. The three issues were: the Quit India movement, Netaji Bose and his INA movement and the Muslim League's communal demand for Pakistan. For all their support of Pakistan, in the mistaken notion that thereby they would win the sympathy and support of the Muslims, Jinnah did not trust them and made no secret of his utter contempt. This is what he said at the Karachi session of the Muslim League in December 1943:[13] "…I find that the cleverest party that is carrying on propaganda are the Communists. They have got so many flags, and I think they consider that there is safety in numbers. They have got the Red Flag; they have got the Russian Flag; they have got the Soviet Flag: they have got the Congress flag. And now they have been good enough to introduce our flag also…". Jinnah, an eminent lawyer, was as sarcastic as he could be about the habit of the Reds to sail under different flags. Whether he committed an error, indulged in tautology or had the historical insight about the eventual break-up of the USSR one cannot say. Possibly the first was true.

Although he was preaching a false doctrine he could see through the Communist game to endear themselves to him by accepting his Pakistan demand and advocating it. Perhaps many of the Muslim League's landlord delegates failed to grasp his sarcasm but he had no use for the Communist support for the Pakistan demand and his two nation theory. Now Comrade Surjeet would perhaps say "we never supported the two nation theory" but like his many statements these days this one would be as likely to be believed as the forecast about the world's doom on the morrow of the predicted doom.

What the Communists did about the immense popularity of Subhas Bose was even more reprehensible. The *People's War,*[14] the CPI's organ during the Second World War, called Subhas Babu all sort of names like "Traitor", "Traitors" for the followers and "Traitor Bose" being reserved for Netaji Himself. The Indian National Army, founded by Subhas in Singapore in 1943, was called "the advance guard of Tojo and Hitler". For those who might have forgotten the Second World War history, Tojo was the wartime Japanese Prime Minister. Although Subhas Bose was treated by him as an equal and behaved so in their contacts, the Communist weekly carried cartoons depicting Tojo as a giant and Netaji as a pigmy. Since the British rulers liked this immensely the *People's War* in their eyes was rendering a useful service and had all the legal permission to circulate. Only the Indian people did not like it a bit and I have seen copies of the paper being torn to pieces after the reader had paid the price for so many copies.

There were, in fact, a number of caricatures of Netaji and today the CPIM has no compunction about admitting the Forward Bloc, founded by him, to the so-called Left Front (of four parties, CPIM, the faithful CPI, the RSP, Revolutionary Socialist Party, and the FB) but they cannot hide the fact that they hated his guts when he was alive and ruled the hearts of the people. They knew that the people all over the country followed the progress of his INA over clandestine radio broadcasts and his popularity was growing every day. The Communists had, however, a case to preach and uphold and this impelled them to believe that the readers of the various Indian language editions of the weekly lapped up every word of it. As staunch party supporters the Comrades had no option but to believe every word of what was printed in the *People's war* but the people in whose name the Communists were speaking did not believe a word of it.

To throw dust in the eyes of the gullible, they also attacked the British rulers although Joshi kept up his meetings and correspondence with Reginald Maxwell. Such deceit comes naturally to the Comrades. The Congress Socialists, through whom the Reds had entered the Congress as we have seen, were the obvious target of the Communists, because they were great admirers of Subhas Babu and also because they were in the vanguard of the Quit India movement. The leader of the Congress Socialists, the incomparable JP, was the butt of their ridicule and the choicest abuses were reserved for him and his Socialists. They did not want the Congress and the Socialists to walk away with the credit for a movement for India's freedom but felt they had a more urgent task to perform, the prosecution of the *People's War*.

JP's men and other supporters of the Quit India movement were referred to as the fifth column, the same way as Franco's Spanish army and the ally of Hitler and Mussolini used to be described. The Comrades had no intention to be part of the national struggle for freedom as they were engaged in what they regarded as their sacred duty of being tools of the British rulers in the prosecution of their war. Today they play their part in support of Sonia Gandhi and against the Vajpayee Government. They have little to do with the defence of India and in fighting the menace of the ISI agents operating in West Bengal and other parts of India but they have views on every issue. The Reds always have a "higher" goal in defence of their main objective.

The manner in which they decried Netaji and his INA meant that they would have no part to play in the defence of the INA men when the British foolishly launched elaborate trials for the "betrayal" of the officers and men of the British Indian army who had surrendered to the Japanese in Singapore and then joined the INA under Subhas Bose. The Congress leaders, Nehru in particular, knew the people's mood and fully exploited the sentiment and served a good cause. The nation was rising as one man in support of the brave men of the Azad Hind Fouz, Indian name of the INA, and only the Communists had to keep themselves away from the mass agitation because, like the British who were prosecuting them, they had been opposed to the entire INA movement. They had no part to play in the INA trials and the defence of the officers and men. Nehru donned the barrister's black robe, without ever opening his mouth in the court martial of Shanawaz khan, Prem Sehgal and Gurdial Singh Dhillon. (How foolish of the British to put on trial a Muslim, a Hindu and a Sikh, at a time when communal tension was at its peak). Bhulabhai Desai did all the donkey's work, assisted by Asaf Ali, and advised by a team of eminent lawyers like Tej Bahadur Sapru.

Nehru knew the people's mood and trimmed his sails to the prevailing wind. He was aware that the Congress, both as a national organization and a political party, must rise to the occasion in defence of men whom the British rulers wanted to punish for their love of the motherland and their patriotism. It must not be forgotten that Nehru had been against Hitler and the Japanese but also knew, unlike the Communists, that the people's sympathy was with the INA men and their leader, Netaji Subhas Bose, was the very epitome of Indian patriotism.

Later, the Reds shifted their ground because they knew that the people of India, and of West Bengal in particular, were extremely fond of Netaji and made compromises with their so-called principles. As we have seen, they even made the FB a partner of their Left Front. As Chief Minister of West Bengal, Jyoti Basu, one of the top leaders of the CPIM, the ruling party in the state, goes out to honour Netaji's statue. Should we call Basu a hypocrite, a turncoat an opportunist or a revisionist for doing so?

Basu is a highly conceited person and if he bows to Netaji now when his party had thoroughly abused him when he was at his prime he does it with full awareness of the situation. He absented himself from the Dhaka airport reception of Atal Bihari Vajpayee in June 1999 to coincide his visit to the neighbouring country on the inauguration of the Indo-Bangladesh bus and when all the dignitaries were present including Sheikh Hasina Wajid, Prime Minister of Bangladesh. Basu had reached Dhaka ahead of Vajpayee and as Chief Minister of one of the Indian states concerned with the bus launch he was duty bound to be present at the airport. Basu may call the BJP as barbaric and communal but cannot escape the performance of his duty as Chief Minister. A BJP leader, K.N. Govindacharya, one of the general secretaries of the BJP, called this a slight to Vajpayee, a violation of the protocol and a result "of the undemocratic and uncivilized mindset" of the Communists.[15]

It they can dishonour Subhas Bose what they cannot do to their own Prime Minister? Subhas had made a unique contribution to the freedom movement, Indian unity and even planning. As Congress President Subhas had set up a National Planning Committee under the chairmanship of Jawaharlal Nehru and with Prof. K.T. Shah as secretary. That was the first time that the word planning was heard in the national context and the seeds of planning were sown which became an important component of Indian life for many years. Today's media are perhaps not informed of Netaji's interest and his contribution to planning because they are only aware of the controversy of the alleged fight between the Mahatma and Subhas and keen about it.

How Subhas escaped from house arrest in Calcutta and headed for Kabul *via* the NWFP, then part of India, and took the flight to Berlin and then made a long submarine journey to Singapore when war was being fought in all its fierceness defies description. He defied all the hazards of this escape and the long submarine journey and soon became the head of the Provisional Government of Free India and reclaimed the Andaman and Nicobar islands from the Japanese. He welded the Indian soldiers and officers into a united army and from being slaves of the British made them into heroes fighting for the honour of India. He mobilized the resident Indian population in Singapore and the entire South-East Asia and made them willing instruments to fight the British. He was aware that the indigenous people of the region regarded the Japanese as cruel colonisers and evoked the highest respect from the Japanese government drunk with success as it was.

What he did for Indian unity was great indeed. He it was who gave us the slogan "Jai Hind"(victory to India) and gifted it *via* Nehru to the entire Indian nation. He evoked the highest loyalty from the Hindu, Muslim and Sikh officers and men as a leader of all Indians. He was also responsible for introducing the Red Fort of Delhi in the national consciousness as a symbol of India's freedom. It was following the slogan of "Delhi Chalo"(march to Delhi) and the symbolism of the Red Fort that Nehru was to introduce the annual practice of the Prime Minister hoisting the National Flag from the ramparts of he Red Fort and addressing the Nation (over radio, first, and later also TV). Thereby he linked India's present and future to its past and united the nation in its quest for freedom and equality. For a Bengali, who often prides himself on his non-knowledge of Hindi because he loves his Bengali language most, he spoke the Hindi-Hindustani lingua franca clearly and made it the official language of the INA.

He himself made a radio broadcast on Gandhiji's 75th birth anniversary and addressed himself to the Mahatma. It is, therefore, a great pity that the media in India are only interested in the so-called controversy of Subhas Bose's conflict with the national leaders. That the Indian Communists who hold in their ranks some of tne brightest men of the past and present should be so innured to a rigid thinking which made them view such jewels as Subhas Bose totally negatively is a tragedy but a historical fact which must be recognised for what it is worth.

The same is true of the Red aversion to JP who was immensely popular when he took up cudgels against Indira Gandhi in 1974 onwards and it ultimately led to her defeat in the 1977 Lok Sabha election. JP was in a state of retirement or hibernation after Nehru's death. It is no secret that Nehru tried his best to induce JP to join his government as his deputy but JP never responded to this offer. However, when the Congress party was losing its elan in the seventies and was deeply involved in corruption JP launched his Total Revolution movement which compelled Indira Gandhi to impose her Emergency in June 1975. JP's health was not in the best upkeep yet he was imprisoned along with a lot of other leaders, from Morarji Desai downwards and locked up in different prisons and some places converted as special prisons. Even the fact that these leaders were imprisoned and the place of their jailing were not known to the Indian public, so rigid was the censorship under the Emergency rule.

The CPI, smaller of the two main Communist parties, was tied to the frocktails of the Congress. The party was for Congress and with such highminded leaders like Bhupesh Gupta notwithstanding the party submitted to the dictates of the Congress rule even before the Emergency and remained loyal to the illegal rule of the Congress during the notorious phase of 1975 June to January 1977. Then Indira Gandhi, lulled by the faithful Intelligence Bureau's forecast that if elections were held then she would get at least 290, out of 543 seats in the Lok Sabha, cut short the life of the Lok Sabha from the seven years it was raised to during her Emergency rule. She reduced it to six years, JP then quickly and hurriedly organized the Janata Party (not to be mistaken for the largely paper party of S. Swamy) and defeated Indira Gandhi. The Congress party won only 150 seats in the Lok Shabha, a record which it fell to the lot of P.V. Narasinha Rao to break in 1996 when the Congress got just 140 seats. Neither during the Total Revolution phase of the JP movement nor during the Janata Party's election campaign the CPIM gave it support. The CPI had cut its slavish bond with Indira Gandhi but even that party did not side with the Janata Party. But in the JP wave the CPIM and its allies came to power in West Bengal in1977. The debt to JP was never acknowledged then or later. Indira Gandhi had used the Communists, both the CPI and the CPIM, when it suited her and discarded them when it did not. The Communists, however, often have the habit of licking the hand that strikes them. Indira

Gandhi had dismissed their United Front governments of 1967 and 1969, formed under the Chief Ministership of Ajoy Mukherjee, had acted, as alleged by them as a semi-fascist, in the West Bengal Assembly poll in 1972, and had put some of them in jail in the Emergency, yet they would not give up their opposition to JP and would not support his Janata Party. Of the CPI's servility to the Congress the less said the better.

REFERENCES

1. *Hindustan Times*, Delhi, June 11,1999.
2. *Communism in India*, p.140, Overstreet and Windmiller; the book quotes 'open letter' from the Youth Congress International to the All-India Youth Congress (a Communist front organisation then) for it, in which the Indian party was asked to dissolve any remnants of the WPP (workers and Peasants Party, another front organisation).
3. *Ibid.*
4. *Ibid.*
5. Overstreet and Windmiller.
6. A senior Soviet journalist, whom the author met, advocated the demolishing of the Himalayan barrier.
7. In states like Kerala, Tamil Nadu, Gujarat and some others, there are Muslim writers of the respective Indian language and the Muslims generally speak the regional language, not Urdu. Jinnah's thesis was negatived by the splitting of Pakistan in 1971 into Bangladesh and Pakistan. In the division language and culture played an important role.
8. See author's book: *The Great Divide : Muslim Separatism and Partition* Gyan, Delhi, for a detailed discussion.
9. *Communism in India*. Overstreet and Windmiller, p. 491.
10. *Ibid.*
11. *Communism in India*, Overstreet and Windmiller, x p.495.
12. *The Only Fatherland*, Arun Shourie, ASA Publications, New Delhi.
13. *Ibid.*
14. *Ibid.*
15. "BJP frowns upon Basu absence at Dhaka Airport", *Indian Express*, Delhi, June 22, 1999.

6
TWO OUT OF ONE
THE GREAT SPLIT

The Comrades have a splitist mentality. They are champions of an ideologial debate and inordinately fond of discussion in order to convince you and convert you to their point of view. Often they carry to excess their fondness and love of debate but they are also great compromisers as the present attitude of the major party, the CPIM, as well as the minor one, the CPI, shows. The CPIM, in particular, likes to fancy itself as the advance guard of the political situation and would compromise even with Laloo Prasad Yadav, join hands with Jayalalitha and play second fiddle to Sonia Gandhi, in order to fight the "communal" BJP. Basu once called Sonia a mere housewife but soon forgot about it because the dictates of the party's interests wanted him to cowtow to Sonia. Thus they are both compromisers as well as fond of the ideological debate. Basu defended the action of the left in supporting the V.P. Singh government from outside while the BJP also was giving it outside support from another side by saying that "at that time the BJP was not that powerful."[1]

So, the BJP is to be attacked when it is strong and likely to emerge as a leader of the government but you can shake hands with it behind V.P. Singh's back when it is not "that" powerful and you do not have to fear it. It, however, becomes a danger when it is powerful and then you have to take the help of the Congress party because it is a national party and of Laloo and Jayalalitha because they are the only ones who would trust the Communists. In the interview, quoted above, Basu was told point blank that West Bengal, which he has ruled for 22 years continuously "now presents a picture of decay."[2] Basu tried unsuccessfully to defend himself: "Do they (analysts, quoted by the correspondent) go to the countryside where our success story lies. Have they seen how land reforms worked..."

So, he admitted that the CPIM rules the state through the villages of West Bengal, not Calcutta where the Trinamul of Mamata Banerjee holds sway.

The split we are talking of came in 1964. The CPI, one of the old Indian parties, well established and well run among the major political formations, split into two, the radical elements going out and forming a new party, the Communist Party of India Marxist, CPIM, in that year. As we have seen, the Communists were always outside the mainstream of India, although they debated at great length their role in the political affairs of India, as they do even now, and often come to wrong conclusions.

For a long time a debate was going on within the party and its various fora on "class collaboration *Versus* class struggle." In simpler language, the issue was whether the Reds should join hands with the Congress party and other parties or follow their own separatist or other line and pursue politics of their own, that is of struggle. This may result in the adoption of violent methods which, for example, saw the birth of the CPI (ML) as we shall see in the next chapter. The ideological debate in the then CPI led to an accentuation of the differences between the two groups, broadly described as the moderates and the radicals among the Communists.

Ironically the CPIM, which favoured class struggle and no collaboration with the Congress party, among others, is today a great advocate of collaboration and the CPI, which was then a real collaborationist, is somewhat less so now but always would follow the big brother, the CPIM, in this vital matter. Even though it fell out with Laloo in regard to seat distribution in Bihar in the 1999 elections, it would still play along with the CPIM after the polls.

To a great extent, the break between the two major Communist nations of the world, the Soviet Union and China, (of course, at that time) had a significant impact on the Indian Communists. The two Communist parties of the giants, the CPSU (the Communist Party of the Soviet Union) and the CCP (Communist Party of China) were the progenitors of the ideological debates and influenced the split. What is forgotten is that the Chinese Communist Party and the one of the Soviet Union were reflecting their major national interests in the ideological debate but the Indian Comrades were unable to see it. Suffice it to say that the radical faction of the CPI aligned itself with the Chinese who were professing radical policies at that time. Now they no longer do, although the Chinese continue the facade of having the largest Communist party in the world and of being a Communist power. They keep their people under the thumb while they fraternise with the multinationals and give them all the facilities they need. At that time the Chinese were keen to get world recognition and the Soviets were a satisfied power and were influencing the destiny of the world as powerfully as they could.

The Communists are often confused and confuse others, specially some in the media of this country who mistake the trees for the wood. They forget that the great Communist nations, at one time the Soviet Union and, of course, the Chinese, are swayed by their national interests which get supremacy of position rather than the so-called ideological debate. In the cold war, the Soviets were inclined to treat each nation as a friend, actual or potential, a neutral country, or a foe, generally reserved for the western nations, and their stooges like Pakistan. In the Soviet eyes India was a friend even though technically this country was non-aligned and outside the Soviet block. The Chinese were brothers as long as they had not fallen out.

The Chinese, on their part, divided the world according to their own light. They thought of India as a friend as long as the bonhomie of Hindi -Chini bhaibhaiship and friendship was in the air, knowing as the Chinese did that this country was among the first non-Communist nations to recognise them and fight for their admission to the United Nations. The moment this bonhomie was over and the border dispute with India boiled over into a regular war and simmered thereafter they had no need for India and looked to the United States and its stooge. They would have gladly befriended India had Nehru gone on with them and not threatened to go to war over their incursions in NEFA (North East Frontier Agency, now called Arunachal Pradesh) and in Ladakh in Kashmir. They recognised late in the seventies and in the eighties that good relations with India were important and continued conflict would come in the way of the multinationals coming into their country.

This brief narration holds an important truth. It is not ideological issue which were mainly responsible for the great divide between the two Communist giants but the conflict of their national interests. The Indian Communists have been rather slow in recognising this essential truth and even Jyoti Basu, who now projects himself as a future Prime Minister of India, once saw the Chinese claims on Indian territory in a favourable light. A number of our Comrades wore the Beijing glasses when China attacked India in October 1962. The need for better relations with a major neighbour like China is well recognized but that does not hide the less than honourable role of many of the Communists in 1962 and even later.

Suffice it to say that the faction of the old CPI which clung to the old party were pro-Soviet and the radical faction which went out of the party, the CPIM, was pronouncedly pro-Chinese although they might not admit it now. The CPIM soon outdid the CPI and became the larger of the two factions and compelled the CPI to obey its dictates. The CPIM became the obvious leader of the Left Front when it was formed in West Bengal in 1967 when they fought the elections and formed a government under the leadership of Ajoy Mukherjee of the Bangla Congress. The CPI had no option but to follow their leadership in the other two states where the Communists have often been in power, Kerala and Tripura.

The account of the Communist movement, its origin and growth, is presented more sympathetically in the book, *Communism in Indian Politics.* According to this book the CPIM was strong in West Bengal, Kerala, Tamil Nadu and Andhra Pradesh,[3] of which only the first two are under Communist rule. Andhra Pradesh first fell to the Congress and later came under the influence of the Telugu Desam, on the question of the Telugu pride since the Congress treated the people of Andhra Pradesh as less than first class citizens. Tamil Nadu went over to the Dravidian parties in 1967 and has stayed there ever since. It is a matter of some surprise that the book, published in 1972, still refers to Tamil Nadu as a region of influence of the CPIM. No doubt, pockets of Communist influence exist in Tamil Nadu even now as in some other states.

According to the book, the CPI had more influence in some of the Hindi speaking areas which is true even today but to a limited extent. The CPI has more pockets of influence in Bihar and Uttar Pradesh where the CPIM influence is at a much low ebb. The CPIM as well as the CPI regularly put up some candidates in both the states pretending that they have influence in those areas. This is typical of other political parties too and has something to do with the faulty logic of the Election Commission which just goes by the total vote secured by each party in the last general election. Naturally the political parties nominate candidates in the hope of gathering some votes, even if they lose, and even if they lose their security deposits. On the total count of each party is based the Commission's final grant of regional or national status which also means that they can boast of the party symbol which is important because large sections of the voters are illiterate.

But outside the three states of West Bengal, Tripura and Kerala the two Communist parties have practically no sway. In Kerala there is a real power struggle between the Congress-led UDF (United Democratic Front) and LDF (Lelf Democratic Front). Both fronts draw a significant amount of their support from communal parties of Christians and Muslims. The sympathetic[4] book, referred to earlier, also tells us that the CPIM in the split drew its support from the lower castes (even the Communists have to recognise castes) while the CPI largely attracted the upper castes. This can hardly be true. People like Harkishan Singh Surjeet and Jyoti Basu, who dominate the CPIM, are themselves members of the upper castes and Basu, in particular, is believed to be well off. In the split there were a few Contrists like the noted leader, EMS Namboodiripad, but later they also joined the CPIM. Generally power and influence have their own attraction and most people go to the faction which holds more plus points of power.

The Government of India, almost exclusively belonging to the Congress party, looked for a long time on the CPIM leaders with suspicions and considered them as agents of China. Many of them were detained and some even went underground, something which comes naturally to the Communists. Among the leaders of the party who were detained were P. Sundarayya, A.K. Gopalan, M. Basavapunisah, and the inevitable Harkishan Singh Surjeet who is now a bosom friend of Congress leaders, particularly Sonia Gandhi. In letters to Prime Minister Lal Bahadur Shastri and Home Minister Gulzarilal Nanda they tried to answer and refute the charge of being pro-China from the prison cell. The Home Minister had even brought out a white paper, Anti-National Activities of Pro-Peking Communists and their Preparations for Subversion and Violence.[5]

During the interregnum between the Chinese attack on India, in October 1962, and the final split in the parent party in 1964 the two factions functioned more or less independently of each other. One of the sidelights of the interlude was a well mounted attack on the most prominent of the CPI leaders, S.A. Dange. This attack was based on some letters allegedly written by Dange while in British prisons offering his services to the British rulers in return for release from imprisonment. The letters were believed to be in the National Archives in New Delhi and although Dange emerged from the controversy more or less unscathed, his image was tarnished which suited the rivals. Elements in the CPIM were believed to be behind the anti-Dange campaign but all this did not affect Dange's control of the AITUC (All India Trade Union Congress). Even to this day the Central Trade Union body remains under the thumb of the CPI. The Congress had set up the INTUC (Indian National Trade Union Congress) in the years when India was about to get its freedom and it has become customary for all political parties to have their own all-India body of trade unions. The CPIM has the CITU (Centre of Indian Trade Unions) and the BJP has the BMS (Bharatiya Mazdoor Sangh). Some of the front bodies are, however, fiercely independent in their approach and are proving difficult for the main political parties to handle.

There were other differentiations. For example, the CPI looked upon parliamentary democracy as a strategical way, as a kind of path it should follow, while the CPIM conceived the democratic path as only a tactical device to be resorted to as a matter of convenience. Such differentiation was more relevant at the time of the split as both have trodden the same path and, at least at present they are both greatly involved in party affairs and elections, seats in legislatures and so on. What is more relevant is that the big brother, the CPIM, has led the CPI by its nose although at times the CPI has tranversed a different course and during the Emergency it was friendly and servile to Indira Gandhi's Congress party while the CPIM was having a running battle. The leaders of the lesser of the two parties have, on the whole, found it conveninent to walk the political path with the help of the big brother, no matter the ideological differences between the two.

The Left Front concept made popular and acceptable by the CPIM has made it obligatory for the CPI to join it whether it likes it or not and it has found it generally agreeable too. When the CPIM decided to support the V.P. Singh government from outside in 1989, with the BJP propping up the government from the other side, the CPI found it convenient to join in. This went on for nearly a year until Laloo Prasad Yadav, then a respectable and much more loved figure, not a buffon and one hauled up for corruption, arrested Lal Krishna Advani, BJP President, in his Bihar state, where he was Chief Minister. Advani was then in the course of his 'rathyatra' which in the opinion of many created communal tension but Laloo should have weighed the consequences of his action. The moot point is that for a whole year the BJP was acceptable to the two Communist parties while they are now determined to root it out and crown Sonia instead.

The CPI is obliged to join the CPIM-led governments in the states under the latter's control because it knows that if it has to exist nationally it has toe the CPIM line. In the 12th Lok Sabha the CPI had only nine members while the Big Brother had 32 and the CPI would be lost in the welter of parties if it did not form a kind of permanent alliance with the CPIM. There is a perceptible difference between the two; in the United Front in 1996-97, the CPI joined the government of Deve Gowda and Gujral while the CPIM controlled it from outside.

When the two parties separated from each other and went their different ways the two had real differences. At that time there was much argument over whether the two Communist parties should follow the path of parliamentary democracy. Now the CPIM leader, Harkishan Singh Surjeet, is considered a pastmaster in the art and technique of political manouevres whether in the end he has to face failure for all his manipulations or not.

For example, he was for the elevation of Mulayam Singh Yadav to the high office of Prime Minister in April 1997 when Deve Gowda had to bow out of power because the Congress did not like his face and would not tolerate him for a moment. And without the Congress support from outside the UF government had no legs to stand upon.

Surjeet, however, failed in the task although he had powerful support in a section of the media and the *Times of India*, a leading newspaper, had almost nominated Mulayam on the strength of Surjeet briefing. The then Congress president, Sitaram Kesri, had given it in writing to the President of India that his party would support the wishiwashy compromise candidate Gujral, a former Congressman, but only seven months later the Congress withdrew support from his government and Surjeet could not prevent the fall of the UF. In May 1996 Surjeet had failed to convince his own party to allow Jyoti Basu to become UF Prime Minister, although Basu was more than willing and Surjeet supported him to the hilt.

Despite such failures, which his friends in the media do not notice, Surjeet was at it throughout 1998 and part of 1999 trying to topple the BJP-led Vajpayee government and install in its place Sonia Gandhi's government. Throughout 1998 he egged on Sonia to topple the Vajpayee government. Sonia was first bitten by the principles bug and did not want to destabilize the government, as she said, but soon converted herself to the politician like frame of mind and sought an opportunity to oust the government by resorting to political manipulations in which Surjeet has acquired quite an expertise. The victories of the Congress party in the state assembly elections in Delhi, Rajasthan and Madhya Pradesh, in November 1998, whatever the reasons, boosted the morale of the manipulators which was somewhat dampened by Vajpayee's Lahore bus trip and the generally favourable budget of 1999-2000 presented by Vajpayees Finance Minister Yashvant Sinha.

But to resume the narrative leading to the division and split in 1964, it is peculiar that while the CPI was sympathetic to the Congress then more so than the CPIM, it follows at times reluctantly the collaborationist course prescribed by the CPIM leaders like Surjeet and Basu. According to the sympathetic book, referred to earlier,[6] the CPI "took a kindlier view of the Congress party than did the CPIM. "The CPI, at that time, said that the role played by the Congress under Nehru's leadership had consolidated and given the Indian independence a mass base. This covered all classes, including large sections of the working class, peasantry, intellectuals, artisans and others. The party, therefore, looked forward to programmatic cooperation with the Congress party while the CPIM did not consider the

Congress a progressive force and regarded the party as one dominated by reactionary elements.[7]

After the CPI freed itself of the enslavement clutches of the Congress after the Emergency it had gone its separate way and the CPIM had trodden a different path. But neither gave a full-throated support to JP's Total Revolution nor did either party join his hastily formed Janata Party. The CPIM and its Left Front owed much of their rise to power in West Bengal to the well-aroused anti-Congress sentiment which swept the whole country in 1975-77. The two Communist parties showed a sympathetic interest in the Janata Party government which came into being at the Centre but again when the ruling party split, largely as a result of the personal ambitions of Charan Singh, the CPIM threw its weight behind him and did not support the faction led by Jagjivan Ram who had replaced Morarji Desai as the leader of the major faction of the party. The CPI was once again showing tendencies of being pro-Congress and since the Congress had brought the Charan Singh government into being (and withdrawn support from it after just 21 days) found it more convenient to back it.

The anti-Congressism of the CPIM is equally phoney. It, no doubt, came to the fore when CPIM was giving outside support to the V.P. Singh government and later when the Narasimha Rao government of the Congress was gobbling up one small opposition party after another in 1991-96. But the CPIM leans on the Congress when it suits it. The outside support of the Congress to the UF government, of which the CPIM was the chief progenitor, changed its outlook. The Congress, for its own reasons, toppled both the UF governments and the seeds of sympathies had been sown and they sprouted and flowered in 1998 and 1999. The banner of ideology is raised by the CPIM when it is convenient and given the go bye later.

The principle of outside support has to be understood in its proper perspective. The CPIM did not enter the UF government because of opposition at the grassroots level to the manipulative politics of Surjeet and Basu. All the same, it was the prime mover of all the political parties constituting it and Surjeet and Basu had seen President Shanker Dayal Sharma even before the UF was formally constituted and a leader was chosen. The Central Committee's opposition and the inverted snobbery of the party, which impresses some gullible mediamen, ensured that the CPIM would not be in the UF government, either under Deve Gowda or the wishywashy Gujral but it had high stakes in the survival of the UF. This entirely depended on the outside support of the Congress party. At the best of times the UF had only 180 Lok Sabha members to back it and sorely needed the Congress oxygen. The CPIM knew this fact more than the others did.

The Congress's real irritation was that while it was the bulwark of the rickety UF government its 140 members did not have even a fraction of the immense powers enjoyed by people like Ramakant Khalap, of the Maharashtrawadi Gomantak Party (MGP), who was the only member of his party in the UF and yet was a minister and the two member group of Sisram Ola and Satpal Maharaj, who chose to continue to be part of the UF simply because they were holding ministerial positions while the two other members of their Tiwari Congress, N.D. Tiwari and Madhavrao Scindia, had rejoined the parent party. Happily, Messrs Khalap, Ola and Maharaj are all in the Congress now.

While people like Khalap, Ola and Maharaj enjoyed immense powers and perquisites Congressmen who were the real power behind the throne could only watch the show from the wings. It was this frustrating wait for the fruits of power which finally impelled the Congress to act rashly and bring about the demise of one UF government after another. Incidentally, the CPI was in the government, represented by two senior ministers, Indrajit Gupta in charge of Home and Chaturanan Mishra of Agriculture. Gupta had no compunction in imposing President's rule in Gujarat and recommending it for Uttar Pradesh while decrying the misuse in both cases of Article 356 of the Constitution but he was reelected, with CPIM support to the 12th Lok Sabha but Mishra who was an effective minister was rejected by his electorate in Bihar. Such is the strange logic of elections where local and regional factors and the effective strength of the party concerned play their part.

The UF was pulled down twice by the Congress and this, logically speaking, should have impressed on the CPIM the need to work against the Congress and finish it off as a political force and if that was not possible to reduce its strength significantly. The CPIM, however, did not pursue either course in the elections to the 12th Lok Sabha. Instead, the CPIM made the calculation that it must help the Congress to come to power in order to fight the BJP. Inverted logic, if it be called that at all, made it pursue a wrong policy and the CPI concurred in it.

Sonia had campaigned furiously to secure maximum seats for the Congress party, of which she was only a voluntary campaigner but in spite of her efforts the party's tally stood exactly where it was in 1996, at 140 seats in the Lok Sabha. This, however, fuelled her ambition to head the government of India in a future set-up. She was invited to try to form a government even in March 1998 when the future of India had to be decided on the basis of the poll results but she had to admit that the Congress party did not have the necessary majority, even with the open support of the CPIM and the CPI.

By that time Sonia had ousted Sitaram Kesri from the office of Congress president and assumed the office herself. She was the inheritor of the supposed charisma of Indira Gandhi and had been the wife of Indira's son Rajiv Gandhi. She had been chairman of the Rajiv Gandhi Foundation which had extensive properties and had been connected with several institutions drawing their influence from the "ruling" family.

In the Congress she was now all in all and the so-called leaders, like Arjun Singh and Pranab Mukherjee, were bending to her wishes. She had acquired the services of Rajiv faithfuls like V.George and invited R.D. Pradhan, a retired civil servant who was known for his loyalty to Rajiv, before he was finally pushed out in August 1999. But by that time Pradhan had done his duty and organised the set-up of the 10 Janpath from which Sonia ruled the Congress party and of 24 Akbar Road which housed the headquarters of the Congress. She exploited the organisation to suit her object of acquiring control over the destiny of India.

Where do the leaders of the CPIM and the servile CPI fit in with this set-up? The wily old leaders of the CPIM, both Surjeet and Basu, being well over eighty, knew of Sonia's ambition to rule over India, which she camouflaged as a burning desire to serve the people of this land. They also knew the people of this land. They knew that the people of India were gullible and would be carried away by the mere fact that she would repeatedly appear before them as the 'bahu' (daughter-in-law) of Indira Gandhi, enough, according to the CPIM leaders, for the people to be swept off their feet. They thought that the Congress could be utilised for putting down the rising BJP, little realising that just as they were findling it now very difficult to fight the BJP they would one day see that the Congress, if it became powerful and was installed in power with their help, would also be very difficult for the CPIM to resist.

It did not matter for the leaders of the CPIM if Sonia was Italian by birth and had not taken Indian citizenship of at least 15 years after her marriage with Rajiv Gandhi. In the permissive culture, preached by the English media, anything was passe and if anybody had a fair skin it was all the more attractive to the semi-starved Indians. The CPIM leaders were as cynical about the matter as many others.

With this end in view the CPIM leaders, with the CPI in tow, egged her throughout 1998 to overthrow the Vajpayee government with their support, such as it was. Sonia knew that thin as the Vajpayee government's majority in the Lok Sabha was it was not vulnerable unless one of the allies of the BJP, principally the AIADMK of Jayalalitha, who was always making personal demands in return for her support, could be made to withdraw from the alliance. Jayalalitha was involved in a plethora of corruption cases, 46 of them, filed against her by the regime of the DMK which succeeded the AIADMK in May 1996 when the AIADMK, along with the Congress, had drawn a blank in the Lok Sabha elections. (The Tamil Nadu assembly was elected simultaneously, and had returned the DMK in strength, the AIADMK securing only three seats in the assembly.)

Jayalalitha openly demanded the dismissal of the DMK government under Article 356 of the Constitution of which Prime Minister Vajpayee's response was 'no' with a loud and clear voice. Jayalalitha thought that she would be able to put enough pressure on the Vajpayee government and make it yield on this major issue and thereafter the court cases against her would be withdrawn and she would be free of all the worries.

Jayalalitha had a weapon, potent and loud-mouthed. Subramanian Swamy was known for his ability to make wild charges against all and sundry. He had, in fact, carried on an anti-corruption campaign against Jayalalitha herself when she was Chief Minister of Tamil Nadu, in 1991 to 1996, and had even obtained the sanction of Governor Channa Reddy who had a score to settle with Jayalalitha being the owner of a highly inflated ego, she could not tolerate another authority over her in the state. Reddy had spent some years as Chief Minister of Andhra Pradesh, had been a Central Minister and finally agreed to be consigned to the garbage heap of governorship. He and Swamy got on famously and Swamy knew the art of getting close to the seat of power.

With the Governor's sanction for the prosecution of the Chief Minister in his pocket Swamy approached one court after another and with a wife practising law in the Supreme Court found it all the more convenient to do so. However, with his amazing slippery nature, he made a complete somersault and one day emerged as an ardent supporter of the 'madam', as Jayalalitha is known by her partymen. The AIADMK is a party to reckon with in Tamil Nadu and only Jayalalitha's writ runs in it. From a Jayalalitha-baiter and tormentor, he turned a close associate of the madam, better known in Tamil as "amma", mother as most grown-up women are called, with respect, and virtually tagged himself to the Queen of Poes Garden as her chief orderly.

His largely paper party, Janata not to be confused with JP's historical if short-lived party, was admitted by Jayalalitha as an ally and was allowed to fight the 1998 elections from the Madurai constituency. The AIADMK had other allies also, namely the BJP, which was trying hard to make inroads into Tamil Nadu, the PMK, MDMK and VK. Ramamoorthy's Tamil Rajiv Congress. Ramamoorthy had once been President of the Tamil Nadu Congress which had broken into two, the TMC, with the effective leader, G.K. Moopanar as its chief. The TMC was the result of P.V. Narasimha Rao forcing the Tamil Nadu congress to have an alliance with the AIADMK when everyone in Tamil Nadu knew that the AIADMK had reached its nadir in terms of popularity. The TMC struck up an alliance with the DMK and the two together swept the Tamil Nadu Lok Sabha elections, leaving nothing for the Congress and Jayalalitha's AIADMK.

By a curious turn of fortunes, for which Tamil Nadu is famous, the DMK-TMC alliance cut a sorry figure in the 1998 elections and secured just nine seats in the Lok Sabha, 27 going to the alliance, the BJP getting three seats and the AIADMK itself getting a much as 18. Swamy, of course, won the Madurai seat, and the PMK got four, the MDMK three and the Tamil Rajiv Congress of Ramamoorthy one. The DMK had brought several well marshalled corruption cases against Jayalalitha but her charisma was at work and the people of Tamil Nadu were responding. The Tamil Nadu politics is peculiar in that the Congress and the two Dravidian parties, the DMK and the AIADMK, know that the voters would not be convinced unless they had formed an alliance. The Congress, therefore, chose either party, depending on the general mood of the voters and the calculations of the parties. The BJP had much strength in North, Western and Central India and had built up quite a base for itself in Karnataka and to a less spectacular extent in Andhra Pradesh too. Tamil Nadu was a virgin area for it (Kerala still eludes the BJP.); so, in 1998 it chose to align with the AIADMK.

Swamy never abides by his pledged word. In terms of his responsibility to the alliance, with whose support he had been elected, he should have been a loyal member of the alliance in the Lok Sabha. He has never respected such loyalties. He has immense capacity for making friends with the media which depends on his dropping of juicy bits of misinformation about the inner goings on in the alliance. The media, which we should once more say refers to a section of the English newspapers, which often influence others, seize every word of his and are ready to take him at his word. If he says that Vajpayee is ill some newspapers lap it up and go mad with front page stories and banner headlines of the Prime Minister's illness. The source: Swamy, of course, which is quoted sometimes and every time he opens his mouth, which is often, the media would report his outpourings.

With Jayalalitha's support he tried to become Vajpayee's Finance Minister, then Minister of Commerce and finally a Cabinet Minister in charge of any portfolio. Vajpayee would have none of it and the reason for rejecting his claims was not far to seek. Swamy had been a Jana Sangh member of the Lok Sabha in 1977 when the Sangh was a part of the Janata Party of JP which had scored a major victory against Indira Gandhi's Congress at the Centre.

Even at that time, Swamy had a keen propensity for party hopping. When the Janata Party broke up in July 1979 he switched on to Charan Singh's Lok Dal, saying ta-ta to the Jana Sangh and the Janata. Later he formed his own paper party, the Janata Party, and tried his luck in Tamil Nadu, to which he belonged but he was elected to Parliament for the first time on the Jana Sangh ticket from north India. The BJP leaders, Vajpayee and Advani, knew him to be thoroughly unreliable, a turncoat and party-hopper. It was, therefore, natural that they would not touch him with a pair of tongs and there was no question of giving Swamy any portfolio, much less Finance, even if Jayalalitha was sponsoring him. The madam would also not go the whole hog to butress him but would still listen to him and even, on occasions, be guided by her.

Swamy, who was in touch with Surjeet as well as Sonia, was now out for double revenge, having deserted the Jana Sangh once and recently having been turned down by Vajpayee for a ministerial berth. The seeds of his disloyalty having been sowed—there is something in him which makes him disloyal by nature—he set about trying one ploy after another to dislodge the Vajpayee government. Not a day passed when he would not tell his faithful mediapersons, men and women, gossip about the imminent fall of the Vajpayee government and sometimes he would even set a date for the happening. If, however, wishes were horses the BJP-led government would have fallen in 1998 and any time before it did in 1999.

Swamy, however, never gave up although his predictions about the imminent fall of the government did not come true in 1998 or even 1999 nor his briefing of a woman reporter of the *Asian Age* of Akbar about the physical collapse of Vajpayee. He was habituated to make the predictions and some newspapers were glibly or knowingly giving credence to him. He had, in fact, revealed his self when he left Delhi when the crucial vote of confidence was about to be taken in the Lok Sabha on March 28,1998. He pretended that he had important business in Tamil Nadu and he even said that the Government was sure to win (even without his vote). The government did win the vote, by 275 to 264 votes, but Swamy was hoping in his heart of hearts that it would be the other way round.

Otherwise, he would not have turned so hostile on the morrow. His turn finally came when he arranged a so-called tea party for his madam, Jayalalitha, at one of the posh hotels in the capital in April 1999 when Jayalalitha must have told him that she was trying to finally topple the Vajpayee government and crown Sonia and people like Surjeet, with the CPI as servile as ever in tow, were clicking their tongues. The stability of the nation, about which Sonia and Surjeet shed many a crocodile tear, was thus thrown to the winds as Sonia went to Swamy's tea party with the specific object of meeting Jayalalitha. They came face to face for the first time for a destructive object.

Events moved fast thereafter and Jayalalitha withdrew her 18-member support and her ministers resigned from the Vajpayee Cabinet. A flutter was caused in the political world and the media. Even respectable papers, like the *Times of India*, not the sensation-loving *Asian Age*, played up the events. The *Times* had been privy even earlier to Sonia's unlimited ambition for power and used the stories in its news columns; in the fast moving events, the DMK had to leave the so-called Third Front of Surjeet who waited on Jayalalitha now to hang on to her round self for crumbs in Tamil Nadu. If the AIADMK was in the anti-Vajpayee camp the DMK could not co-exist with her and had, of necessity, to switch its loyality to the BJP-led alliance.

If the Third Front was thus disintegrating, only Surjeet and the faithful CPI had to take the entire blame. The DMK leader and Chief Minister of Tamil Nadu, M. Karunanidhi, knew that Vajapyee had not dismissed his government although Jayalalitha, in the thirteen-month of her membership of the alliance had constantly pressed the Prime Minister to do it. He told Surjeet that if the choise before him was between communalism and corruption he would prefer the first. By corruption, he meant Jayalalitha who was the obvious choice of Surjeet in his toppling game. Surjeet knew that the AIADMK had 18 members in the Lok Sabha while the DMK, his partner, had only 6 and he knew that 18 was three times that of 6. In the cynical calculations of the politicians the numbers matters more than principles and Surjeet is above all a politician.

The Telugu Desam, the National Conference of Jammu and Kashmir and the Asom Gana Parishad, the ruling party in Assam, had lost faith in Surjeet long ago because of his open preference for the Congress. To this expanding list was now added the DMK, the original member of the National Front in 1989 when the V.P. Singh government was installed in power. In their singleminded devotion to Sonia the CPIM duo of Surjeet and Basu had not much sensitivity for the Third Front partners and the front was now lying by the wayside. Surjeet even accused the Telugu Desam and the DMK of betrayal. When you betray your partners you can always turn around and say that they betrayed you. Surjeet knew that the DMK and AIDMK could not sit on the same side and if he befriends the AIADMK he was aware that the DMK would bid good-bye to him.

Surjeet's manipulative powers were now joined by the unfathomable venality of Jayalalitha and Swamy's machinations and if in the process communism has been abandoned nobody raised this question. The CPI was the epitome of compromise and, in any case, being pro-Congress came naturally to it. The party's leadership, like that of the CPIM, which it followed in all major respects, was old and having more memories than other things, they could do Surjeet's bidding. But there was a snag. The two smaller parties in the Left Front, the RSP and the FB, would not vote for Sonia under any circumstances.

Sonia's applecart was upset as these parties, having between them seven Lok Sabha members, and Mulayam Singh Yadav with 20 Samajwadi party MPs behind him, said[6] no to Sonia when she accepted President Narayanan's invitation to try and form an alternative government after the Vajpayee government was defeated in the Lok Sabha, 269 votes for it and 270 against it, on April 17. Mulayam was pressurised by Surjeet but the Samajwadi leader would not budge at all. He knew that Sonia was after his Muslim vote bank in Uttar Pradesh where Sonia had drawn a blank in 1998 and the Congress believed, with the support of the gullible media, that it was on a comeback trail. This was a danger signal for Mulayam.

In the Confidence vote on April 17, six votes were manipulated by the opposition, Sonia and Surjeet. Five BSP members, who had, according to the plighted word of their leader, Mayawati a day earlier, decided to abstain in voting, suddenly on the crucial day changed front and voted for Sonia. The sixth vote belonged to the Orissa Chief Minister, Giridhar Gomang, who had gone over to his state more than two months earlier to head the state cabinet there in the Congress party's internal reshuffle, and had taken no part in the proceedings of the Lok Sabha. Due to a faulty provision in the Constitution and its faultier interpretation, one could cast one's vote even after becoming Chief Minister of a state.

That happened on April 17. Now the more difficult part, that of installing an alternative government in place of Vajpayee government that had been pulled down. The BJP and its allies had taken precautionary measures but their efforts fell just short of success Apart from getting the DMK on its side, the BJP had managed to get the votes of all the four members of the INLD (Indian National Lok Dal) of Haryana and some unattached members or those from very tiny parties or unattached members. But all these efforts were not enough to secure the future of the Vajpayee government.

But Vajpayee and his colleagues had the satisfaction to see that Sonia and even Basu who was now ever willing to become Prime Minister, could not succeed in their endeavour to place a government in place of the one they had pulled down. Sonia and Basu, Surjeet and Jayalalitha now realised that to build something was difficult, not as easy as destroying something which had been built by others.

Soon after the confidence vote was lost in the Lok Sabha, President Narayanan, a former Congressman himself, called upon Sonia to explore the possibility of forming an alternative government. Sonia began with a fanfare and claimed, much to the delight of the section of the media which was mesmerized by this Italian woman, that she had a strength of 279 members in the Lok Sabha, just enough to enable her to form a majority government. How she claimed this number is still a mystery because Mulayam Singh Yadav, who had with him 20 MPs, had said 'no' to Sonia because he did not wish to commit harakiri which Surjeet wanted him to do. Also, the seven-member block of the RSP and FB had made it clear that while they were with the opposition in throwing out the Vajpayee government they had no intention to see Sonia in Vajpayee's shoes.

Surprisingly, a couple of days later after she had claimed the support of 279 members, Sonia told the President that she was not able to get their support and all the support she could muster totalled 239 members. Obviously, apart from the 20 Samajwadi MPs and seven of the RSP and FB, there were six other members who did not wish to be counted as Sonia supporters, provided she had made some calculations before meeting the President on both occasions.

Surjeet had failed and Swamy and his madam had both failed. Surjeet blamed Mulayam and in a typical Communist outburst told him a few things and Mulayam returned the compliment with equal vehemence and with characteristic boldness. Mulayam was often referred to by mediapersons, who claimed to be knowledgeable about Left party affairs, as in Surjeet's "pockets" but he now resisted his efforts to reduce him to be at the mercy of Sonia and ultimately did not yield. He had no desire to support a foreigner and had no intention to lose his Muslim votebank to Sonia.

Surjeet and Basu could not make Mulayam bend to the wishes of Sonia nor did they get their Left Front partners to budge from their resolve.

We have referred to one mystery that of the missing six members who did not agree to support Sonia. There was, however, a greater mystery: who were all the 239 members who supported Sonia, as she claimed. The mediamen did not ask her, nor when she claimed suspport of a majority members nor when she said the number had come down to 239. The President ought to have asked her to specify but there is no knowing, except that in his final communique Narayanan said Sonia had not been able to convince him she could command a majority.

Narayanan was willing to be impressed and was favourably inclined as he had seen her to the door of his study, an honour Narayanan had denied to other claimants. But he had a reputation to keep, for fairness and for taking the right decisions. So, Narayanan dissolved the Lok Sabha on April 26 after the cabinet recommended it to him. Was it wise to plunge the country in yet another poll, within a year and two months of the last ? Narayanan must ask himself and should have asked Sonia Gandhi who had taken the initiative in toppling the Vajpayee government.

Basu and Surjeet, however, made a last ditch move to see if by default or otherwise Basu could be Prime Minister. On April 25, the day following Sonia's throwing in of the towel, the CPIM Politburo met in the pre-lunch period if their 32-member party could win the outside support of the Congress and of other "likeminded" parties to enable Basu to form a government. The CPIM Congress, at its October 1998 session in Calcutta, had ruled that the CPIM should not form a government with just 32 members. The Politburo, ignoring the decision of the party Congress, wanted the Congress Working Committee to see its way to support Basu in the same fashion as the Congress had extended outside support to Deve Gowda and Gujral in 1996 and 1997.

The Politburo retired for lunch and the customary siesta (both Basu and Surjeet being above eighty needed rest after their lunch) when the phone rang in Basu's room in the Banga Bhavan in the Capital. Sonia was on the line to tell Basu that the CWC had "unanimously" decided not to back Basu for the office of Prime Minister. Basu's hopes were dashed to the ground. The CPIM's Somnath Chatterjee, who is by no means a pleasant speaker in the Lok Sabha where he was leader of the CPIM group in the 12th Lok Sabha, told a foreign TV channel, claiming to be Indian, Star TV, that the Politburo had okayed Basu's candidature. As though Basu had the necessary majority, with just 32 members. Obviously, Sonia had herself voted against Basu in the CWC because she said the committee was unanimous. This was yet another lack of feather in Surjeet's cap.

After the President dissolved the Lok Sabha he ordered fresh elections and the Election Commission of India got busy to hold the polls. The stark summer and a wet monsoon which could make campaigning difficult was ahead as the house had been rendered non-functional at the end of April. The BJP and its allies pleaded for early elections, late in June although by then the monsoon would have set in parts of the south of India, like Kerala state, while the Congress and parties of the Left supporting it strongly urged the Election Commission to postpone the polls to the end of the monsoon period, some time in September and October. The BJP and its allies wanted to avail of the sympathy which would accrue to the ruling alliance because the Congress and the Left parties had forced an early election on the country and failed to install an alternative government after toppling the existing one.

The Election Commission, which is supposed to be impartial, ultimately ruled in favour of the Congress and the Left parties. It had, of course, consulted the government officials on the deployment of Central forces, who have to supplement the efforts of the state police and are trusted by the electorate. All the deployment called for a Herculean effort but the Congress and the Left were overjoyed as if the Commission had ruled in their favour.

The BJP and its allies were naturally dejected. But they did not know that two other extremely favourable factors were to intervene soon. First in the middle of May, three important members of the CWC, Sharad Pawar, who was a top leader of the party but always unfavoured by Sonia Gandhi, P.A. Sangma, a top leader who had been Speaker of the Lok Sabha when the 11th house was in session, and Tariq Anwar, one of the General Secretaries of the party, raised the question of Sonia's foreign birth and thereby a storm in the party. They were finally expelled in May itself and in June they formed a new party, the NCP, Nationalist Congress Pary, and caused a disruption in the party on the eve of the polls.

Later in May, yet another, a major, development occurred when it was discovered that Pakistani regulars and some of the terrorists, aided and abetted by her, had entered Kargil in Kashmir, in the Ladakh region, and the Air Force and the Army were ordered to throw therm out by what was referred to by many in the media as a "caretaker" government. There is no such thing as a caretaker government and in any case a period of nearly six months, before an elected government is installed, is too long a period for a "caretaker" government to carry on. The Kargil operations ended in a glorious military and diplomatic victory for India and a defeat for Pakistan and its people called this a misadventure. However, the Congress and the

Left parties, joined in by some others, tried to weaken the government and reduce the importance of the nation's victory. They knew that the nation had come to look upon Atal Bihari Vajpayee as almost a hero and this was bound to reflect favourably on the prospects of the National Democratic Alliance, NDA, which had been formed out of the BJP and its allies at the instance of the BJP. They tried their best during the Kargil operations and after, during the poll campaign, to denigrate Vajpayee and made many allegations against him.

Swamy was a cog in the wheel which was being operated by Surjeet. It would, therefore, be appropriate if we spend some time here and deal with the anti-climax of the Swamy story. After the failure of the Sonia and Surjeet endeavour to place the crown of India's Prime Minister on Sonia's head, failing that of Jyoti Basu, Swamy had lambasted both the Congress and the CPIM. He, in particular, lambasted the Congress leaders for trying to form their own government. Jayalalitha and Laloo knew that once Sonia was installed as Prime Minister they would press on her their claims but it was left to Swamy to weep in public over the split milk. What he was lamenting was the lost opportunity for him to become a minister in the Sonia cabinet, provided she formed one.

Jayalalitha had other ideas. She knew that the AIADMK would need the support of the Congress in the elections to 13th Lok Sabha but would deal with the Congress and the crumb-seeking Left parties in her own imperious way. In the seat-sharing negotiations she had decided to simply cut out Swamy and that would be revealed at the proper time. Talks with the Congress were proceeding at somewhat leisurely pace. They had been initiated by Sharad Pawar who was said to have a good rapport with the Poes Garden madam. Pawar was, however, expelled by Sonia after staging a weeklong drama of "resignation" from the office of Congress president and stage-managed pro-Sonia demonstrations in the Capital.

Jayalalitha was getting impatient and told the Congress she would spare no more than six seats for the Congress to contest out of 40, 39 for Tamil Nadu and one for Pondicherry, at her disposal. In the negotiations, conducted by Manmohan Singh and Antony, one a real man of integrity (Antony) and another having that reputation, but both unwanted by Jayalalitha who was charged with monumental corruption. In the talks, Jayalalitha went up to only ten seats for the Congress to contest. This was galling for a party which used to get as many as 26 Lok Sabha seats from the state to contest under the so-called MGR (M.G. Ramachandran, the late, who was the founder of the AIADMK and a former Chief Minister of Tamil Nadu who was a great actor of the Tamil screen and often a co-star of Jayalalitha in her acting days-formula. MGR had a special relationship with the madam but the Congress appeals fell on her hard-headed nature. In a final bid, the Congress madam phoned the Poes Garden madam and the later said "12 and no more." The Congress which had drawn a blank on Tamil Nadu in 1996 as well as 1998, had to accept the humiliating deal. Jayalalitha also threw two crumbs at the CPIM and another two at the CPI. She also provided a seat to a faction of the IUML (Indian Union Muslim League). Incidentally, the Congress which is leading the UDF (United Democratic Front) in adjoining Kerala has a regular alliance with the IUML. The Congress is boosted as a "secular" party by the CPIM and some media although it has an alliance with the Muslim League and some Christian parties in Kerala.

Where does Swamy fit in with this story? Jayalalitha wanted to teach him a lesson, apparently for having misled her in withdrawing support and not being able to find a place in the imaginary Sonia cabinet. In the last election in 1998, she had given Swamy the Madurai seat to contest and with her party's support Swamy had even won. He thought that since then he had served the madam well he would be allotted the same seat in the 1999 poll also. He apparently did not know his own madam. She had cut out his name and refused to see him until after the seat allotment was completed. (In the exercise, the AIADMK had the lion's share.)

Swamy gave up in the end. He was utterly frustrated. He had served his madam well but he did not realise that he was gifted as part of the deal a Lok Sabha seat now being defended by him as an independent. He had led the madam up the garden path (not Poes Garden path, where the entry was barred for him now) and while the Vajpayee government was dismissed no alternative was found possible and Jayalalitha was left without any ministers at the Centre. In her system of heads being rolled, it was now the turn of Swamy to become the "bali ka Bakra", the proverbial sacrificial goat.

"Swamy severs ties with Jayalalitha" screamed a headline in the *Pioneer* of Delhi and Lucknow and the Jaya favourite, the once staid *Hindu* of Chennai and several other cities shouted "Swamy assails Jayalalitha".[9] The sum and substance of these newspaper stories was that Swamy was fuming and fretting but was not able to do much about his discomfiture. He, of course, resorted to his familiar tactics of making charges and said "Jayalalitha was not her own person and her decisions were under the control of a coterie."[10] As long as Swamy himself was part of the decision making coterie it was, of course, all right. Before long, he would be defeated from the Madurai constituency and would be at his favourite pastime of making charges which need not be against the madam.

His condition was akin to that of the proverbial dog of the washerman "neither the dog belongs to the washing place nor to the washerman's house". The dog in the proverb tags himself on to the washerman but Swamy was more than that. Jayalalitha had used him as much as he had used her. For all his exertions, he deserved better at the hands of his madam but all of them must meet their fate sooner or later. Swamy served the madam with inside information and the ways of Delhi because none of her 18 MPs would have dared to approach her with these tidbits even if they had access to them. He it was who had made it possible for Jayalalitha to meet an equally vain female in the effort to topple Vajpayee. But Jayalalitha had other objectives in mind which the failure of Sonia and Surjeet had frustrated.

In the entire process the CPIM cut a sorry figure and with the declining fortunes of the Third Front the chances of Surjeet dominating the Indian political scene once more had evaporated. In the run-up to the polls, the Janata Dal, the hardcore of the UF in 1996 and 1997, broke up and the Janata Dal (United - JDU) became part and parcel of the BJP-led National Democratic Alliance. There was great reluctance for the merger and the alliance in the Karnataka unit of the BJP but it had to bow to Vajpayee's wishes in the end as the Prime Minister was keen on the JDU joining the NDA and the Lok Shakti in Karnataka and the Samata Party in Bihar had already joined the JDU and the BJP had an alliance with two parties in the respective states.

From the Akali Dal in Punjab to the DMK in Tamil Nadu the BJP has alliances and electoral or seat sharing arrangements with the number of parties. It has its own strength and hopes of it once more emerging as the largest single party in the Lok Sabha, crossing the 200 seat barrier for the first time, are high in the 13th Lok Sabha poll. With the wider acceptance of the BJP in the world of the Indian political parties, even the staid *Hindustan Times*, not known for friendship for the BJP, took note of these developments. In an article a senior editorial writer of the paper, known to be a staunch critic of the BJP, had to admit that the BJP, under Atal Bihari Vajpayee, had matured. "Maturing of the BJP" was the title of the article.[12]

It is futile to expect the CPIM, with the servile CPI in tow, to follow the course taken by a number of former Socialists. There is a certain incompatibility between the Socialists and the Communists. The strange consequences of the split of 1964 are yet to unfold.

REFERENCES

1. Interview of the Week, Jyoti Basu, by Ashis Chakrabarti, *Indian Express*, Delhi, Sept. 5, 1999.
2. *Ibid.*
3. *Communism in Indian Politics*, Bhabani Sen Gupta, Columbia, 1975.
4. *Ibid.*
5. *Ibid.*
6. Sen Gupta.
7. *Ibid.*
8. *Hindustan Times*, Delhi, April 18, 1999.
9. *Pioneer*, Delhi, July 16, and *Hindu*, Chennai and other cities, July 17.
10. *Hindu*, July 17, 1999.
11. The proverb is *dhobi ka kutta na ghar ka, na ghat ka.*
12. *Hindustan Times*, Delhi, July 19, 1999.

7
CPIM REBORN AS CPI (ML)

Along the foothills of Darjeeling, near the trijunction of India, Nepal and Bangladesh (then still East Pakistan), not far from the border with Bhutan, lies the village of Naxalbari in West Bengal. Here, in May 1967 the peasants rose in revolt. The uprising was led by members of the CPIM who broke away from the main party in two years to form a new party, the Communist Party of India, Marxist Lininist, CPI (ML). The uprising was crushed by the police, aided by the cadres of the CPIM itself. The movement spread to other parts of the country in adjoining Bihar, Srikakulam in Andhra Pradesh and parts of West Bengal where the movement was not strong at the outset. The leader of the movement, ardent exponent of the theory of violence through which, he said, the Communists would capture power was Charu Mazumdar. He died of cardiac asthma but his followers said police persecution was responsible for his death at an early age. It goes without saying that he was a great admirer of Chairman Mao Dze Dong (Mao Tse Tung) like the violent Naxalites then and later.

We have seen how unequal is the struggle of the small farmers and even to an extent of the middle farmers also against tenancy laws. Since agriculture is a state subject, different states have enacted laws to protect the farmers against illegal extractions and lay down a framework for the land tenure system. India's food production has gone up more than four times, from 50 million tonnes in 1950 to 204 million tonnes in 1998 and the country is self-sufficient in food but the farmers are not a happy lot and to a substantial extent the land tenure system and the inadequate implementation of land reforms are resposible for that state of affairs. The rural economy is predominantly dependent on agriculture and despite the massive growth of irrigation, farming is still largely dependent on rainfall.

Lawyers play a role in getting the land reforms in several states not implemented and litigation by the landowners has the effect of putting obstacles in the way of the politicians and the bureaucrats, often unwilling and reluctant, and the entire state machinery not doing enough for the small farmers. Lawyers are known to get many a criminal off the hook by bailing him out, during which he is free to commit more crimes, and this expertise is used by legal brains to exploit the loopholes in the tenancy and land laws and add to the worries of the state machinery if it is really interested in the welfare of the farmers.

Some of the states have solved the problem and are going ahead in agricultural production but the rural problem is far from solved in most states. But is armed insurrection an answer to it ? In no circumstances can armed action and taking law and order in their own hands be an answer to the problem we encounter in the villages. In the name of helping the farmers, it is well known, that big and middle rank farmers are reaping the benefits which all political parties seek to confer on the farmers. These include incentives like subsidies on fertilisers and pesticides, extensive credit facilities through rural banks and cooperative societies, even free supply of electricity or supply at highly subsidised rates. Many of the big and middle level farmers also control the votes of the small and landless farmers, these classes are pampered even more since seventy per cent of the votes come from the villages.

The CPI (ML), born of the womb of the CPIM, has now turned a new leaf in its career and it is like any other party making promises and seeking votes, having renounced violence. But that does not mean that Naxalite groups, who believe in and practise violence and use arms have ceased to operate. Whether they have any ideology at all it is difficult to say. Possibly they have none. Vagabonds and unemployed youth, out for fun or easy enrichment, abound in the ranks of the so-called Naxalites. But the armed groups do exist in several parts of the country and where the farmers are said to be under the influence of the armed men or just fear of arms is the motivating factor these groups are not being tackled in the right way. Both firmness and a social approach are necessary if the Naxalite problem has to be solved. Bihar is an extreme example because the administrative machinary has virtually broken down or has no will power and motivation to meet the challenge. Laloo Prasad Yadav is capable of only sweet talk but neither he nor his semi-literate wife, whom he has installed as Chief Minister, has a grasp of the depth of the problem nor do they wish to help the small farmers. Even the landowning classes include many who are small and middle rank landowners and are afraid of both the police and the armed groups and the RJD government does nothing to allay their fears.

In 1967, the situation in parts of rural West Bengal was far from satisfactory. There were hot-headed CPIM men who were intent on doing something for the tenant farmers and believed that the newly installed coalition government, in which the CPIM and other Left elements had a big hand, would protect them in their struggle against the landlords. There were many young men and women who wanted to do something for the farmers. They were bright in their studies and some people, even outside West Bengal, joined the Naxalite movement out of the simple desire to do their part in support of the peasants as they believed, often mistakenly, that armed action was the answer to the problem, the only answer. After the rising in Naxalbari there was a virtual underground movement in several parts of the country to join these armed groups. It was more a case of frustration and misplaced idealism. This phase was shortlived but the movement lived on in several parts of the country and no solution has been found so far.

A journalist, who participated in the Naxalite movement in West Bengal, Sumanta Bannerjee, has given an account of the rise of the movement and the birth of the new party in "In the wake of Naxalbari"[1], a kind of history of the movement. He has quoted extensively from the articles and books he came across to prove that the land tenure system was totally unfair to the poor cultivators. "Even in those states where the law protected his (peasant's) rights to some extent he was invariably deprived of his due share. Thus in Punjab, both the Punjab Security of Land Tenure Act passed in 1953 and the Pepsu Tenancy and Agricultural Land Act, passed in 1955, provide the maximum rent payable by a tenant in respest of the land leased by him should not exceed one-third of the produce of the land or the value of such produce, as the case might be. But according to a survey carried out in three districts of Punjab, it was revealed that cultivators had to part with half of their produce."[2]

This is generally illustrative of the kind of information gathered by the book. Instances of forced labour or of bonded work by the tenant farmers have also been cited. These instances and information are also available to the Planning Commission which seeks to ameliorate the conditions of the rural folks in different states. Much water has flowed down the rivers of India since the instances were quoted and, as we have noted, the production of agriculture has gone up substantially, although the problem exists in an acute form in some areas and in much milder form in some other at states. The rural people are subject to considerable deception, as indeed are those living in urban areas, by politicians who promise them the moon at poll times and forget their promise or the benefits, intentionally or otherwise, go to the wrong recipients.

But the solution to the farmers' problem does not lie in violence. It is, however, equally true despite the wisdom of this observation the votaries of the thesis of violence abound. What happened in Naxalbari in May 1967 which made it noticed by many in the country and even outside and some look to it even now with a feeling expectation? Naxalbari, together with Phansidewa and Kharibari, are said to be three important centres of farming in the Darjeeling district of West Bengal. The area is spread over 300 square miles equivalent to 767 square km. The farmers were mainly tribals, Santhals, Oraons and Rajbanshis. The landlords, called "jotedars" in West Bengal, employed them on contract, that is, they cultivated the land while the owners provided them with seeds, bullocks and even ploughs and gave them a limited share of the produce. In the adjoining parts of the district there are extensive tea gardens whose workers were also tribals who worked on the tea garden land, stealthily kept by the owners of the tea gardens aside for paddy cultivation since the tea gardens are not even now covered under the land ceiling act. Paddy land is, of course, subject to a ceiling. The area is strategically important but that does not seem to have been at the back of the organisers of the movement of the peasant revolt.

A farmers' conference organised by the CPIM activists in the Siliguri sub-division, (in which Naxalbari is situated) was a pronounced success. This had helped the activists to organise the peasants and, if sympathetic accounts are to be believed, more than 15,000 of them were enrolled as activists. Peasants were organised in committees and also armed. Soon they occupied the land they had been cultivating as tenants in the name of the committees, burnt all records of tenancy and high interest loans, looted the arms of the landlords and also equipped themselves with their conventional weapons of bows and arrows. They also set up their own administration to look after the villages and attend to their needs and problems.

Now permission was necessary to enter the area as some of the adjoining villages were also captured by the activists. The CPIM was in the famous UF mode in West Bengal then with Ajoy Mukherjee of the Bangla Congress, an offshoot of the Congress party. But they knew their limitations and knew that they, part of the UF government, could be instantly dismissed for supporting violence and if there were sufficient grounds to believe that they were behind the uprising. Ideologically also the CPIM leaders were averse to such action which they dubbed as adventurism on the part of some CPIM cadres. Charu Mazumdar, Kanu Sanyal and some other leaders of the violent movement were all CPIM cadres but they knew that the party leaders had disowned them, although even among the top leaders, people like Harekrishna Konar, Revenue Minister in the UF government and a veteran peasant leader, were sympathetic to the revolt.

The CPIM did not look back. It used its full weight in the government and as a party to crush the Naxalbari revolt. There were thus clashes between the revolt leaders and their supporters on the one hand and the police and the CPIM cadres on the other. Many students in Calcutta were with the Naxalites and rose in revolt against the CPIM on account of its failure to stand by the Naxalites and even oppose them. The Centre was then ruled by Indira Gandhi and her Congress party and would have enforced President's Rule in time if it was not satisfied that Ajoy Mukherjee on his own was acting strongly against the revolt. The CPIM party secretariat opposed the repression but the party leadership knew that it had to stand by the Chief Minister. Otherwise the government could be dismissed.

China, which was then promoting extremism at home, was overjoyed at the Naxalbari revolt as it saw in it signs of Maoism succeeding in India. In June 1967, Radio Peking described the Naxalbari revolt as "the front paw of the revolutionary armed struggle lanched by the Indian people under the guidance of Mao Tse Tung." For a time the CCP (Chinese Communist Party) was at loggerheads with the CPIM which was known to be more inclined towards China while the CPI was rated as pro-Soviet. But almost from the outset the CPIM had adopted the parliamentary path. It knew that capturing power through the ballot box was much easier than armed action and ballot boxes can be manipulated.

The Naxalbari movement was destined to fail because it depended, among others, on widespread support of the peasants, their willingness to take up arms under the leadership of the cadres of the CPIM, the availability of arms, and above all, the state being utterly powerless to resist the depredations of the Communist leaders. No government worth its salt could tolerate an open challenge to its authority and had to summon all the weight at its command to fight the menace. This police action, however, in West Bengal did not prevent the movement from acquiring strength in other parts of India because the land problem needed a solution, but the Communist expectation that it would spread like wild fire was dashed to the ground.

The Naxalite movement spread from West Bengal to adjoining Bihar and Srikakulam in Andhra Pradesh. After some years the fire in Srikakulam was quenched but the movement is even today active in the Telengana region of the state where in the forties and fifties the Communists had organised as major rebellion and which gave birth to Vinoba Bhave's Bhoodan (land gift) movement. The Reds lost virtually all their Political influence in Audhra Pradesh due to their faulty policies. When the state opted for the Congress the Comrades hitched their wagon to the Telugu Desam star which rose phenomenally in Andhra Pradesh on the issue of Telugu pride. But that was to receive crumbs from the TD table. When, however, Surjeet chose open alignment with the Congress and with its Italian chief, Sonia Gandhi, the TDP left the CPIM's Third Front and supported Vajpayee's BJP-led government.

The leaders of the Naxalbari revolt analysed their failure and drew some conclusions, apart from the CPIM's tactical reasons. "When all the peasants were armed and the jotedars and other vested interests fled the village, we assumed that the base area had been created. We took the armed people for an armed force... In one or two cases we formed small bands and snatched away (the) guns from the jotedars but we did not make this the main form of the struggle and assumed instead that (a) gurrella force would be built upon the spontaneity of the masses. In many cases we were impressed with the militant attitude of the vagabonds and made them leaders for building up armed force." Kanu Sanyal[3] is quoted as citing some of the reasons of the failure of the movement.

Neglect of the task of redistribution of seized land was indicated as another reason for the failure of the movement. Among other reasons were the attacks on the jotedars in their homes rather than seizing their land and the conflict between the poor peasant and the middle peasant. The absence of a powerful mass base, the usual tendency to underestimate the enemy, that is the power of the state, are among other reasons the analysis give for the failure of the Naxalites. The organisers of the revolt did not expect the UF government in West Bengal to go 'that far'. They scarce realised that the CPIM, the dominant element in the UF, would face action under Article 356 of the Constitution which empowers the Centre to dismiss a state government under certain circumstances and the subsequent use by Delhi of the superior fire power of the army and the central paramilitary forces and, worse still from a Communist point of view, the danger of the CPIM being outlawed. As already stated, the CPIM considered the Naxalite movement as adventurism although there was no dearth of sympathy in CPIM ranks for the movement.

As indicated, the Naxalbari movement spread from West Bengal to other parts of India and is even now active in the Telengana area of Andhra Pradesh and in certain parts of South and Central Bihar. Deep forests in Telengana are ideal for the depredations of the Communists, masquerading as Naxalites, and in Bihar it is the utter failure of the administrative and police machinery and extreme politicisation of the machinery and the entire system. Bihar has been ruled for the past nearly nine years by Laloo Prasad Yadav, or his semi-literate wife, Rabri Devi, installed by him, and he has the support of the Congress chief, Sonia Gandhi, and the CPIM leaders, Surjeet and Basu. Laloo specialises in slogans to lull the public and make them forget their utter poverty. The masses in Bihar, one of the richest states in terms of resources, are steeped in penury and the average Bihari, a hard working and intelligent person, is encouraged to defy law while many have to seek employment in other states.

The region in Bihar, where the Naxalite Communists operate, also holds some thick forests but the main reason for the growth of the movement is failure of the Laloo regime to enforce land reform legislation, the politicisation of the police who lack modern arms and are generally reluctant to act against the armed Communists. As a consequence, the landholders, which term would include many poor farmers who have no desire to support the violence and have no faith in the administration, have organised their own army, the Ranbir Sena. This results in massacres and counter-massacares and the Naxalites becoming bold on occasions like the 1999 elections when they killed policemen and officers at will, some forty men.

The Naxalbari movement led to the formation of a new Communist party, the CPI (ML), Communist Party of India, Marxist Leninist. Although the name would perhaps indicate some connection with the CPI, the weaker of the two Communist parties, in reality it was an offshoot of the CPIM. In the course of time, the CPI (ML) also became a parliamentary party, with its main limited strength in Bihar. The party was formed in Calcutta in April-May 1969. When elections were held to the West Bengal Assembly in 1969 and another UF government was formed, with the CPIM holding a dominant position and Ajay Mukherjee being made the Chief Minister once again, "one of the first acts of the new government was the release of Kanu Sanyal, Jangal Santhal and other leaders of the 1967 Naxalbari uprising..."[4] Any of the reasons, cited by sympathetic writers could have impelled the new government to take the decsion. The movement had failed in achieving its main objectives and things were more or less quiet. The Chinese were, of course, all praise for the revolt but they knew in their heart of hearts that it had left no final impact. Many of the Naxalite

Communists, following the leader of the movement, Charu Mazumdar, went about saying that "China's Chairman is our Chairman".

The CPIM also did not like the leaders of the movement to wear the halo of martyrdom which would have happened if a leader like Kanu Sanyal remained longer behind the bars. On April, 22 of 1969 the new party was formed and its formation was announced at a May Day rally, organised in Calcutta by the Naxalites, by Kanu Sanyal. It hardly occurred to the rallyists and the CPI(ML) leaders that May Day was originally an American institution. The practice of observing May Day was borrowed by the world Communists and the Indian Comrades, without knowing its implications, followed suit.

Naxalites in their violent form are active in some parts of the country, as we have said, and the CPI(ML) exists as a separate Communist party which has very limited following and is now a parliamentary party like its bigger sisters, the CPI and the CPIM from whose womb they originally sprang. The Naxalism that we find in some parts, particularly in Andhra Pradesh and Bihar, is an apology for the original movement and which represented a significant development, although somewhat misconceived and not particularly relelvant. All the same, the original Naxalite movement had a historical role and raised a debate. What we find today is an aberration.

It is doubtful if the peasants in whose name the terrorists operate are really benefited by their armed action. The peasants are not part of the movement which is carried on in their name and on their behalf. In Bihar, the present government has, one suspects, a tolerant attitude towards the Naxalite Communists and one cannot accept that the small and marginal farmers are at all benefited or are involved in any manner. The Laloo regime has no option but to allow them to carry on because the police or civil administration has neither the will or wherewithal to counter them. The well to do farmers and those small ones who live under their protection are looking after themselves and the Communists indulge in periodical massacres in retaliation or just to impress on the populace their importance. There is widespread suspicion that the RJD is using the armed men on occasions, like the large-scale violence they engaged themselves in on September 18,1999.

The Naxalite are believed to be active in Andhra Pradesh, Madhya Pradesh and Maharashtra which are contagious and the armed men can flit about at will. But it is in the Telengana region of Andhra Pradesh where the Communists armed men are in some strength and can prove to be a real danger. The state administration is also taking them on and giving them a real battle and the armed men sometimes attack the police stealthily and cause a sensation.

We have seen how early in the original Naxalite movement in West Bengal the leaders were concerned with the infiltration of "vagabonds", the young people who joined the movement, more out of fun than any ideological commitment, to enjoy life, to end the boredom of their existence and their state of unemployment. The so called Maoists in Telengana, organised the PWG (People's War Group) formations and sometimes running courts of their own, face the problem of "vagabonds". This is sometimes in a more acute form than the original Naxalites encountered if a reliable report in a leading newspaper is to be believed. "PWG punishing 'erring' militants"[5] is the title of the story. It gives us an insight into the doings of the armed groups, armed with weapons they have seized from the police in their raids, purchased from the arms bazar (the Reds travel long distances to buy these weapons) and those supplied to them by the ISI agents of Pakistan and other foreign friends.

Coming to the report, the paper tells us that the Maoists have begun a process of cleansing their ranks by ridding themselves of undesirable elements or 'punishing' them so that the excesses committed by them do not bring a bad name to the PWG. The punishment is awarded to the guilty by the "praja courts' (people's courts, or kangaroo courts), which are nothing but PWG-dominated rough justice organisation where the so-called justice is meted out to these "vagabonds" brought before the courts. The report says the excesses committed by some of the members of the PWG brought a feeling of hatred towards the Naxalites in the villages. They indulged in "large-scale extortions and giving of biased and onesided verdicts (in disputes sorted out by them)"[6].

In the instances quoted by the paper the erring militants were summoned and meted out punishment... "at least three Dalam (section) commanders have been charged," says the report.[7] And what were some of the crimes committed by these dalam commanders? One militant had raped a girl and killed her, in the time-honoured tradition in which the rape victim sometimes faces the danger of being killed by the rapist. And the punishment? The militant was beaten up and a fine imposed on him! If a girl is raped outside the Naxalite camp, the Communists will raise hell demanding police action and exemplary punishment to the rapist. Rightly so, as would other activists and social workers. But the stark difference is between an accused facing IPC (Indian Penal Code) treatment and one in the four corners of a PWG dalam. Another Maoist had extracted Rs. 10,000 from his victim and when his demand for more money was refused he burnt alive the victim, a woman. We are not told what punishment, if any, was inflicted on the guilty but it could not have been heavy because another section commander who misbehaved with women colleagues was "shifted to other area".[8]

The peasants, are, no doubt, subject to all kinds of extractions by the landlords who have political and bureaucratic patronage. But when they are subjected to such depredations there is at least the law, the media and political agitations, by the Communists and others. But in the remote jungle area, dominated by the Naxalite communists, armed and ruthless, there is no guarantee of such measures. The 'praja courts', when they finally get together, they mete out paltry and ridiculous punishment to the criminals in their own ranks, fines for rape and murder and at the worst expulsion from the movement. It is typical of the inverted sense of fairness that while doing a service in bringing to light the existence of such crimes the reporter had nothing to say about the ridiculously light punishment. The same reporter would have gone into many a fulmination and pretended demands for justice being meted out if a rape had to be reported in the streets of Hyderabad city.

The CPI (ML) is, as we have said before, a parliamentary party and its General Secretary (the communist tradition is being observed here, since there is no chairman) is Dipankar Bhattacharya who succeeded Vinod Mishra when he died. Mishra was highly spoken of by party men. But in the state where the CPI (ML) is active, Bihar, there are Maoist groups of Naxalites, some belonging to the MCC, Maoist Coordination Committee, also called the Marxist Coordination Committee.

REFERENCES

1. *In the Wake of Naxalbari*, Sumanta Banerjee, Subarnarekha, Calcutta,1980.
2. *Ibid.*
3. *In the Wake of Naxalbari.*
4. *Ibid.*
5. *Hindu*, Delhi, Chennai and other cities, March 19, 1999.
6. *Ibid.*
7. *Ibid.*
8. *Ibid.*

8
CONFUSION WORST CONFOUNDED

"CPIM gets ready to jettison ideology"[1] screamed a headline in one of the Delhi dailies, not particularly noted for its fondness for the Communists but one which wants to project all kinds of political activity. The paper was reporting the briefing given by Harkishan Singh Surjeet, General Secretary of the CPIM, on the two-day meeting of the party's Politburo in Delhi on the electoral alliances of the CPIM for the forthcoming 13th Lok Sabha poll and the usual camouflague the party resorts to.

In the process, the CPIM has confused and confounded everyone of its admirers and friends, except the gullible in the media, about the lack of any ideological ballast. In the place of ideology the party has substituted a single-point programme to bring Sonia Gandhi to power, by hook or by crook, no matter how disdainfully she treats the Reds. Surjeet may talk of the revival of the Third Front, by throwing dust in the eyes of some mediamen about a hung house,[2] but all the while he is working on his pet objective of installing a Congress government in power. He is fully aware that the Third Front is dead as the dodo and is not a practicable proposition. The smaller sister CPI General Secretary said some time ago that the theory of equidistance between the Congress and the BJP, a Communist slogan for some time, is not a sustainable proposition. So Surjeet knows that he will have a role to play after the polls just as he tried his best in April 1999 to crown Sonia Gandhi but failed.

Why did he go on bended knees to Jayalalitha, soon after the failure he encountered in April, to get just two seats to contest in Tamil Nadu and why did he have an alliance with the equally disreputable Laloo Prasad Yadav even when the CPI his sister, had broken off negotiations with Laloo over seat sharing in Bihar?

Such questions can be asked by the dozen and it is true other political parties may also find it difficult to answer when similar questions are raised about their behaviour. The only difference is that others do not pretend too much about their moral scruples while the CPIM constantly talks about them. It holds up itself as a spotless white, genuine party, drawn from the top drawer of political formations. But, as we have seen, the CPIM, and its associate CPI, have less scruples than an ordinary political party, talks more about principles and ideology but behaves in a grasping manner and achieves pretty little in the end.

The ideological bankruptcy of the CPIM is, however, noticed on occasions. The Calcutta newspaper, the *Telegraph*, in an article referred to the periodical exercise indulged in by Chief Minister Jyoti Basu of West Bengal of flaying the cadres of his own party for their many failures and asked Basu:[3] "Why blame these poor fellows for having sunk to ideological illiteracy? What kind of education have the party leaders been providing them through puerile writings in their party journals and by their dodges and subterfuges in explaining away recent developments in the Communist world? Or by their newly acquired stake in a splintered polity at home, their fear of confronting their own past and their habit of opportunistic shifts in policies with fatty layers of old rhetoric? According to some observers the CPIM has lost the stake as recent events show."

The article also referred to the failure, and refusal, of the Communist leaders to acknowledge the demise of the Russian Revolution and of the cataclysmic changes in China which have placed the erstwhile Communist nation in the forefront of market-based economy and which some of the Indian Comrades interprete as "socialist market". China, as the knowledgeable are aware, has built itself as a home of the multinationals which have brought in foreign capital in a big way. This is in sharp contrast to the failure of the CPIM in West Bengal which is often described by many Bengalis as a decaying state. This state has been under CPIM rule for 22 years at a stretch and would remain there if the people tolerate the electoral rigging the CPIM resorts to on a large-scale. The Bengalis, as a people, are industrious and possess vast intellectual resources but have been taught a wrong work culture which encourages laziness and laxity which drives out industry to other states.

What happens in China throws light on the state of affairs in a Communist country and should open the eyes of many of our Comrades. While West Bengal is afflicted with labour militancy China laid off seven million workers of the white elephants, thousands of public sector enterprises, in 1999. Several million dollars would be expended on giving them social security but the hard-headed Chinese recognise that if the multinational are to be attracted in a big way and foreign capital must be brought into the country the giant public sector must be first liquidated.[4]

The Chinese have also opened the insurance[5] sector, considered worth many billion dollars, to foreign capital and to permit foreign firms to compete with state run Chinese insurance companies. This is precisely what India has proposed to do but the Communists oppose it tooth and nail. They instead encourage the Insurance employees in India to go on strike to resist the national policy and register their protest against it. India also wants to set up an insurance Regulatory Commission just as China has done and its chairman, Ma Yongwei, envisaged the issue of more licences to foreign companies in order that China would be successful in its bid to enter the World Trade Organisation (WTO).

The chairman of the Chinese Commission said that he would not wait for the domestic industry to fully prepare itself to face the competition from the multinationals. He said, on the other hand, "foreign institutions will be admitted at an appropriate time to create pressure on home companies to increase their awareness of self-improvement."[6]

"The collapse of the Soviet Union and the fast-paced economic reforms in China, to which multinationals are rushing have not taught a lesson to India's left parties," says an article in the *Hindu*. The article refers to the case of Casabianca who stood on the burning deck of his ship exactly the same way as his father had left him and observes: "Perhaps the Indian Leftists principally the two Communist parties, are reposing a similar steadfast faith in Marx, Engels, Lenin and Mao Zedong despite their ideologies having met with a fate much the same as Casabianca's ship".[7] The article contrasts the developments in China with what is happening elsewhere and says: "What is astonishing is that the "faithfuls", new rulers of China, are rolling out the red carpet to the capitalist MNCs who are seeking out the country with their billions of dollars. China seems to have foreseen the need for making a U-turn in its economic policy in the late seventies itself when there was no inkling of what was going to happen to the Soviet Union and when India could not sniff out the winds of change and would not have dared to think of the reforms which were forced on it from mid-1991".[8]

It would be interesting to analyse the Chinese going in for widespread economic reforms in order to bring a semblance of economic benefits to its teeming millions while maintaining a tight regimen of political repression of the worst kind. In India we have halting economic reforms while there is unlimited political freedom. The Chinese seem to have learnt the basic lesson in economic reforms combined with political repression from another Chinese of great eminence, Lee Kuan Yew of Singapore, who ruled the island nation for nearly thirty years from 1959 onwards. Lee is now retired but retains a lively interest in the fate of Singapore from his retirement and lays down the law in crucial matters. The only difference, if it can be so called, is that while China has no need for even a showcase democracy Singapore maintains the showcase.

When the question is about taking a U-turn, the Communists can take a U-turn in politics but not economics. For a number of years they maintained a sham or real anti-Congressism stance but when the BJP was about to come to power at the Centre, and finally when it did, they suddenly changed their stance and they chose to be great devotes of their goddess, Sonia Gandhi. They would do anything to crown her queen of Delhi and demolish the BJP, even when many erstwhile Socialists and their Comrades in the third front, the TDP and the DMK and even the Trinamul Congress, their *bete noire* but proudly "secular", join hands with the BJP. These elements may find the BJP not communal and may have no objection to associating with it and share power with it but the lilywhite CPIM must demolish the BJP and in its place put Sonia in power. Even if Sonia's obedient Congress MPs, including Manmohan Singh who prides himself on being a clean politician, toe Sonia's line in Parliament.

If the Congress, supposing for the sake of argument, comes to power with the support of the Communists and virtually follows the same economic policies what would the Comrades do? They would perhaps launch a Congress demolition programme and the cycle would thus go on. They would not instil a brand new culture among their cadres and teach them the rudiments of discipline. They would, if they did so, be able to call back industry to West Bengal and help Indian polity in a big way. What happens today is that they are fond of "secularism" and forgive Laloo for all his sins of omission and commission because he wears secular clothes. If the criterion is, prefer the label of "secularism" and corruption and lack of development can be overlooked, the Communists and whoever they can influence are going to get stuck in deeper and deeper morass.

There is a myth, especially among the gullible media, that the Communists are incorruptiable. If Mamata Banerjee is to be believed this is entirely untrue and myth is a mild word for the phenomenon. In April 1999, a CPIM minister of West Bengal,was "censured" by the party[9] for an ostentatious lifestyle and lavish spending during his daughter's wedding which had then taken place and could have been attended by partymen as well as other officials and guests. The partymen however closed their eyes to the affair of the daughter's wedding and the lavish spending but they could not overlook the complaint of the Bangladesh Communist party about what happened during Bidyut Ganguly's visit to that country. The CPIM considers itself close to the Bangladeshi Communists because the fellow feeling generated by Bengali Bhaibhaiship is something to be believed when you see it. Whether it is Jyoti Basu or the winner of the Nobel prize in economics, both of whom were born in Bangladesh, they are subject to the same sentiment.

Ganguly was called to the CPIM headquarters in Alimuddin Street in Calcutta when the party general secretary in West Bangal and a Politburo member, and Sailen Das Gupta, chairman of the Left Front, were among those present. Since the Communists do not believe in the bourgeoisie practices of other political parties (they are great adherents of scruples) they follow the "difficult" way of chastisement and not of public obloquiy and court cases which the other parties often practise although cases of corrupt politicians brought to book in the end are still not many. But then these politicians have the discomfiture of going through courts, incarceration in police custody or even judicial custody, as in the case of Jayalalitha and Laloo, both dear to the CPIM, and other indignities. The Communists do not subscribe to such methods which they leave to the other parties to practise.

The CPIM minister Ganguly who had recently visited Bangladesh was found to be unstable, a result of too much drinking obviously, and was not behaving normally while attending programmes in his honour arranged by the fellow Comrades of Bangladesh. He had celebrated the wedding of his daughter in Calcutta, an occasion in which partymen in West Bengal had taken part. He had spent lavishly, as do many Congressmen, but then they have to face the opprobrium of public criticism and condemnation when they are caught and the media make a howl about it. Here nothing of the kind happened and since corruption is not a crime in the eyes of the Comrades so they did not notice it when they took part in it as guests at the wedding. Even otherwise, the CPIM men would have come to know about his doings but they chose to connive at it until the Bangladesh Communists complained against his behaviour.

There was no punishment and the Minister was let off with just a censure which he would put in his glass in the evening and enjoy his drink all the more. What are the other steps the party would take against an erring member? It is said there could be more"drastic" measures like condemnation, which a cynical minister would care nothing for and ouster from the post which would, of course, hurt him because the extra income as a minister would no longer be available to him. Then would follow his loss of the party membership and formal expulsion from the CPIM. These are, in any case, smooth ways of dealing with a corrupt minister. But then the CPIM does not admit that it has any corrupt persons in its ranks. When Ganguly spent lavishly during his daughter's wedding the party bigwigs should have asked him where he got all that money from. A CBI inquiry into his assets and whether they were within his known sources of income would have brought to light the facts of his corruption or proved him innocent if he had other sourcs of income from which he could afford lavish spending.

Jyoti Basu has, however, a reputation for seeing no corruption and hearing no corruption charges. Another big leader, Indira Gandhi, used to laugh at corruption charges because she said it was a global phenomenon. It is said when a female Congress employee complained of sexual harassment at her job, she had her promptly dismissed. Did not a British author advise women to enjoy the rape if they could not do anything about it. The dismissal would seem to be a better way to get out of a difficult situation because the source of harassment would be eliminated, but then you would lose your job. In this scheme of things you do not have a right to complain.

The mention of Indira Gandhi recalls to mind what the *Call*, journal of the RSP (Revolutionary Socialist Party), now defunct, had said early in 1970, when the CPI as well as the CPIM were engaged in saving Indira Gandhi from the "clutches" of the Syndicate leaders. The CPIM may complain bitterly about Indira Gandhi, or for that matter about any present Congress leader but it cannot fail to rise gallantly in her defence when she is besieged by "reactionary" leaders. The *Call* had observed... "The first and the most interesting development[10]... is the eventual veering round of the CPIM to an open pro-Indira position. It is no longer opposed to the formation of a United Front, at least with a section of the Indicate..". Congressmen supporting Indira Gandhi were called by the Communists Indicate.

By her slogan "Garibi Hatao" (abolish poverty) Indira Gandhi had charmed many a Communist in 1970 and 1971. In 1972 the CPIM was to bitterly complain of the terror let loose by Indira Gandhi and her henchmen in West Bengal and the manner in which they tried to finish the CPIM in the state assembly elections. This did not prevent the gallant CPIM men from coming to her rescue, particularly if she gave attractive slogans. There is a time to complain and denounce and there is a time to rise to her defence. A Congress-oriented correspondent would tell us in July 1999, when the electoral battle for the 1999 poll was getting into full swing, that the Congress, under Sonia Gandhi, was going to adopt the deceptive slogan of "garibi hatao" once more.[11] Nothing of the kind happened, of course.

To come back to the corrupt CPIM minister. Bidyut Ganguly. In a way Ganguly chose well to cause the CPIM endless embarrassment when he died in mysterious circumstances at his home in Bhatpara in the North 24 Parganas district, adjoining Calcutta,on one Sunday evening on April 30, 2000.[11a] As we have seen, the CPIM was shaken from its root in West Bengal, where it is strongest and where it has ruled continuously now for 23 years, when first Ganguly was reported against by fellow Communists in brotherly Bangladesh. By then the comrades had noted his lavish spending at his daughter's wedding earlier and wanted to hide the whole thing and push the scandal under the carpet.

They had reprimanded the minister but could not admit that he had committed acts of corruption because such a word does not exist in their vocabulary and they are chummy with known corrupt figures like Laloo Prasad Yadav of Bihar and J. Jayalalitha of Tamil Nadu. By now the AIADMK boss has been convicted in one corruption case and has been awarded a year's hard labour in jail. Laloo has often been imprisoned as an undertrial and before long he would face the day of reckoning but the comrades who value his presence in their "secular" front would protest against such high-handedness.

From the moment of Ganguly's death the CPIM, headed by Jyoti Basu, said that Ganguly had died of depression. Actually he had suffered 92 per cent burn injuries and his home was full of petroleum fumes. The doctors post mortem report came in four days and the same formula was repeated by Basu and other Comrades that Ganguly was suffering from depression. They knew that the Trinamul, the BJP and even the Congress would exploit the mystery death of Ganguly in the municipal elections to the Calcutta Municipal Corporation and polls to nearly eighty other municipalities around West Bengal. There were prestigious polls because the CPIM and their fellow comrades had to make up for the loss of two per cent votes which they had suffered in the last Lok Sabha elections. Per contra the Trinamu–BJP and the Congress together had gained a higher percentage than the entire Left Front which induced Mamata to propose a "Mahajot" (grand alliance) of the three parties and although the West Bengal Congress was almost unanimously in favour of the concept, Sonia Gandhi and her henchmen in Delhi rejected the proposal. They trotted out the excuse that by going into the Mahajot the Congress would have to work with the hated BJP and thereby its "secularism" would be jeopardised. The real reason, of course, was that Sonia needed the CPIM's support at the national level and it could ill afford to antagonise that party.

We will come to that later but the 64-year old Ganguly had upset the CPIM's applecart and despite Sonia's 'no' to the Mamata Mahajot it would haunt the CPIM in the municipal polls and even the Panskura by-election. The fact was that Ganguly had taken to heart the admonition of the West Bengal CPIM over his corruption and wanted to put an early end to the charges. Bidyut Ganguly had been chairman[11b] of the Bhatpara municipality for more than two decades before being elected to the state assembly for the first time in 1991. He was immediately made a minister of state and perhaps because of his earlier administrative experience and his performance as a minister of state, he was made by the CPIM a full fledgded cabinet minister and given charge of Commerce and Industry in 1996 when he was re-elected. He was, of course, entirely unhappy with the loud-mouthed Somnath Chatterjee, leader of the CPIM in the Lok Sabha, being given excessive importance by the party because the Delhi media gave him undue coverage. Chatterjee was made by the CPIM chairman of the West Bengal Industrial Development Corporation besides his parliamentary duties.

The Trinamul and other opposition parties demanded that the Communist regime hold a judicial inquiry but the demand was not conceded. If the suicide theory was right and there seemed to be no other reason for the death and for the 92 per cent burns suffered by Ganguly whose clothes bore signs of having been soaked in petroleum—questions could arise why a communist minister had to end his life in this manner. The theory of depression was relevant and handy to the leaders of the Red party. But the question still remained: Why did Ganguly have depression when the whole West Bengal was crying for bread and a comrade had in theory to meet the demand.

Jyoti Basu and another top leader of the CPIM, Sailen Dasgupta, chairman of the Left Front created by the CPIM as a device to rule the state with the help of some likeminded parties, did not visit the CPIM party headquarters in Alimuddin Street where Ganguly's body was kept for the usual "darshan" by the public before cremation. Normally the top leaders go to Alimuddin Street to offer "Lal Salam" (traditional communist way of offering homage) and the media refer to Alimuddin Street as though the CPIM owned the whole street. Simply because the party headquarters is located there the media love to identify the party with the street, just as in Delhi 10, Janpath is identified with Sonia Gandhi. She, of course, lives there without paying any rent. Such VIPs work for the "poor" so much so that V.P. Singh's kidney treatment cost the nation more than a crore of rupees but he lives to serve the poor.

The CPIM is naturally worried over the fallout of the entire Ganguly episode. They know that some 21 municipalities are to go the polls in the dead minister's area and the alleged suicide of Ganguly would upset the voters not only of the town of Bhatpara but of the other municipalities as well. They know that last year Ganguly was called to Alimuddin Street headquarters of the CPIM in Calcutta and perhaps told that he would not be nominated again in the 2001 assembly elections when the Trinamul hopes to capture power in West Bengal.

It is possible that the Trinamul, if it succeeds in its effort to capture power, it may unravel the mystery of the death of Bidyut Ganguly. The CPIM regime has something to hide and for that reason it would not think of ordering a proper probe into the mystery. But there is no doubt that his death has raised many doubts among the followers of the party and it is bound to be reflected in the voting pattern in the coming days. There is yet another angle to the Ganguly death apart from the corruption aspect. He was close the West Bengal Transport Minister, Subhas Chakraborty, who is generally taken as a dissenter in the ranks of the CPIM and whom the party bigwigs tolerate because there could be a virtual revolt if any action is taken against him.

In fact, the CPIM is now engaged in an exercise to win over Chakraborty and not taking action against his open defiance as well as of the CPIM former MP, Saifuddin Chaudhry, who had made quite an impact during the time he was in the Lok Sabha until the party put an end to his tenure. How this would all end remains to be seen.

Reference was made in this book to the disruption of an Indo-Pakistan cricket match at the famous Eden Garden in Calcutta February 1999. A senior editor of the *Hindustan Times*, noted for his strong anti-BJP views but an alumni of the prestigious Calcutta institution, the Presidency College, said: "And the Calcutta crowd too has demonstrated (like the Shiv Sainiks) twice in three years the same penchant to indulge in hooliganism if it cannot have things going its way." Exposing the myth that Calcutta was safe for couples, the elderly and women, who could walk back home from a night show, the author says: "All that changed in the sixties when frightening stories circulated of a woman having been dragged away from her husband after the two emerged from a cinema late in the evening and of women being molested at the end of a musical show in South Calcutta. It is not only that Calcutta's tradition of night life came to an end during the Naxalite "period", as the late sixties and early seventies came to be known, an atmosphere of violence also gripped the city."[12]

That was well before the BJP came to Calcutta and West Bengal and Basu called the BJP "barbarous". That was at a time when the CPIM rose to be supreme in the life of Calcutta and West Bengal. Violence is part of any great city's fate but in Calcutta, under the CPIM, there are frequent clashes first between the CPIM cadres and Congress activists, then between the CPIM cadres and Naxalites, who were all CPIM activists until the other day, and now between the CPIM and the Trinamul Congress of Mamata Baerjee and the BJP.

Mamata Banerjee is the rising star of West Bengal and her mercurial nature adds to her strength and influence. She realised long ago that the CPIM menace must be faced if West Bengal were to be saved. The Communists had promised much when they came to power first in 1977 but being fundamentalists of a different kind they went against the very essence of the Bengalis who love freedom. Mamata thought the Congress would be able to fight the CPIM and regain power in the state and, therefore, for a long time she remained a loyal Congresswoman. But she gradually realised that the Congress was no match for the CPIM's machinations and also saw that there were too many factions in the party and the top leadership in Delhi were patronising them. Her forte was her personality and she broke away from the main party and even Sonia Gandhi, who took over the leadership of the party from the unwilling hands of Sitaram Kesri in March 1998, could not bring her back into the Congress.

She had also realised that if the CPIM was to be effectively fought she had to take along with her the fledgling BJP which, despite all its faults, was the answer to Bengal's need for dynamism and an able ally in countering the CPIM. While she ridiculed the Congress in West Bengal as the B team of the CPIM she also defeated the Congress in her very first election exercise. In 1998 she won seven seats in the Lok Sabha, helped the BJP win one, and allowed the Congress only one seat. The Communists however, won the rest of the 42 seats of the state, 33 of them. She had an uneasy relationship with the BJP-led government at the centre but she realised that the future lay with Vajpayee whom she repeatedly proclaimed leader of the country.

Now Mamata is much more powerful and is likely to snatch some of the rural seats from the CPIM. The outcome of the poll for the 13th Lok Sabha would be interesting not only from the overall point of view but the results in West Bengal may be totally surprising.

C.R. Irani, the boss of the *Statesman*, of Calcutta and Delhi,is not noted for his writing ability although he is the editor of the paper. Often he writes his "Caveat" column (he is himself an unsuccessful lawyer) in the paper over which he presides with an iron hand, not dissimilar to a dictatorial approach. But it cannot be denied that when he speaks of the CPIM rulers of West Bengal, whom he should know like the palm of his hand from his Chowringee perch in the *Statesman* house in Calcutta, it should make interesting reading:

"It would be a gross understatement to say that the Left are in a sorry state, not because of the ideology, but as a consequence of the greed of their leadership which are anxious to advance their bargaining power at the Centre after the elections, by crook, if not by hook. Hence the new addition to the political lexicon, the CPIM and CPI are "allies" all over the country but they will have different, even contradictory, "seat adjustments" with the others in different states, depending on the "ground situation", whatever that may mean to the author of the proposition, the evergreen Harkishen Singh Surjeet. That these will make the Communists the laughing stock does not worry him."[13]

REFERENCES

1. *Indian Express*, Delhi, July 27,1999.
2. *Ibid.*
3. *"Ideological illiteracy", The Telegraph*, Calcutta, March 11,1999.
4. "*China to lay off 7 m workers in 1999," Hindustan Times,* Delhi, April 15, 1999.
5. "China opens insurance in bid to join WTO", *Times of India,* Delhi, March 29,1999.
6. *Ibid.*
7. "The Intrepid Casabiance", C.V. Gopalakrishnan, *The Hindu,* December 21, 1998.
8. *Ibid.*
9. "CPIM censures minister for Industries," *Hindustan Times,* Delhi, April 15, 1999.
10. *"The Economic Times,"* Delhi, October 15, 1998.
11. "Congress revives 'garibi hatao' plank," *Times of India,* Delhi, July 28, 1999.

11(*a*). "Police to probe West Bengal ministers death," *Hindustan Times*

Delhi, May 2, 2000.

11(*b*). "Jitters in CPI(M) over Minister's suicide," *National Herald*, Delhi, May 21, 2000.

12. "No garden of Eden, Amulya Ganguli on West Bengal's decline," *Hindustan Times*, Delhi, February 28, 1999.

13. "The decline and fall of the left," C.R. Irani, Caveat, *the Statesman*, Delhi and Calcutta, July 28, 1999.

9

NDA EMERGES VICTORIOUS: REDS SHOCKED

The CPIM General Secretary Harkishan Singh Surjeet had played a leading part in toppling the Vajpayees government in April 1999. But despite all his efforts to put the crown of Delhi on the head of Sonia Gandhi he dismally failed. Neither Sonia nor the second best, Jyoti Basu, Chief Minister of West Bengal, could come to power. Failure was gall to Surjeet who poured scorn on people whom he had expected but did not stand by him and was beside himself with grief.

But the wise men of politics do not waste much time on grief. They do not believe in mourning while there is work to do and new goals to be laid and met. President K.R. Narayanan at heart a Congressman, who gave more than the required time to Sonia Gandhi whom he did not question as to how she was going to make up for the support of a large number of MPs when she was herself not one and the Congress party in the Lok Sabha had only 140 members. She claimed the support of 279 MP's but failed to substantiate her claim in the three days allowed to her by a pliant President to do so. She had to admit that she was falling short of the magic figure by a substantial number. Even more irksome was her failure to Surjeet and the CPIM as a party which tried unsuccessfully to project the aged Basu as a prospective Prime Minister for a few hours after Sonia handed over the Presidential mandate back to Narayanan.

Surjeet after a day or two of mourning and emptying his heart of bitterness went to Jayalalitha at her palatial hotel residence and applied for AIADMK support. In politics no party should be untouchable, although the Communists try to portray the BJP as such. Having secured Jayalalitha's support for the CPIM he next knocked on the doors of the plebian Laloo Prasad Yadav. The object in his mind was still the crown for Sonia Gandhi.

He believed that the Congress and the Left had scored a major victory when another constitutional authority, the Chief Election Commissioner, Dr. M. S. Gill, ruled that the early polls which the BJP and the NDA wanted were not feasible and the September-October period which the Congress and the Left had opted for was the real period. Elections were held in the country and in a major state like Gujarat in June (the Gujarat assembly was elected in June 1975 and very soon Mrs Indira Gandhi had proclaimed the Emergency) but neither did he nor the Congress nor, indeed, the Left had noted that the longer the BJP and NDA were to remain in power in the Centre the Congress and its allies could not relish it and it was not to their benefit. Nor did they realise that there could arise many a contingency like the Pakistani failed enterprise in Kargil in Kashmir.

Mrs Sonia Gandhi fulminated against the BJP in the numerous election rallies she addressed on the Kargil issue; the electorate which came to those rallies in large numbers thought that she was not in favour of India's victory in the Kargil war. This was to be reflected in the votes cast in favour of the Congress candidates eventually but little did Sonia Gandhi and the coterie of her close advisers realise that and they felt no need for a midterm course correction. Anti-BJPism and anti-Vajpayeeism come naturally to her because she craves to wear the crown of Delhi and the average Congressman then thought that she was their best bet to get into the seat of power. Comrade Surjeet also thought so and still thinks along these lines, although like many Congressmen his faith in Sonia has dwindled somewhat.

The Left naturally tried its best to maintain its position in the Lok Sabha. Although most media have not yet realised that, this writer long ago came to the conclusion that the Left strength in the country is inflexible. It could decline but there are no visible signs that the strength could be enhanced. Once more the Reds failed in their attempt to increase their tally in the Lok Sabha polls. Their total number, along with the supporting parties, was even less than the usual quota. The 1999 elections to the 13th Lok Sabha gave the CPIM 32 seats, the CPI only four, the RSP 3, the Forward Bloc its normal quota of 2, and one of its allies in Kerala one seat. The Left failed to come anywhere near its target of 50.

The Congress even fared worse. Despite the vigorous campaigning by Sonia Gandhi, who floated from rally to rally to read out anti-BJP and anti-Vajpayee speeches written for her in Roman Hindi in bold types to the usual crowd of expectant Congressmen and some voters, the Congress tally was only 112 instead of the strength of the party under the old man Sitaram Kesri when it was 140. The loss of 28 seats was difficult to explain although the media were kinder than usual. They had projected Sonia and her charming daughter, Priyanka, as the saviours of the weaker sections in certain areas and even speculated on the daughter's permanent entry into politics.

The Congress had done well in some areas of the country, like Karnataka and Punjab, and eventually managed to capture power in Maharashtra in the company of the expelled Sharad Pawar-led Nationalist Congress Party (NCP). But it drew a blank in Delhi, Haryana and Himachal Pradesh where the BJP scored over it capturing all the seats and dividing the ten seats in Haryana with the INLD (Indian National Lok Dal). The Congress opened its account in Uttar Pradesh, India's most populous state, where it had not got a single seat in the 1998 election when also Sonia had campaigned for the party.

The BJP did very well in several states like Madhya Pradesh, Rajasthan and playing its cards well got in several states like Orissa, Andhra Pradesh and Tamil Nadu as a second fiddler to the regionally strong parties like the BJPD (Biju Janta Dal), the Telugu Desam and the DMK. Incidentally, the indefatigable maker of accusations, Subramanyan Swamy, lost his security deposit. He was refused a nomination by his patron Jayalalitha who was angry with him over his failure to provide for an alternative government after toppling the Vajpayee government in April 1999. Like the proverbial washerman's beast of burden, he neither belonged to the home of the washerman (in this case Jayalalitha) nor to the washing place (the Lok Sabha).

The BJP suffered a severe blow in UP where its aggregate came down from the impressive figure of 60 seats in 1998 to less than half that, 29 seats. The main beneficiary of this debacle was the Samajwadi Party of Mulayam Singh Yadav who had defied Surjeet in April 1999 and refused to support Sonia Gandhi in her bid to form a government. Sonia wanted to steal his Muslim votebank in UP and yet hoped to get his support in forming a purely Congress government on her strength of 140 seats. Mulayam had rightly refused to toe Surjeet and Congress line and had in the bargain actually been rewarded by the Muslim voters of UP in the 1999 elections.

The NDA did extremely well and secured an absolute majority, nearly 300 of the 543 seats in the Lok Sabha. The 70 strong Vajpayee cabinet was sworn in by President Narayanan on October 13, 1999. Despite the media evenhandedly projecting both the NDA and the opposition the NDA in the first year in office of the government withstood the pressure of some of the allies of the BJP in the NDA coalition, particularly the Telugu Desam, the Trinamul and the JD (U), to rollback the subsidy cuts in the budget of 2000-2001. The budget was passed and the long Parliament session for the budget was successfully negotiated.

What is more, the media hype for Sonia was fast coming to nought. Instead of the usual media madness for the European lady, now the media reported from day to day the attacks on Sonia by prominent Congressmen and the virtual revolt in the West Bengal unit of the party. Leaders of the party in the state were all for the Mahajot (grand alliance) concept propounded by the Trinamul leader, Miss Mamata Banerjee, despite the fact that the grand alliance had under its umbrella the BJP with which the Trinamul had an electoral alliance. Mamata is Railway Minister in the Vajpayee government and her party is a member of the NDA. In the 1999 Lok Sabha polls the two parties, fighting the elections together, had increased their tally by two, Trinamul going up from 7 to 8 and BJP from 1 to 2, one seat each for the two parties and together with the Congress had managed a total vote tally higher than the Left Front of the CPIM.

That was the rationale and justification for The Mahajot plan of Mamata. West Bengal Congressmen saw the point and opted wholeheartedly for it. They realised that thereby the party could still be intact and the old Congress dream of defeating the Leftists in West Bengal could be realised simultaneously. Their experience of the success of the Trinamul-supported nominee in the biannual elections to the Rajya Sabha from West Bengal on May 28 was before them. Then many Congress MLAs in the assembly had voted for the Trinamul-supported independent candidate and defeated their party nominee who had been chosen by Sonia herself. Jayant Bhattacharya was the Trinamul-supported candidate (who later formally joined the party) and the defeated Congress nominee was former minister in the Narasimha Rao government at the Centre, Pal).

This convinced almost all the Congress activists and leaders in West Bengal that the future in the state for Congressmen was with Mamata Banerjee. If they had to fight the Left juggernaut and give shape to their dream to see the Left out of power in their Bengal they had to strengthen the hands of the only leader who looked like giving the Communists a run for their money. The state leaders were convinced but not the Central leaders of the party keen on retaining the confidence of the Reds. The Congress president knew that if her ambition to become the Prime Minister of the country was to be ever realised, it must be through the instrumentality of the CPIM. For that reason, Sonia was opposed to the Mahajot idea and so were her henchmen in Delhi while the West Bengal Congress was all for it.

To understand the significance of the Mahajot concept and the fondness of the average Congressman for it one must delve a little deeper into the politics of the state. After the death of Bidhan Chandra Roy, who was a leading Congressman of Gandhian vintage and an eminent physician in Bengal and became the Chief Minister of West Bengal at a critical period in the life of the state and remained in that office for ten long years, the state was in the grip of the Reds. The youth of the province had taken a leading part in the violent movement against foreign rulers and the Communists of Bengal were in the forefront of the communist movement in the country.

As long as Bidhan Babu was alive the Communists had little hope of coming to power in the state. The story was different after his death. In the 1967 elections several Congress governments in states suffered defeats and in West Bangal also a United Front government of the Bangla Congress and the Communists led by the CPIM, came to power. There were mid-term elections two years later and once again the same combination came to power. Jyoti Basu was Deputy Chief Minister both in 1967 and again in 1969. In the wake of the blazing success of Mrs. Indira Gandhi in the 1971 Bangladesh war in December 1971, the Congress had a resounding success in the mid-term poll to the state assembly of West Bengal in 1972.

That was all the success the Congress was having in the state because in the anti-emergency wave against Mrs. Indira Gandhi's Congress the Communists came to power in West Bengal in 1977 and remained in that position dashing all Congress hopes to the ground. Rajiv Gandhi was immensely popular until Bofors led to his downfall and he tried his hand at the 1987 assembly elections in West Bengal also. Nothing, however, worked and the people of West Bengal had to live with the Reds.

The Congress had a measure of influence in the urban areas of the state but the Reds had a stronghold in the rural areas, apart from some influence in the urban. We have seen the electoral special arrangements made by the CPIM-led Left government in West Bengal for success in the elections. In the face of such effective power structure built up by the Reds, there was little hope for the Congress to come to power. The BJP had begun to make an impact in some areas but the real answer to the CPIM rule came when Mamata Banerjee left the Congress to form her Trinamul (grassroot) Congress early in 1998 after the state Congressmen would not acknowledge her primacy in the affairs of the state.

Immediately she made impact and knowing the importance of the BJP she entered into an alliance with it. This had the desired effect in the parliamentary polls in February 1998 and although her association with the BJP at the Centre was never an unqualified success, she stuck to the alliance and in the elections to the Thirteenth Lok Sabha this was reflected when she once again humbled both the Congress and the Reds, although the CPIM and its supporting parties had a majority of seats.

Mamata was until then known as a rabble rouser and a street fighter but she proved the equal of Joyti Basu as an orator in Bengali and as Railway Minister in the Vajpayee cabinet she proved equally effective as an administrator and a planner. She became the hope that the Bengalis were looking for and a symbol for the restoration of the pride that the Bengali was seeking. What is more, she offered the people of the state a promise that under her leadership they could overthrow the Marxists and achieve real democratic rule if all the non-Communist forces united under her leadership.

Sonia Gandhi, who has a link with the CPIM, resisted Mamata's effort at bringing all non-Communist parties under a common platform. She took the plea that the Congress could not join any alliance with the BJP in it. The West Bengal Congress had, however, no objection to the arrangements because they realised that only under Mamata there was hope of overthrowing the CPIM regime. A. B. A. Ghani Khan Chaudhury and his predecessor, Somen Mitra, were called by Sonia Gandhi to Delhi originally to explain the cross voting in the Rajya Sabha biennial election that the Congress MLA's had indulged in. This was not a simple matter and the state Congress leaders took up the question of the Mahajot with Sonia and gave a virtual go-by to the cross voting which normally speaking must be taken seriously as it affected party discipline.

Sonia had the support of people like Ghulam Nabi Azad who is not normally concerned with West Bangal as the state of West Bengal is allotted to another General Secretary of the All India Congress Committee, Prabha Rau. But he is known as a Sonia loyalist and is keenly anti-BJP. So is the only West Bengal party leader, Priya Ranjan Das Munshi, who was nominated by Sonia as Working President because A. B. A. Ghani Khan Chaudhury had not been keeping good health and could not bear the burden of day-to-day work. But the Mahajot concept brought out the best in him and he rose to the occasion until his spirits were somewhat dampened by sonia's anti-Mahajot move.

As we have seen, Sonia's main consideration was not to offend the CPIM, its main prop in her bid to capture power at the Centre, and the concern not to mix with the BJP only a minor objection. Even there, the main concern was that the CPIM would take it amiss if she were found to cohabit with the BJP through the Trinamul. Her primary concern was not to offend the CPIM not realising that both in West Bengal and Kerala, and even in Tripura the third state where the CPIM was in power, the main rival of the CPIM was the Congress, now of course, the Trinamul which is an offshoot of the parent body. If the CPIM has to be fought effectively in these states, the Congress has to gird up its loins.

In Kerala, the Congress has been heading the UDF (United Democratic Front) which often alternates with the CPIM-led LDF (Left Democratic Front) which is in power in the state and would remain there until 2001 when a new Kerala assembly is to be elected as in West Bengal. Congressmen in Kerala are keenly aware of the coming contest and are trying to win parties and individuals from their alliance with the CPIM and the LDF dominated by it. Recently, a controversy in the state is concerning the IUML (Indian Union Muslim League) which is an important force in Kerala's life because the Muslims are 21 per cent of the total population. The only representatives of the IUML in the Lok Sabha come from Kerala and they are usually two in number.

Ever since the first Prime Minister, Jawaharlal Nehru, said that the Muslim League in Kerala was different, meaning it was not communal, the Congress has embraced it and included it in the UDF. If anybody in India has to be called communal it is the IUML, not because of its name and its ancestry, but also because it meets the accepted definition of a communal party. It does not admit any non-Muslim as its members and is thus exclusive. Strangely, the BJP is described as communal by the CPIM and the Congress, both of which seek to woo the IUML, but the BJP has a number of Muslims in its ranks. One of its senior leaders is Sikander Bakht, a former Delhi Congressman, who also became a Union Minister and was leader of the Rajya Sabha in the 1998 Vajpayee government. Even in the Thirteenth Lok Sabha, the BJP has a minister from the Muslim community, Shah Nawaz Khan of Bihar, a minister of state and several of its important leaders in the party are Muslim. Its Vice President in West Bengal, Muzaffar Khan, is a Muslim and like Sikander Bakht a Muslim Minister of State was in the previous Vajpayee cabinet, Mukhtar Naqvy.

It suits the CPIM and the Congress, headed by a Roman Catholic, to dub the BJP as communal. We have referred to the role of several BJP leaders in the demolition of the Babari mosque in Ayodhya in Uttar Pradesh and condemned it in unequivocal terms[1]. But it has to be acknowledged that in spite of it a number of experienced administrators and former leading Congressmen like Lt. Gen. (Retd.) J.F.R. Jacob, Governor of Punjab, the Deputy Chairman of the Planning Commission, K.C. Pant, who held several ministerial berths under one Congress government or another, T.N. Chaturvedi, a member of the Rajya Sabha, and Jagmohan, a minister in the previous Vajpayee government and even in the present NDA regime, and elected as a BJP representative to the Lok Sabha, have been attracted to the party. This is apart from several others who have joined the organisation for various reasons.

But the party is not only the effective opponent of the Congress at the all-India level and has made a success of the governance it was entrusted with in 1998 and again in 1999. In foreign policy and from the point of view of national security it has achieved notable successes which makes the Congress and the CPIM even more jealous of the party.

For the CPIM, the BJP has been a thorn in its side for more reasons than one. Apart from the BJP's Babari past, which like Sonia the CPIM would like to recollect again and again, it knows that the BJP, as part of its all-India drive, has been cutting into the CPIM's preserves like West Bengal, where the BJP has won two seats, previously held by the CPIM, and is well on the way to become a significant force in Kerala, apart from other areas. What is more, the BJP has stolen the CPIM's thunder of the United Front.

This has been dealt with in a separate chapter but it would be relevant to recall the CPIM General Secretary, Harkishan Singh Surjeet's remarks of his expectation that the Telugu Desam in Andhra Pradesh coming back to the Third Front. The Reds are now talking of it as an alternative to the UF concept that they had fathered and brought into being in 1996 for a couple of years. But it would be pertinent to point out that the TDP was driven out of the UF by the CPIM itself when it wanted to support the Congress which ultimately it did when the Vajpayee government was toppled in April 1999. There is little point in projecting the old and tired Jyoti Basu, who has been given by the CPIM time until the elections to the West Bengal assembly in 2001 after which he would retire at the age of 87 years, as the leader of Third Front. The out-of-work ex-Prime Ministers in their wily ways may proclaim him as their leader but they have no political support base of any kind. V.P. Singh gives false hopes to slum dwellers of Delhi but his rallies have had poor attendance.

Thus both the Congress and the CPIM found the BJP unpalatable. For one (the Congress) it is a rival at the all-India level and a stumbling block in Sonia's ambition to become the ruler of India. It would be no small gain for an Italian to head the government of India and it should be remembered that the Italian media came rushing in like butterflies attracted to honey when they saw some flicker of hope for this ambition to be realised. For the CPIM, the BJP has to be hated through and maligned as a fascist organisation and, in Jyoti Basu's language, as uncivilised and barbarous, because it acts as a thorn in its side and spoils its plans to project their leader as a future Prime Minister of India. In both cases, the BJP is standing in the way of the unfulfilled ambitions of Jyoti Basu and Sonia Gandhi.

But what is the actual situation at least concerning Mrs. Sonia Gandhi? She was hailed by the media when she first came to the fore to lead the Congress campaign to capture power at the Centre. Knowing her, one could not imagine that she would be a thundering success as a party leader and eventually as the Prime Minister of India. When she was accompanying her husband, the then Prime Minister, Rajiv Gandhi, on his frequent tours of India, she was at the Hyderabad airport once when the person seated next to her was P. Upendra who had become a cabinet minister under V.P. Singh and then quietly joined the Congress and was even elected once as a Lok Sabha MP as a Congress candidate but failed the second time.

As the Prime Minister's wife and as someone who was about to reprimand Upendra, Sonia should have made sure of the person she was going to speak. She did nothing of the kind and upbraided the then National Front spokesman for maligning her Italian relations on the Bofors issue in Parliament. Upendra had done nothing of the kind and was aghast at the sudden outburst of the then Prime Minister's wife. What had happened was that Sonia Gandhi had mistaken Upendra for Unnikrishnan of the Congress (S), who was also like Upendra a minister in the V. P. Singh government. Both then had a somewhat similar build but there the comparison ended because one was as different from the other as chalk is from cheese.

Vasant Sathe, a former minister under Indira Gandhi and even Rajiv Gandhi, and Chairman of the editorial board of the Congress journal, *Sandesh* (the message), was one of those who attacked Sonia in the middle of the year 2000 when Sathe referred to "a crisis of confidence"[2] in the Congress party under Sonia Gandhi. In a subsequent interview[3] he referred to Sonia's known inability to know many individuals and perhaps this story, which I reported for the Mumbai paper, *Afternoon Counrier and Despatch*, and which was confirmed by no less a person than Unnikrishnan, who happened to be in Mumbai on the day the story appeared, fits in with what poor Sathe had to say of Sonia. For those who might not know even though they may be working in the media, let me add that Sathe is well known to the Indira Gandhi family. When Sathe was Minister under Indira

Gandhi, Sonia was nobody in the household and Sathe used to walk into the house without an appointment.

Sonia came to the Congress at a time when the partymen had given up any hopes of the Congress coming back to power. Twice, the Congress had pulled down the United Front Government of H. D. Deve Gowda and I.K. Gujral, in 1997, and when elections were ordered by President Narayanan, the first of the mid-term polls he had committed the nation to, they were at their wits end as they saw no light at the end of the tunnel. The Congress faced a somewhat similar position in the middle of the year 2000 when Congress leaders and activists gave up hope that they would be able to seize power under Sonia. Defiance of the party president had begun early. In May, 1999 when the party should have put its best foot forward because the 1999 elections to the 13th Lok Sabha were at hand the party expelled one of its top leaders, Sharad Pawar, along with the former Lok Sabha Speaker, P. A. Sangma, and one of the AICC General Secretaries, Tariq Anwar. Sharad Pawar was known to be a rival to Sonia for the leadership of the organisation and had the position of Leader of the Opposition in the outgoing 12th Lok Sabha by virtue of his position as leader of the Congress party in the Lok Sabha. He was thus an important leader with considerable influence in his native Maharashtra. But Sangma had been known to be a faithful follower of Sonia, being also a Roman Catholic and universally respected in the north-east of the country. It was all the more a matter of some surprise that Sharad Pawar had such distinguished company and Sangma felt as strongly about Sonia's foreign origin as did many others, some of whom had openly expressed themselves, as did Pawar, Sangma and Anwar.

That the three leaders and the Nationalist Congress Party (NCP) which they formed soon after their expulsion from the Congress did considerable damage to the election fortunes of the Congress was proved by the results. Sonia had thrown tantrums soon after the expulsion and refused to withdraw her resignation of the post held by her until hordes of Congressmen sycophantically fell on their feet and begged her to withdraw the resignation. How sincere they were was proved in the poll results which proved, if any proof was needed, that wailing partymen are not sincere in the piteous appeals they make.

Soon after the debacle of the party in the elections there was a hue and cry and a demand for some heads to roll but with the advice of the coterie she was clever enough to appoint a committee of introspection under the cleanest Congress leader, A.K. Anthony, former Chief Minister of Kerala and a former central Minister. The introspection came to nothing as everything was state-managed. Sonia remained ensconed as Congress President and her coterie remained safe in their positions and no harm came to anybody. It is typical of the Congress that even after a major debacle nobody was made to step down from his or her safe perch.

The Budget session of Parliament came and the Congress MPs staged many walkouts and held protest dharnas and rallies, some of them poorly attended despite Sonia addressing them, and some mediamen saying in advance that she would address a huge rally. Came the crucial time to pass the budget and Sonia was found wanting as a leader of the Opposition. A time came when a known Sonia apologist[4] cried out "where is the Opposition?" and described the Congress as comatose. The Congress had not brought up a single motion of symbolic opposition, the cut motions as they are called. The Congress had been outwitted by the government which got the budget passed by the Lok Sabha and endorsed by the upper house as the Congress members were busy with their walkouts and protests but the inexperienced leader of the Opposition, now Sonia herself, was not there to tell them what they should do.

Just before the budget was passed, the Congress party was begulied into juxtaposing their leader, Sonia, with the experienced and eloquent Prime Minister in the Lok Sabha. The opportunity came as the debate over the motion of thanks to the President to the joint session of the two houses of Parliament, was to end. This should have been gone through much earlier but because of the frequent walkouts was postponed to the second half of the Budget session. Vajpayee simply floored the Congress chief and some of the media said it was an unequal fight. Unequal it was; a master of oratory was pitted again against a novice who simply read out her speech which is not normally allowed in Parliament but was tolerated as a matter of concession. But then who told the Congress party to place their inexperienced leader side by side with the Prime Minister and who told them to choose an inexperienced leader in the first place?

Congressmen choose the leader and the media describe her as 'inexperienced'! What Vajpayee had done to twit the Congress was to ask Sonia to explain the inconsistency in the party's stand on the nuclear deterrent issue. When Congress president and some of her closest advisers met the American President Bill Clinton in March, 2000 they had told him that the Congress supported a minimum credible nuclear deterrent policy for India. Pranab Mukherjee who briefed the media after the meeting told them in so many words but he was contradicted the next day by the party spokesman, Ajit Jogi, when it came out in the media that the Congress had come out in support of the BJP-led government's policy.

Mukherjee did not like such contradiction a bit and some media reported it and Sonia appointed a committee to examine the party's nuclear policy but the inconsistency remained and Vajpayee was able to tease the party over the issue. That Sonia kept quiet when Vajpayee asked her about it in the open house was noted by the media some of whom were kind enough to her and attributed her silence to her inability to reply extempore. This was not true because Sonia could speak in English or Hindi if she wished.

All this combined with the Budget session coming to an end without the Congress party making an impact and the continued dissensions in most of the state units, unleashed a plethora of adverse comments in the media which naturally came to the view that the party was getting tired of its Indira Gandhi family member as leader. The dynasty was seen losing its charisma as though much charisma was left and much of it was in evidence in the Lok Sabha or the continuing assembly elections. In this climate of criticism and media assault came some of the strongest criticism of the Congress president by some of Sonia's closest colleagues which was seen by the media as signs of growing disenchantment with the leadership of Sonia Gandhi.

REFERENCES

1. This issues has been dealt with at some length in the author's book *The Great Divide: Muslim Separatism and Partition*. It was brought out by Gyan, Delhi. The former U.P. Chief Minister, Kalyan Singh, was in power at the time and was pulled up by the Supreme Court of India and a case has been registered against some BJP leaders. The real issue, however, is the abandonment of the authority by the Congress Prime Minister, P.V. Narasimha Rao, who just watched the mosque, from his safe perch in Delhi, being demolished and India earning a bad name. The Congress was punished in election after election by the Muslim electorate and perhaps the party has not been forgiven yet. The Muslim mobs in India, Pakistan, UAE and London and even Bangladesh made the demolition of the Babari mosque an excuse for destroying some 150 temples, a fact which is not even taken into account.
2. *See Hindustan Times,* Delhi, May 18, 2000, "Crisis of Confidence," by Vasant Sathe.

3. *Hindustan Times,* Delhi, May 21, Interview with Vasant Sathe, "The CWC is not performing its role; it hasn't helped Sonia". The interviewer was Kalyani Shanker, a senior journalist.
4. "Where has the Opposition gone", *Hindustan Times*, Delhi, May 20, 2000, Bharat Bhushan, Executive Editor of the paper, known for his pro-Sonia and anti-Vajpayee views.

10
DECLINE OF CONGRESS

In the summer of 2000, the Congress leadership was suffering from a crisis of confidence. Not only Vasant Sathe wrote about it in the Congress journal, *Sandesh,* there were others expressing doubts about Sonia's capacity to hold the party together and give it an effective lead. She was, of course, continuing her anti-BJP blast as usual, something in which she excels as she reads out the prepared speeches from a raised podium with declining attendance at the rallies. She was 'however' not able to convey her thoughts and the thoughts of the Congress party and it was a pitiable sight to see Kapil Sibal, the eminent lawyer, who acted as her mouthpiece during the crucial electoral campaign period before the nation went to the polls in September-October 1999 to elect the thirteenth Lok Sabha, throwing charges at her Despite the many charges flung recklessly by Sibal at no less a person than Vajpayee and his government and the BJP the Congress suffered an ignominious defeat.

Kapil went back to his legal practice at the Supreme Court of India after the polls and occasionally made an appearance in the Rajya Sabha as long as he continued to be its Congress member. He was, in fact, the first Congressman to throw doubts about Sonia's ability to lead the party to achieve any notable success, much less to get the party back to power at the Centre. He was, however, soon forgotten as others jumped on to the bandwagon. Even people like Balram Jakhar, a former Lok Sabha Speaker known for his sycophantic utterances, took a few swipes at the party leadership, meaning Sonia Gandhi. Although the Congress won a notable assembly victory in Rajasthan in November 1998, in the Lok Sabha election about a year later from the state the party had suffered some notable defeats and Balram Jakhar was among the Congress candidates who had the misfortune to be routed. Although a Punjabi, he had migrated to a Rajasthan Lok Sabha constituency at a time when the Punjab terrorists made life difficult for people like Jakhar. Even Buta Singh, once Home Minister under Rajiv Gandhi, and himself a Sikh, had to choose a Rajasthan contituency as a Congress candidate or masquerading as an independent. For a few months he even became a Minister in the first Vajpayee cabinet in 1998 but was compelled to resign when action was demanded against his continuance by that epitome of "honesty", Jayalalitha when one of her own ministers, S.R. Muthiah, was chargesheeted in a Chennai court. Muthiah was ultimately convicted and perhaps Buta Singh's turn may be coming soon when judgment is pronounced in the JMM bribery case. That Jayalalitha, after the Chennai court's conviction of Muthiah, dismissed him and several other top personalities of the AIADMK in 2000 is, of course, a different matter.

After the end of the Budget session of Parliament, however, the dam burst in the Congress as Sonia's deficiencies were seen by Congressmen themselves, many of whom were genuinely alarmed at the erosion of Sonia's authority and the future of the party. Under Vajpayee's wise leadership and the umbrella of protection and security which he spread out to all those who needed it, the Vajpayee rule was making the average Indian safe and secure. There was a large measure of freedom for the people to do what they liked and express themselves in a variety of ways in the arts, media, entertainment and the like. Prices had, of course, gone up, largely because of the subsidy being cut but the people did not complain about it much as long as the employment situation was under control. The Trade Unions of the CPIM often thundered and tried to undo the economic reforms brought in by Vajpayee but despite their fulminations and occasional strikes called by them, the work culture preached by them of absenteeism and less and less work was not finding general acceptance. With the NDA partners releasing that they had as much stake in the coalition as the BJP, the country was for the first time in several years experiencing stability.

No wonder the thinking elements in the Congress party were truly concerned by the developments because they saw the futility of the Congress playing any significant role in national affairs. They naturally expressed lack of confidence in Sonia being able to provide effective leadership at this critical juncture for the party. Some like Vithal Gadgil, a former Congress Minister at the Centre, found fault with Sonia denouncing the Hindus all the time in the name of condemning the BJP. It is customary for Congressmen to wear the secular label and in the process run down the Hindus who form the backbone and the bulk of the Indian population. Sonia and her followers forget that the Hindus constitute the bulk and the hardcore of the people of India and if you denounce them from the party platform the people naturally look at you with some suspicion.

Others did not understand the implication of Sonia's routine condemnation of Hinduism and spoke in general terms of her ineffectual leadership, her inability to grasp the essence of India and Congressmen losing faith in her leadership. Vasant Sathe, in an interview after his editorial criticism of Sonia blamed the Congress Working Committee not being able to help the party president. In a way, this was more a reflection on Sonia's leadership rather than a criticism of the CWC. After all, the committee consisted of her nominees and she had shown a strong propensity for the CWC to tell her what she wanted. Witness the expulsion of Sharad Pawar and his two colleagues in May 1999 after they told her in no uncertain terms that she was not fit to lead the party and aspire to become the Prime Minister of India being a person born of foreign parents.

Whatever way Congressmen looked at her she was proving an utter failure as Congress party president who had to come often to the party's rescue. Sonia always acted through intermediaries like party spokespersons and party leaders in Parliament most of whom were content to carry out their duties as Her Majesty's loyal servants. When, as we have seen, Pranab Mukherjee said something on nuclear weapons which was quite clearly the truth but which did not suit the party for the time being he was disclaimed by a regular party spokesperson who incidentally was under Mukherjee because he was the boss of the Congress media department.

But when the dam burst and the party was full of anger against her over her failures the partymen did not bother about such niceties. One of the party's middle ranking leaders has a position of his own because he is sought out by the media for explaining the party's point of view. That is because he has often more than the platitudes to project. As a secretary of the AICC in charge of the party's economic policy, Jairam Ramesh was often liked more by the media than by the party itself. Partymen who take a narrow view of their duties and responsibilities are often critical of Ramesh and of his going over to the party's enemies as they view them. When the computer-savvy Chief Minister of Andhra Pradesh invited Ramesh to join his economic advisory council, Ramesh showed inclination to do so. But the party's Andhra Pradesh men strongly opposed it and finally scuttled it when they represented it to the party boss as a violation of the party discipline.

To compensate Ramesh for the loss of the job and prestige, the Congress Chief Minister of neighbouring Karnataka, Ramesh's home state, made him deputy Chairman of the state planning board. This was poor compensation for the lost opportunity of serving the Andhra Pradesh Chief Minister, N. Chandrababu Naidu, who has an international image and who has made Hyderabad a veritable Cyberabad. Soon Ramesh was to be in the limelight in a different context when the *Asiaweek* of Hong Kong approached him for his views and Ramesh expressed himself rather freely.

As usual with the media, there was some exaggeration in the interview and some words of Ramesh were interpreted rather liberally. But there was no doubt that Ramesh had said many critical things about the Congress party and about its leader, Sonia Gandhi. He told the weekly that the Congress could not come to power for another fifty years. This was rather a liberal interpretation of Ramesh's prediction that it could take the party years before it could ever aspire to be in power. The average Congressman wants power here and now and Sonia tried to gain power for herself in April 1999 and failed miserably in the effort.

What Jairam Ramesh did say was even more condemnatory of Sonia. He said in the interview that those Congressmen who were earlier hoping to get "Nirvana" from Sonia were now getting "Narak". Nirvana is literally extinction when the individual soul loses its identity by merger with the Universal soul. Popularly it means blissor the ultimate joy. Narak 'of course, means hell, although in north India it is wrongly spelt as "Nark", although the meaning is the same. To say that many partymen who earlier hoped to be gifted by Sonia with bliss now were afraid that they would be sent to hell by her was a strong denunciation of the party president.

A big howl went up in the pro-Congress media and others saw in Ramesh's admission a sign of the weakening of faith by many Congressmen in the capacity of Sonia to lead them to success. In a way, the Ramesh interview heralded the avalanche of criticism against the party leader and for the first time it was categorically stated that she had failed to provide effective leadership to the party. The Sathe article appeared after the contents of the Ramesh interview were known. Dissensions, directed against Sonia's nominees in the party and in state governments under Congress control, began to grow in intensity and acquired more substance.

Ramesh, of course, made his peace with the party boss and wrote a letter in which he expressed the usual sentiments and was perhaps forgiven by Sonia, more out of necessity than otherwise. When a general tidal wave rises and is likely to engulf the organisation prudence requires that you show mercy, or at least make a show of it, rather than take disciplinary action against the individual because that may further aggravate the situation.

An expression of lack of faith in the party leader now became the fashion as the Uttar Pradesh Congress which was a hotbed of dissension and intrigue seemed to overflow. Jitendra Prasada was the dissident leader but Sonia had throttled him and thrust on the state party her own nominee, Salman Khursheed. He was normally resident in Delhi but he had to find a constituency for which UP offered unlimited scope. His father had served as governor of Karnataka for a long time and was ultimately ousted by the National Democratic Alliance (NDA) government. His main qualification was that he was a son-in-law of the late President, Zakir Husain of revered memory because Zakir Husain had worked with Gandhiji.

Salman Khursheed was chosen by Sonia to head the UP unit of the party which was in "a bad way", the Congress having been completely wiped out in the 1998 Lok Sabha elections. The party in the state assembly had broken up and the larger part was supporting the BJP led government while a smaller section was still with the party. In the wake of the Congress party's success in the assembly election in Delhi, Rajasthan and Madhya Pradesh in November 1998 there was a strong feeling in the Congress that the party was on the way back to power. Some indications that the Muslim voters in UP, who constitute about 15 per cent, were returning to the Congress were seen and Sonia was in great spirits. So at least the Congress party and Sonia loyalists thought.

This expectation was proved completely wrong when ballots for the Lok Sabha elections were cast in September-October 1999 and Mulayam Singh's faith in his own leadership and his steadfast refusal to toe the Sonia Line in the crucial days of April 1999 was borne out. The Muslim voters had by and large remained with Mulayam Singh's Samajwadi party and consequently he improved his position in the Lok Sabha from 20 seats in the previous house to 26 in the Thirteenth Lok Sabha. He considerably strengthened his party's position, which could stand him in good stead in future, particularly the crucial state assembly elections in the middle or later part of 2001 when the new UP assembly is to be elected.

The Congress, no doubt, improved its position in the state where it had drawn blank in the previous year. Now it scored 10 seats from UP, not just opened its account. But that figure includes the Amethi seat won by Sonia. On the whole, however the party had put up a much improved show but it did not take its tally beyond 112 seats, the lowest ever recorded by this 115-year old party which brought freedom to India from colonial bondage. Several factors played their part. Sonia's inability to provide a substitute government when she helped Surjeet to pull down the Vajpayee government and an obliging President Narayanan gave her clear three days to put together an alternative. One of the reasons for that dismal performance was the deduction made by Indian electorate that the Congress could no longer rule the country.

The appointment of Salman Khursheed was made by Sonia because she did not have confidence in Jitendra Prasada who had served Narasimha Rao as Political Secretary. But Sonia has bad memory and she did not remember that Prasada had also served her husband as one of the key figures of the Congress Centenary Committee. Many of our friends in the media would not be guilty of knowing it either. In fact, Prasada was a mere MP from Uttar Pradesh before he was given that position and because the Committee was headed by a nondescript woman, called Sheila kaul, whose work as Urban Development Minister was to bring nothing but scams to the party. While making Salman president of the UP Congress, she should have told the new incumbent to keep Prasada informed and consult him and generally not to antagonise him. Unfortunately, the Congress tradition is for the new broom to sweep everything done in the past and the party boss encourages it.

When Jitendra Prasada organised two rallies, at Jhansi on May 21, Rajiv's death anniversary, and at Lucknow on May 24, he left no one in doubt that he wanted the scalp of Salman. Remove Salman as UPCC president, Sonia was clearly told by the two successful rallies. He invited Rajesh Pilot to attend and address the two rallies and both raised the question of inner party democracy. No political party tolerates any of its partyman raising his head but such expression of views is being tolerated to a limited extent. Rajesh Pilot has often protested without any particular target in mind and often he chickens out at the last moment when he should be demonstrating that he means business. However, there were hints in his speeches and his defiance of the party discipline in attending the two rallies of Jitendra Prasada a without the sanction of the UP Congress boss that Pilot might throw the gauntlet at Sonia.

Whether the rallies were sanctioned by the Congress or not, they were a symbol of the growing defiance of the UP Congress President and many Congress leaders were even ready to face the show cause notice. Sonia Gandhi's authority was suffering rapid erosion little to ward it off. The Salman episode was a particularly nasty one because an old party loyalist like Jitendra Prasada was suffering neglect in his home state. Sonia's preference for Salman could also be because of his being a Muslim. She shows a particular liking for such men as Ahmed Patel who has lost election after election in his home state of Gujarat but has the reputation of being a clean man and what is more he merges his identity with that of the Congress president.

It is quite possible that despite all these developments the Congress party could be back to its favourite devices and go to Sonia on bended knees. That would be a real disaster for the party and a tragedy for the nation because the country could ill afford to see such an established party go to pieces. The Congress has many good points but its sycophantic habit of humouring a member of the dynasty and surrendering its judgment to him or her is proving very costly. Sonia was chosen the Congress President in the expectation that the dynastic principle would once again prevail with her return. She was, in fact, offered the seat, which had fallen vacant because of the unfortunate death of her husband in an LTTE attack. Then she had rightly refused the crown being totally unacquainted with the ways of politics and not confident of acquiring the rudiments ever. But years of hibernation in 10 Janpath gave her some hope and the more urgent was the need for her to acquire some direct or indirect control over the government so that she could stop further probing into the Bofors deal in which even Rajiv Gandhi was an accused.

Then, as Sitaram Kesri, was proving an utter liability she managed a coup in the AICC with the help of people like Arjun Singh and Ghulam Nabi Azad and ousted the unwilling Kesri and assumed command. While Atal Bihari Vajpayee was climbing the steps of Rashtrapati Bhavan, she snicked into the Congress President's *gaddi*. Vajpayee has stayed put in his 7 Race Course road house by virtue of his Prime Ministership, and Sonia has occupied 10 Janpath by virtue of the strange Delhi phenomenon that once you get hold of a government bungalow you are there for the rest of your life. There are dozens of houses under VVIP and VIP occupation, on nominal or no rent, and there are a large number of bungalows occupied by the mushrooming political parties all of which want a New Delhi address. The Congress party can afford to hire helicopters and even planes at will but wants a government house for the use of its party president. Of course, most other parties do so and there is thus a glaring misuse of government facilities. At one time, there was in New Delhi no other accommodation than houses built by the government for its staff and all political parties eyed these houses. Now the situation is different and there are any number of attractive houses all over the capital for which, of course, the required rent has to be paid. But if the government can be pressurised into giving you a house, you not only save on the huge rent you would otherwise be paying to the landlord but you can live in a government house without having anything to do with it. Think of the prestige that accrues to you if you live in a government house. The average Indian still has an aura of all that is connected with the government.

Sonia not only ousted Kesri but had a grip on all the assets of the Congress in Delhi just as she had illegally acquired prestigious houses in the name of running the Rajiv Gandhi Foundation. With her keen possessive sense, she not only occupied the houses, with the Congress or Congress-supported governments looking on, she also became life Chairman of a trust formed in a high cost area of New Delhi. This was the Indira Gandhi Centre for the Arts close the Memorial Arch, popularly called the India Gate which has possibly the highest land value in a terribly costly New Delhi. The Centre is notable for the large number of books it has acquired, although arts are at a discount. With a gift of high cost land and a financial cash grant the trust is of immense value to whoever controls it and Sonia had made it sure that she did this "duty" to her late mother-in-law.

By virtue of an executive decision, during the Prime Ministership of Narasimha Rao, who missed no opportunity of pleasing Sonia with government decisions although he really hated her because in her late husband's days Rao was rendered a non-entity and he had to bow to Sonia as well, Sonia who was merely a chairman of the board of trustees got herself a lifelong post. She ensured that her family's favourites also became life trustees. This situation was intolerable to the BJP-ruled Vajpayee government although its Human Resource Development Minister was also now one of the Trustees. Murli Manoher Joshi could hardly bear to see people like Sonia occupying a seat of honour and taking major decisions while he, a minister, only could be a witness to them.

The matter went to the Delhi High Court and then the ball was set in motion. It was only a PIL, Public Interest Litigation, which was brought before the High Court and Sonia and her henchmen were now on tenterhooks. A PIL has a greater public interest if the issue covered by it is one of greater public interest and some top lawyers offer their services in the expectation that they can earn good publicity and make up for any montary loss of earnings in other cases. The court allowed the government to effect any changes in the trustees and promptly the government dis-appointed Sonia and her henchmen and took control of the property.

When Congressmen themselves lost faith in Sonia's leadership the CPIM General Secretary, Harkishan Singh Surjeet, could not be blamed for losing his own. For the first time in May 2000, when the crescendo against Sonia's Congress President status was building up, Surjeet, with Jytoti Basu acting in tandem, expressed himself in favour of his old theme, the

Third Front. Jyoti Basu was sought out by the out-of-work and rudderless four former Prime Ministers. Chandra Shekhar was given Congress backing for four months in 1990-91 when he ditched V.P. Singh and formed a government with only 65 Janata Dal men many of whom later deserted him. But Rajiv Gandhi gave him support just as his mother, Indira Gandhi, had supported Charan Singh against Morarji Desai. Indira's support for the Chaudhuri was withdrawn only after 21 days while Chandra Shekhar remained in power with Rajiv's outside support for four months and two months for the elections to be held.

It was during this electioneering interlude that Rajiv Gandhi was cruelly assassinated by the LTTE. Both H.D. Deve Gauda and I. K. Gujral became Prime Ministers by courtesy of the Congress and when Sitaram Kesri (the then Congress President) pulled the rug from under their feet they were toppled and their governments were no more. Except V. P. Singh, who saw the 12th month of his regime rising before he was ousted, the others ruled for less than a year, Chandra Shekhar remaining in the saddle for the shortest time. Chaudhuri Charan Singh remained in power a little longer because the elections were held in December while he was toppled by Indira in August 1979.

The four out-of-job ex-PMs tried their best to rope in another former Prime Minister, P.V. Narasimha Rao, but he proved as elusive as ever and never attended any of their get-together nor lent any support to them in their inexplicable mission to put Jyoti Basu of the CPIM in the seat of the Prime Minister. Basu had really speaking told his party that at the age of 86 years he needed rest and at the second persuasion the party had agreed to allow him rest after the 2001 West Bengal assembly elections when they said Basu would campaign for the party but would not be a party candidate for an MLAs position which was essential if he were to be the party's nominee for the Chief Minister's office for a record sixth time. That he would campaign was also because of the Trinamul Congress leader Mamata Banerjee's threat of ousting the Communists from power in their citadel of West Bengal.

Basu was thus in the retirement mode, although he knew that Mamata was a real challenge and he would have to meet it in West Bengal. While this threat was growing in strength, the Deputy CM, Buddhadeb Bhattacharya, allowed to be Deputy Chief Minister by the CPIM at Basu's insistence, announced suddenly that Basu had been chosen by the ex-PMs to lead the Third Front. This front was non-existent and the Prime Minister's office was also not vacant. But there is no harm for any party to day-dream and if the CPIM, the premier Communist party in the country was known for its hardheadedness, it was also known for pursuing chimera.

For a long time, over two years, the CPIM General Secretary had made it his one-point programme to make the Congress leader, Sonia Gandhi, Prime Minister of India. That both Surjeet and his official shadow Jyoti Basu as well as Sonia failed in their effort has been narrated in this book and is part of history. Surjeet had now put his faith in Jyoti Basu, the old semi-retired Communist leader, who attended his office as Chief Minister for only an hour, as had the cynical ex-PMs who wanted some free publicity for themselves and some media attention even if it was for the media's fun.

Even while proclaiming Basu as a future Prime Minister (thankfully he was not made the PM straightaway), the two CPIM leaders left a loophole for individual Congressmen to join the Third Front and strengthen it. How this could be possible even while the Congress party was in tact is beyond ordinary intelligence but the ways of the Communists are somewhat inscrutable at times and they know that they can count on media support or media gullibility. The four ex-PMs seemed to be determined as they held a seminar after a rally to garner political and media support for their foolhardy venture. They seemed to have washed their hands of the Congress but not the principal ally, the CPIM, which still had some faith left in that rickety organisation.

What the degree of that faith was it was difficult to say because the leader had not inspired any degree of confidence among her own followers by her actions. Take the case of two states Haryana and Bihar one medium sized but extremely go ahead and another a large, India's No. 2 state, with unlimited resources but the administration in a rundown condition and law and order totally non-existent and development at an abysmally low level. Let us take up first Haryana where the usual Congress policy of opposing every move of the BJP was employed. If the BJP was withdrawing support from the Bansilal government the Congress naturally had to support it, however unpopular the government might have been.

That was in 1999 and having extended support once the Congress realised its folly and withdrew support. The result was the Bansilal government fell and the Congress was blamed for it by the people. Then the Sonia-led establishment in the Congress party thought it has a good chance of coming to power in the state when Om Prakash Chautala, the newly elected Chief Minister, dissolved the assembly and declared elections. Held simultaneously with Bihar and Orissa, where the Congress was in power, the party performed miserably in all three states, losing power in Orissa and not being returned in Haryana and Bihar, where it had no hopes.

Not only was Om Prakash Chuatala returned to power and he continued to be the Chief Minister of the state but he could dispense with the outside support of the BJP if he so wished. That he did not do so was a political move. The Congress party under Sonia failed to hold power in Orissa and the BJD (Biju Janata Dal, founded by the Oriya leader, Navin Patnaik, who could not speak Oriya but was still popular with the people) formed the government with the BJP who played second fiddle to the BJD.

So long, Sonia had supported the RJD (Rashtriya Janata Dal) in Bihar despite several massacres in the state after one of which in February 1999 Sonia had even issued a statement and condemned the Rabari Devi government saying it had lost all moral right to rule. In spite of this strong condemnation Sonia kept on supporting the government and the ruling party in the Lok Sabha polls in September-October 1999. This was also done by the CPIM, which has only a few pockets of influence. The results of the Lok Sabha polls were however poor both for the ruling RJD and the Congress. So the Congress severed its ties with RJD and fought the February 2000 elections to the assembly on its own. The result was no different; the Congress getting only 23 seats in the 324-member assembly.

The results were somewhat startling as the RJD, despite the setback it had suffered in the Lok Sabha polls when it had secured only seven seats (Bihar has 54) instead of the 17 seats it had won in 1998. The Congress, however, reversed its stand at the prospect of sharing power with the RJD, which formed the government in Bihar once again after a brief stint by Nitish Kumar of the NDA. Not only the leader of the Congress block got for himself the post of the Speaker of the House, but all the remaining 22 Congress members became ministers. Naturally all of them would be grateful to Sonia and would profusely thank her for the favours.

That is what all Congressmen want their leader, Sonia Gandhi, to perform— to win for themselves the perks and privileges of office. Alas, Sonia is not able to do it. She neither gets the votes needed for the party to win a majority in the Lok Sabha without which even a friendly Narayanan cannot invite her to form a government and without which even another friend, Harkishan Singh Surjeet, cannot do obeisance to her in season and out of season. However much Surjeet may wish to see her in the seat of power, he cannot wish it by the magic wand. Sonia has to achieve it by dint of her work and her perorations all over the country where she reads out prepared speeches from boldly typed Hindi texts have failed to achieve it for her.

As a seasoned journalist observed: "According to a veteran leader, Congressmen can live with a lack of democracy which has been always denied to them, but they cannot live with a leader who cannot get votes. Mrs. Gandhi's tactics have not undergone any transformation in spite of her losing the charisma of being a vote catcher and of one who can lead an alliance to help the party come to power. It is this inability that is not acceptable to her partymen and is making even the traditional Congressman turn."

Sonia Gandhi is fond of being an emperor even if she like a later Mughal emperor had no more jurisdiction than the periphery of the Red Fort. She has all the paraphernalia of a court with Vincent George telling Congress leaders of the eminence of Arjun Singh, Ghulam Nabi Azad, Madhavarao Scindia, Ahmed Patel and others like them what they should tell the madam so that she is happy. If they tell her, as she would fondly like to listen, how Vajpayee slipped in his bungalow, even if he did nothing of the kind, she would be happy and would listen to their tale of woe more willingly and interestingly. If on the other hand they were just to tell her that drastic action must be taken against Rajesh Pilot, she would get easily bored and would go to sleep. George may have a lot of problems with the CBI for his alleged possession of assets disproportionate to his known sources of income but he is still close to the 'madam' who takes her along with her on trips by planes and helicopters. After all, George has been with the Rajiv Gandhi and Sonia Gandhi couple since the days when Rajiv had his first lessons in politics in the 24 Akbar Road offices of the AICC before he became Prime Minister on that fateful day of October 31, 1984. From those early days George has been with the ruling couple and when Rajiv lost power he was still with the former Prime Minister. Then, on his tragic assassination George reverted to the 'madam' and has been with the imperious lady from those days in May 1991. But, alas, power has eluded the lady and her Roman Catholic Private Secretary and his dreams of being the shadow of the Prime Minister once again have not seen the light of the day.

Vincent George's confrontation with Abhishek Verma, son of the late Shrikant Verma, the propagandist of Mrs Indira Gandhi, are well known is and need not be recounted here. The CBI's files are full of the tales and one day will enlighten us on George's acquisition of wealth in which his wife is allegedly involved although she has little inkling of her husband's doings.

Such is the lady of 10 Janpath whom Rajiv Gandhi described as having no interest in politics. He told this in an interview to Simi Garewal on

Doordarshan before he laid down his office of the Prime Minister of India. How suddenly she sprang to life after his death, that too seven years later, is a mystery to most mediamen who have made little effort to probe the matter.

Surjeet tried even less because Jyoti Basu and he had accepted her from the beginning just as she was and for their purpose the less she knew of India and Indians the better for Surjeet and Basu because her Italian pronounciation made no difference and caused little problem to the two Communist veterans. For all her imperial pomp she could not forget her early days which required her to trudge long distances on foot in her London days before she married into the "royal." family of India. Neither the two veteran communists cared very much for her days soon after the defeat of her mother-in-law in the general elections of 1977 when she was at a loose end in Delhi and advised her husband, then a junior pilot in the Indian Airlines, to migrate to Europe and get away from this "madding crowd". The seasoned Communists cared less for such outpourings of a lonely heart but they bothered about her failure to get votes and secure power for the Congress party. Her failure to secure the office of the most important political figure had upset their calculations and made them turn to the mythical Third Front.

11
A SHIFT IN CPIM STRATEGY

As indicated in the previous chapter, the sure shot that Harkishan Surjeet and Jyoti Basu had imagined Sonia Gandhi to be had let them down and the Congress party itself was losing faith in her leadership. If one day the Congress party lost confidence in her vote-catching ability and discarded her with the dynasty she is supposed to represent what would the Comrades do? They had now opened their options wider than the single-point programme of installing Sonia in the Prime Minister's chair and went about casting their net to let in the mythical Third Front, a modified version of the United Front which lost power in 1997 when I.K.Gujral was eased out of office by Sitaram Kesri pulling the rug under his feet.

Surjeet had suddenly put his faith in the Third Front but the ex-PMs threw the bait of Prime Ministership at Jyoti Basu and his nominated deputy, Buddhadeb Bhattacharya, promptly announced that Jyoti Basu would lead the front. That was pure and simple day-dreaming and the Indian Communists are known for indulging in it and living on it for long periods. The hard-headed Communists which they are when they are not day-dreaming know it for certain that the NDA governments is safe and secure in the saddle and Atal Bihari Vajpayee's stock as a national leader is up and up. The allies of the BJP know that they have as much stake in the government of India as the major party.

This was proved in the first week of June 2000 when coming out of the Cabinet Committee on security, to which he was specially invited, Murasoli Maran, DMK leader and Commerce Minister in the Vajpayee cabinet, said categorically that the DMK was part of the NDA government and it had no differences with the government on the Sri Lanka issue.[1] That was in the face of the DMK president and Tamil Nadu Chief Minister, M. Karunanidhi, saying a few days earlier that Sri Lanka should be divided into Sinhala and Tamil regions just as Czechoslovakia was divided by mutual agreement as the Czech and Slovak nations. The Sri Lanka government had violently reacted to the Karunanidhi's statement even going to the extent that India would be divided in that event. Murasoli Maran is Karunanidhi's nephew and a trusted aide and almost his guide on all-India affairs.

As everyone knows, the original statement of Karunanidhi was intended for the consumption of the Tamil voters in next year's assembly polls which are crucial to the continuance of his government and to the future of the state. That he should not have made a statement of this sort still is the proper all-India reaction and for the NDA which has to stand united at all times. Due to the regional considerations of Tamil Nadu, which has close affinity with the Tamils in Sri Lanka and from where refugees continue to enter Tamil Nadu state during the fighting between the Sri Lankan army and the LTTE, the NDA's Tamil Nadu allies, the DMK, PMK and MDMK, which between them and the BJP, have more Lok Sabha MPs than their rivals, have natural feelings for the Tamils in the island republic. They have, however, to bear in mind the repercussions of their utterances on the policy of India as a whole on Crucial issues in the world areas.

There is indeed no possibility of an NDA partner rocking the boat of the Central government as did the AIADMK supremo, J. Jayalalitha, in April 1999 when, under Sonia's inspiration and Surjeet's instigation (and the manipulations of Subramanian Swamy) the Vajpayee government lost power by a single vote. But Sonia, despite Surjeet's and Swamy's efforts to the utmost, was not able to offer an alternative government although President Narayanan allowed her more time to do so.

But there in no harm in building castles in the air and day-dreaming if that happens to be a part of one's policy. While Surjeet said that the Third Front was to be revived Jyoti Basu's deputy said that he (Basu) would be the leader of the front, as deemed by the ex-PMs. In his own reaction Basu still left some scope for Congressmen (obviously meaning Sonia) to come into his parlour of the Third Front. How, while being good Congressmen (or women) they could still be part of the mythical Third Front beats one's imagination. Possibly Basu meant that like the Congress sustained the two United Front governments into power in 1996-1997, it should again come to the rescue of the Comrades.

For that to happen, the Janata Dal should be united and should form the focal point of the conglomerates which would constitute the United Front in future too. Are there any such possibilities ? First Laloo Prased Yadav broke up the JD in June 1997. He was facing the CBI scam cases of more than Rs.1000 crores swindled in the name of the dumb animals of

Bihar when he was holding the portfolio of finance and was simultaneously Chief Minister of Bihar, almost continuously since March 1990. It is morally high sounding to talk of secularism, as does the CPIM and some of the media which always support it , but one should not forget that the party has supported to the hilt Laloo and his semi-literate wife Rabri Devi whom be installed as Chief Minister of Bihar when he had to step down because he was about to be arrested in the first of several animal husbandry cases against him in the end of July 1997. The CPIM has stood by him in the Lok Sabha elections of 1999 and the assembly poll of February 2000 although it has extremely limited stakes in the Bihar assembly just two seats in a 324-member assembly.

But Laloo has seven members in the Lok Sabha whose leader makes enough noise for all the opposition all the time. The CPIM needs all that and thinks Laloo is an effective supporter of the Third Front concept of the CPIM. He is able to hoodwink the CPIM and the media which stand by taking the name of secularism and fighting the communal bogey while the CPIM gives comfort to the Bangladeshi illegal immigrants and woos the Muslims of Kerala and tried to hijack them from the Congress-dominated UDF (United Democratic Front). The Bangladeshi immigrants many of whom are enlisted as voters by the CPIM activists themselves, are no threat to Indian secularism and the Kerala Muslim League is not a communal body although by its very constitution only Muslims can be its members. This is only a small example of the warped thinking of the Communists in general and the leading party of the Reds, the CPIM in particular. It must, however, be said of the smaller CPI, although it is the original party, that they have decided to shun Laloo Prasad Yadav for some time since the middle of 1999.

In any case, the JD of yore has to be united which means that not only Laloo has to give up his RJD but the two factions of the remnant JD, one led by H.D. Deve Gouda the JD(S), as it is called, and another by Sharad Yadav, the JD(U), have to come together. Is it possible in the present circumstances? Sharad Yadav, like Ram Vilas Paswan , is safely ensconced in the Vajpayee cabinet as minister. No doubt, Deve Gowda is among the ex-PMs out to rescue Indian democracy from the clutches of the NDA and has sought the help of Jyoti Basu as leader of the Third Front, if Buddhadeb Bhattacharya is to be believed. The UF of 1996-97 was built on the bedrock of the JD which had 55 members in the 11th Lok Sabha, dissolved by Narayanan in December 1997.

Then there is the Samajwadi party of Mulayam Singh Yadav who had a brief honeymoon with Laloo, another Yadav like him, when the RJD and

Samajwadi parties came together. Now they are poles apart but politics is a strange game and anything could happen. But Mulayam is sure of one thing, he would have noting to do with the Congress which is his enemy number one. He has repeatedly said that he would support the Third Front once the CPIM gives up its love for his Congress. He fell out with the CPIM and its leader, Surjeet, in April 1999 when Surjeet did his best to sponsor Sonia Gandhi and the Congress party and Mulayam refused to toe the Surjeet line. He knew the Congress had tried to steal his Muslim votebank in Uttar Pradesh (and failed) but he was opposed to it tooth and nail. He maintains the opposition to the Congress party still and now he says that Sonia's Congress has done nothing to mobilise the opposition parties to oppose the NDA government.

In other words, Mulayam's 26 MPs are not available to the CPIM in its quest for power. The CPIM General Secretary had once referred to the Telugu Desam party as a likely source of support to the Third Front concept. It should be recalled in this context that the Telugu Desam leader and Andhra Pradesh Chief Minister, who was a kind of Major Domo in the CPIM-dominated United Front but had broken away from him on the issue of his fascination for the Congress after the election for the 12th Lok Sabha in 1998. In fact, it was a crucial factor which shattered the UF dream of the CPIM. Later he drove out the DMK from the combined opposition and virtually forced it to befriend the BJP-led National Democratic Alliance. That was on the issue of Surjeet falling for Jayalalitha's charm and the famous words of Karunanidhi that "communalism is preferable to corruption" are to be recalled in the same context. The DMK had , in fact, joined the BJP-led alliance in the crucial vote of confidence in April 17, 1999 when Jayalalitha had toppled Vajpayee by a solitary vote in the Lok Sabha.

Surjeet himself had thus broken up the Third Front by driving out such solid supporters like the Telugu Desam and the DMK which had stood by the alliance through thick and thin. This is a new line of thinking—that Surjeet himself is responsible for the decimation of the Third or United Front—but it is nothing sensational if the main thing is borne in mind. The Third Front was built on the CPIM's leadership of a united front the need for which is felt because the Communists by themselves are incapable of coming to power through democratic means. That they cannot come to power by violence has been demonstrated by the failure of the Naxalites to capture power. The Naxalites are Communists to the core and came into being in the Naxalbari area of West Bengal in 1967 The CPIM saw the threat to their domination from the violent Naxalites and ruthlessly put them down. If they are active in Bihar it is because the administration is too weak and Laloo Prasad has mastered the art of keeping his family in power no matter whether Bihar goes to the dogs. If Jyoti Basu had his way, the Bihar Communists who resort to violence from time to time would be finished in a reasonable time. Laloo would have nothing of it and the CPIM is fully backing him and at the same time watching the Naxalites gain an upper hand in some areas.

The point is that the CPIM has tried to fashion the United Front, now called the Third Front, in its own image as a conglomeration of regional parties willing to be moulded as the CPIM leaders, Surjeet and Basu, wish to mould them. They sometimes refuse to be guided by the CPIM, as for example, when Surjeet wanted the Telugu Desam to accept the Congress or the DMK to accept the corrupt Jayalalitha. These parties and even the Samajwadi party were ready to be guided by the CPIM upto a point. When the Surjeet line went against their grain they revolted and left his nest. Surjeet called them deserters and the gullible media also reported all that.

Just as Sonia has faced a virtual revolt against her leadership from within the party itself, Surjeet faced a virtual revolt against his domination from the powerful regional parties. Both Sonia and Surjeet (read Basu in this case) faced a serious challenge from Mamata Banerjee of the Trinamul Congress who demonstrated her prowess when the candidate nominated by her won the Panskura by-election to the Lok Sabha defeating a sesoned parliamentarian like Gurudas Dasgupta of the CPI who had been put up as the combined candidate of the CPIM-dominated Left Front. "Red Fort breached" was the banner headline of one of the capital's prominent papers.[2] Mamata had suffered a setback of sorts in the Municipal elections when in May 2000, when 79 municipalities went to the polls and the Congress following Sonia dictates rejected Mamata's Mahajot, the grand alliance concept which Mamata had put forward. Virtually everyone in the West Bengal Congress had accepted it; they were overruled by the Delhi leadership of the party.

Mamata had advanced the Mahajot idea and the West Bengal Congressmen were convinced about it because she saw it as the ideal solution to the misrule of the CPIM in West Bengal as she called it. The Congress which had been trying to give the Reds a pushover for 23 years without getting anywhere at once realised that here was a solution of the knot they had so long faced in West Bengal and had failed to cut it. As we have seen Sonia was too much under the spell of the CPIM to allow her partymen in West Bengal to join hands with the Trinamul leader and through her party with the BJP.

Mamata Banerjee overcame the setback in the municipal elections which had caused some despondency in her party and the BJP in West Bengal which is aligned to her Trinamul but all that was forgotten the moment the results of the by-election in Panskura came. This was a CPI seat which the party had won in all elections beginning with the one held in 1980. The sympathy wave generated for Gita Mukherjee whose death had caused the by-election failed to help the candidate of the CPI and he bitterly complained of rigging by the Trinamul. It was a kind of joke when, led by Dasgupta's outbursts, Surjeet himself talked in Delhi on June 9, the day following the declaration of the result, and in Calcutta Jyoti Basu, who should know the ground realities better, denied there was any rigging.[3] There was indeed rigging in the Panskura by-election by the CPIM standards because the party had mastered the technique of winning elections and now there was a formidable force in the form of Mamata and the polling officers and the state police saw in her the future Chief Minister of West Bengal and would not let the CPIM do its tricks as in the past.

On May 18, less than three weeks before the Panskura bombshell shattered the calm and ended the joy of the CPIM, Surjeet told the press in the capital that it had modified its strategy somewhat to allow it to join a Third Front government. He was briefing the mediamen on the updating of the CPIM programme, for the first time since the Communist movement split and the older party the CPI was left to fend for itself. He told the media that the party's Central Committee had felt that its strategy of actively associating itself with the government, in other words participating in the government, in West Bengal and Kerala would also be relevant at the Centre. Put simply, the CPIM Communists were now ready to take part in the government at the Centre also, something it had denied poor Jyoti Basu in 1996 and which he later called a historical blunder.[4]

Alas, there[5] was no readymade vacancy for Basu because Atal Bihari Vajpayee was firmly in the saddle and Surjeet was too enamoured of his party's rhetoric to accept the media's objections on this account. As often pointed out in this book, the CPIM indulges in day-dreaming which it often calls as providing for all contingencies. Surjeet told the media that the CPIM would not be averse to joining the Centre if the political situation warranted it. The whole updated programme was to be placed before an appropriate forum, possibly the party Congress or a special convention in October and hopefully approved by it. Surjeet was not only day-dreaming but taking the party rank and file for granted and its approval as a sanction in advance.

He of course, hedged and said the party's approval was necessary which can be understood. But if that was so the programme could have been presented to the media without the usual varnish and the media told plainly that this was only a proposal for the approval of the party Congress.

The document, released by Surjeet, emphasized the decline of the Congress (galling to Surjeet) and said that the so-called reactionary and counter-revolutionary forces like the BJP were trying to fill the void created by the Congress. It is good to find Surjeet admitting that the Congress was in decline but surely Surjeet expected the media to eat out of his hands when he expected them to believe that the BJP was only filling the void. Why did the electorate in 1996 give the BJP 162 seats in the Lok Sabha (in the eleventh house) and the Congress only 140 seats? In other words the BJP was gaining ground even while the Congress was losing it. It was not as though there was a void which the BJP was rushing in to fill as the Congress was in decline.

Even when Surjeet and the West Bengal Chief Minister Jyoti Basu were backing the Congress to the hilt and Sonia was eagerly seeking the crown from the willing hands of President Narayanan (who could not, however, gift it to her) they should have realised that the Congress was being badly led. It was not as though "the counter-revolutionary forces" were just occupying the space vacated by the Congress. Not only was the Congress in incompetent hands and with the untimely death of Rajesh Pilot a likely challenge to Sonia's leadership was extinguished, the Congress by itself was no longer capable to lead the country and it was refusing to take allies with it. Even when Sitaram Kesri was at the helm in the Congress and Sonia was just allowed to campaign for the party when Narayanan dissolved the eleventh Lok Sabha, the Congress managed to get only 140 seats and did not increase its tally even by one seat while the BJP added significantly to its total of seats in the Lok Sabha in the 1998 elections.

In that poll the BJP went up from the total of 162 seats it had held in the previous Lok Sabha to 182 seats. True the BJP could not raise its tally by even on seat in the Thirteenth Lok Sabha when elections were held in September-October 1999 and had a severe setback in Uttar Pradesh, but it should also be remembered that it was constantly expanding in hitherto virgin areas like those in the south and east of the country. No doubt, the decline of the party in the major region of UP was a matter of serious concern to the leaders of the party and one hopes that before long some action would be taken to rebuild the party in that vital base. But the Congress was wiped out almost completely in many areas of the country like the national capital and even in Tamil Nadu where it could manage a solid block of fifteen to twenty MPs in the worst possible days.

The BJP, in any case, stood its ground and achieved a tally of 182 seats while the Congress total went down from 140 to 112 seats. This decline becomes difficult to explain when you note that Sonia addressed rallies in every nook and corner of the country in the campaign to the crucial polls. And there is another point in Surjeet and the CPIM's strategy when they talk of the BJP as representing the counter-revolutionary forces. Do they seriously mean that the Congress represents and constitutes the revolutionary forces? If their statement is read correctly the revolutionary forces come from the Congress and the BJP stands for counter-revolution and is trying to rush in to fill the void created by the departure of the Congress.

If that is the case, one has to give the writers of the CPIM document much credit for sycophancy for calling the Congress revolutionary. Revolution indeed because the party has turned its face against all that the wisdom and good sense deem it necessary for the country. In 1990 the BJP stood by the V.P. Singh government while the left parties also gave the regime its backing from outside. The two together brought the government much needed support which lasted for a whole year until Chandrashekhar broke up the ruling JD party and with the support of the Congress formed a government for a brief period of four months. Laloo Prasad Yadav, then Chief Minister (actually), also arrested Lal Krishna Advani in Bihar. He belong to the JD which the BJP was supporting at the Centre. The BJP with draw then decided to its support from the government.

The Congress then had played a real "revolutionary" role and had toppled first the V.P. Singh government and then the Chandrashekhar government. The CPIM just looked on from the sidelines almost hopelessly while "revolutionary" players like Rajiv Gandhi and Chandrashekhar, who was assisted by another "revolutionary", Subramanian Swamy, brought about a revolution. The CPIM, when it talks of a revolution in India, one is not sure what it means. The Reds speak in language difficult to follow for ordinary mortals who have a reasonable meaning for such terms as revolution. The Congress always plays "revolutionary" games and topples well constituted governments when there are no prospects for it to ascend the throne. The list of the Prime Ministers from Charan Singh to V.P. Singh and Chandrashekhar and from Deve Gowda to I.K. Gujral and not forgetting Atal Bihari Vajpayee, whom the party had a hand in toppling along with the arch revolutionaries, like Subramanian Swamy and Surjeet, is indeed impressive. In its efforts at toppling, the Congress is not concerned with the ideology and the complexion of the regime it is overthrowing but the fact that the party is not able to accommodate the "revolutionary" party like the Congress.

The CPIM is not bothered about the instability that the Congress has caused because it deems the Congress as revolutionary and the BJP as counter-revolutionary. It talks of the growing discontent against the Congress in recent decades leading to its decline. Who brought about this discontent which the CPIM dubs as growing? It refers to the "RSS having access to the instruments of state power and state machinery" with the BJP in power. What are the instruments in the hands of the RSS when the BJP is in power? In states like Karnataka, Maharashtra and Madhya Pradesh as well as Rajasthan, the Congress is in power by itself or in partnership with the NCP (Nationalist Congress Party). The Telugu Desam is a friendly party of the BJP but it is zealously protective of the minorities and at the fall of a hat or pin it is threatening to withdraw support from the NDA regime at the Centre if it finds that the RSS has a hand in disturbing the peace in Andhra Pradesh.

Law and order is a state subject and while the Union Home Ministry coordinates the activities of the states in this area the real instruments of police power are in the hands of the states many of which are in the hands of parties like the Congress. In Bihar, under the Rabri Devi rule, controlled effectively by Laloo Prasad Yadav, the Congress is an ally of the regime and while the Congress demanded and got some of the key portfolios it never wanted the crucial Home portfolio for any of its ministers. The RJD has a vice-like grip over that portfolio as also in the adjoining state of West Bengal the control of the police is in the hands of the deputy of Jyoti Basu, Buddhadeb Bhattacharya, who is besides being Deputy Chief Minister also the Home (Police) Minister and would remain in power until April 2001 when he is likely to be overthrown by Mamata Banerjee's Trinamul.

So in large areas of the country Congress, RJD, TD and CPIM itself is in power. In Tamil Nadu it is again a friendly party of the BJP but one which is extremely mindful of the minorities and their interests. Both the TD in Andhra Pradesh and DMK in Tamil Nadu are alive to the problems of the minorities. But in the BJP, in Gujarat, Uttar Pradesh, Himachal Pradesh, Punjab and Orissa where it is in power by itself or in association with other parties which are friendly to it, have the minorities suffered in any real sense? Has the BJP rule caused large scale riots of a communal nature as for example under Congress rule in Bihar, Uttar Pradesh, Gujarat and some other states? Has any of these states where the BJP is in power by itself or in association with other friendly parties witnesses Malliana, Bhagalpur or Ahmedabad and Baroda when ghastly scenes were inacted?

The Bahujan Samaj Party, which seeks to speak for the downtrodden sections, the Dalits who are the former untouchables, openly claims that it wants frequent and unscheduled elections from which one day it would emerge victorious and capture power at the Centre and some of the states. So far, it has come to power only in Uttar Pradesh, and that because the BJP in its own interest wanted the BSP in power rather than other parties. The BSP, however, goes on in its quest for the ultimate although in it has not succeeded in the effort. In the Lok Sabha its representation has gone up to a maximum of six MPs and in the UP assembly it has secured 67 MLAs many of whom later defected to the BJP to form a coalition with it.

When the CPIM pursues the mirage of power at the Centre it banks on the Congress at times and the Third Front at others. It also, in the style of the BSP, believes in upsetting the arrangements and is convinced, falsely according to some, that in any election it would get the support of a definite number of CPIM lovers in West Bengal, Kerala and Tripura, and with that it could carry on, no matter whether the Congress or the Third Front comes to power at the Centre. This belief in its own power is dangerous and the Election Commission of India is likely to issue a show-cause notice to it as to why it should not be de-recognised as a national party. It is well known that the CPIM has limited pockets of influence in Bihar and Tamil Nadu and little or no influence anywhere in the country. Merely on the strength of the three bastions of its stronghold—West Bengal, Kerala and Tripura—it cannot pass off as a national party. Apart from the great prestige accruing to a national party, its nominees in any state or parliamentary election get the party symbol if the CPIM is a national party.

So, not only the CPIM, particularly its General Secretary, Harkishan Singh Surjeet, is a destroyer of the Third Front (which seeks to modify as it suits it), it is also interested, like the BSP, in frequent and unscheduled elections. It believes that its turn would one day come, as does the BSP. It, therefore, seeks to overthrow the Central government as often as it could so that an obliging Narayanan would dissolve the Lok Sabha and order fresh elections. With sections of the media, gullible and often willing to support the line of argument advanced by Surjeet and Basu, spinning out a plausible line is not much of a problem. That is the difference between the blatant propaganda of the BSP and the well argued but not difficult to discern propaganda line of the CPIM. One is openly boastful of the strength of its ideology while the other weaves a tale of revolution and camouflagues it as a credible story to the gullible media.

The CPIM, like all Communists, has a cadre of devoted men and women many of whom treat the filthy lucre with contempt. They cannot be easily corrupted and often have a Gandhian way of life, simple living and high thinking. They would not give credit to Gandhi but the fact remains that at a time when many in politics tend to be corrupted by the effect of power some of the CPIM men in power have refused to be so. That is not true of a number of CPIM ministers and we have seen the corruption that has set in the ranks of the CPIM in West Bengal and in some other states where the party has wielded power. The real danger lies in the popular concept associated with the CPIM as a party of supposedly incorruptible men and in the revolutionary tale which it spins out from time to time.

We have seen how the CPIM is a destroyer of the Third Front which it claims to build and is really interested in creating conditions of instability at the Centre so that one day it would come to power, by itself or as the dominant element of a United Front or Third Front. It was this purpose in mind which made the CPIM make a change in its 1964 programme and seek a place for itself in a UF coalition at the Centre as announced by Surjeet. He was supremely confident that the rank and file of the party, at the special session, either of a party Congress or special conference in October 2000 to be held at Calcutta, would endorse his reasoning.

The rank and file of the party is gullible like a section of the media which swallows the party line hook, line and sinker. The updating of the 1964 programme also refers to the international situation and regrets the decline of socialism, really speaking Marxism, in the world with the dismantling of the Soviet Union. On the dismantling, one has to remember, Russia emerged as a powerful country after the decline of the Soviet Union. It should be noted that despite the split in the ranks of the Communist world, India has continued to enjoy a special relationship with the Russians. In many matters, specially in defence, Indo-Russian cooperation has actually grown since the dissolution of the Soviet Union. Russia was a dominant member of the confederation formed by the Soviet Union and while Indian relations with the Central Asian Republics have been excellent, India has continued to occupy the same centrality in the Russian view of the world whether the country is stable under Putin or a little unsteady under Yeltsin.

Of the rest of the world, there are three Communist countries—Vietnam, China and North Korea. There is Cuba, of course, but it is faraway and is actually in the non-aligned camp. So far as Vietnam is concerned it is as friendly towards India under Vajpayee as when Deve Gowda, I.K. Gujral or even Narasimha Rao was at the helm of affairs. The CPIM fails to note on the basic tenets of international relations that the foreign policy of a nation does not change with the regime in power. The same is true of Russia after the break-up of the Soviet Union. India has undergone a big change after the decline of the Congress but the relations with Russia have continued to enjoy the primacy that it had when the Soviet Union was still in existence.

The CPIM makes the same mistake when it alleges a shift in India's foreign policy from non-alignment to a pro-United States policy which, it says in the updated programme, has been heightened with the BJP coming to power. Well, so far as the Vajpayee government is concerned it claims that it is being guided by the common agenda of the NDA (National Democratic Alliance) which is really in power. It should not be forgotten that one of the key portfolios, that of Defence, is held by George Fernandes, president of the Samata party. This is an offshoot of the old Janata Dal and although the party is almost exclusively based in Bihar, from which even Fernandes is elected (he should really speaking face the electorate in Karnataka), it has an outlook which embraces all of India. There are other equally important portfolios, like Commerce, Communications and Civil Aviation, which are headed by the other allies of the BJP which, of course, has a leading role adorning such portfolios like Home, External Affairs and Finance, apart from the office of the Prime Minister.

So the foreign policy pursued by the NDA government is only a continuation of the policy pursued since India became free. If it is not the policy of strict non-alignment; it really means that the policy that has evolved over the years has also moved away from that pristine policy of strict neutrality. Even in the days of Jawaharlal Nehru there were major deviations when out of the self-interest of the country he deliberately chose to tilt on one side or the other, in fact, tilt only towards the Soviet block. The first of this tilt came when the Hungarians fought for their freedom and even while Nehru acknowledging that it reminded him of the atmosphere of the days when India fought a non-violent battle with the British rulers did not raise his little finger to help the Hungarians against the Russians, then still in the Soviet Union.

When Indira Gandhi signed a friendship and peace treaty with the Soviet Union in August 1971, four months before the Bangladesh war with the Pakistani military regime, was it not actually the end of the non-alignment policy? What Indira did was in the interest of India and every country has a right to protect its interests, but if you ask anyone why the non-alignment policy was abandoned the answer is national interest and nothing else. The CPIM and the Left world kept quiet, as did most of India at that time they knew that India was going to tilt on the side of the Soviets and that was all right for the Reds.

India's non-alignment has undergone a sea-change over the years and the change began as we saw in the days of Nehru himself. To accuse the NDA government, in the name of attacking the BJP, of going and leaning towards the Americans is a CPIM attempt at disguising things and presenting them as facts when the facts are otherwise. In this world, if you have to survive, you have to recognise reality and adapt yourself in such a way that while you do not abandon your principles you also protect your national interests. Even the leaders of the Soviet block, or rather the descendants, have accepted the reality which is that the Americans are too powerful and it has become a unipilor world. To the extent possible, India takes its stand on various issues on the basis of non-alignment not caring whether the stand offends the Americans or not. But when the real interests of the United States are involved it would not allow the UN Security Council or anybody else to come in its way and the Russians and Chinese, two of the five permanent members of the Security Council, know that as well as does India.

The Americans are fully involved in solving world problems like peace and security in West Asia and Kashmir. Yet India has held its own in Kashmir and the US policymakers have accepted the Indian position that the issue is strictly a bilateral one between India and Pakistan and unless requested by both sides which means that India has to make the request as well as Pakistan. The Americans have changed their stand on Kashmir so much that from a pro-Pakistan tilt they have come to chide Islamabad to give up its policy of cross border terrorism and supporting the Kashmiri terrorists.

When India's interests, as in Kashmir and the nuclear tests, were concerned the Vajpayee government did not hesitate for a moment to think whether the Indian position was going to annoy the State Department in Washington or not. It went ahead and surprisingly the CPIM, acting in the interests of China rather than India, criticised the Indian tests and to this day have not changed the standpoint.

From Nehru's days, the foreign policy was beyond the scope of partisan politics and all Indian parties supported the first Indian Prime Minister. It is only now, when the Vajpayee government is in power that foreign policy issues have acquired a peculiar dimension and the Left has its own approach and the Congress party its own, always opposed to the government's. The non-partisan approach to foreign policy has somehow been given up by the Congress party which attacks the NDA government often without rhyme or reason. The Congress has a so-called Foreign Affairs section and a former minister of state, Natwar Singh, who wants to show off and also prove his loyalty to the Nehru-Indira Gandhi family, shoots off his mouth on every possible occasion.

Naturally, the Vajpayee government should be pulled up when it deserves to and if necessary the government should also be attacked in the Lok Sabha and Rajya Sabha. Unfortunately, what we see happen is that in session and out of session the foreign policy is flayed and the Vajpayee government is found fault with on every occasion when foreign governments and their representatives in India find India opposing many US moves and, of course, supporting some. Natwar Singh used to sit on the floor before the descendants of Nehru and his daughter and take pride in his loyalty to them. There are photographs showing Singh in that stance. What can you expect from the Congress party when their spokesman on foreign policy matters is bristling with loyalty to the dynasty?

Objectivity suffers in situation of this kind. However, a peculiar phenomenon occurred when the Congress delegation met the visiting US President, Bill Clinton, in March 2000. Briefing mediamen after the meeting, Pranab Mukherjee, once Congress government's External Affairs Minister and one of the best spokesmen of the party on wide ranging issues said the Congress delegation, led by the Congress president, Sonia Gandhi, had told the US President that India must have a minimum nuclear deterrent for its security. This was contrary to the Congress stand on the subject as it had opposed the nuclear blasts of the Vajpayee government in May 1998 and afterwards.

The issue had not been resolved till June of that year and the Congress has appointed a committee to sort out the issue as the official spokesman of the party, Ajit Jogi, had contradicted Mukherjee on the day following Mukherjee's briefing. Jogi's contradiction was, however, not accepted by the media and Mukherjee resented being contradicted by one who is supposed to take orders from him..[6]

The Left suffers no such predicament and the CPIM, which is pro-China in India's foreign policy (not on other issues like China's open welcome to the multinational and its introduction of a new work culture in the country) has only to hear the alarm bells ring from Beijing to oppose the Vajpayee government. Alas, the writ of the CPIM no longer runs in Parliament although it makes enough noise for a party about to lose its national status.

The lack of credibility suffered by Surjeet now affects the entire party and whether the party shifts a little bit or more, the masses are no longer affected.

There is much that is wrong in Indian life and the political parties have to play their role in setting it right. The CPIM could have played a useful role but it lost that opportunity a long time ago.

REFERENCES

1. See prominent newspapers of June 9, 2000 which carried the reports of the previous day's cabinet meeting at the end of which Murasoli Maran said that the Tamil Nadu government was in full agreement with the NDA government's Sri Lankan policy.
2. "Red fort breached," *Hindustan Times*, Delhi, June 9, 2000.
3. "No rigging: Basu," *Times of India,* Delhi, June 10, 2000, while on the same page, the paper carried Surjeet's statement "Panskura polls rigged, says Surjeet".
4. All noted papers of May 19 carried reports of the previous days press conference of Surjeet. *The Pioneer* of Delhi said: "CPM changes gear, but shifts are minimal," while the *Statesman* of Delhi carried the report under the heading "CPIM ready to share power at Centre."
5. In this connection, Chandra Shekhar's statement *Third Front a media creation, Says Chandra Shekhar*, reported in the *Pioneer*, Delhi, of June 16, 2000 is relevant. The entire report is reproduced in full in the annexure.
6. *The Pioneer,* Delhi, May 19, 2000.

12
TRIPURA IN TROUBLE

One of the three states under CPIM rule is Tripura which for a five year term had gone under Congress rule but was back in the Comrades' hands in 1998. As we have seen, the area of Tripura was once ruled by a Maharaja and the tribals were in a comfortable position in the state. After independence, it merged with the Indian Union and following the usual process it became a full-fledged state. After a period under the Congress the state came under CPIM spell. The veteran leader, Nripen Chakraborty, was a true Gandhian in his lifestyle and for that reason or some other he was dislodged by the party hierarchy which did not like his ways.

Nripen had set up in 1982, the Tripura Tribal Areas Autonomous District Council and from its very inception the CPIM emerged on top. Despite occasional trouble, the tribals adhered to CPIM leadership and gave it their confidence election after election. Until 2000 when the Communists lost power for the first time in May that year. They won only ten seats in the Autonomous District Council out of 30, 18 seats going to the Indigenous People's Front of Tripura, a tribal party which was the political front of the main terrorist outfit, the National Liberation Front of Tripura. This body has in recent years caused terror among the Bengalis, indigenous as well as the immigrant Bengalis, mostly Hindus, from the erstwhile East Pakistan, now Bangladesh. The Bengalis who form a comfortable majority rule the roost in Tripura and the tribals resent it.

For a long time, the CPIM had the leadership of Nripen Chakraborty and then for a time Dasarath Deb, a tribal himself, who was a Communist. The opposition TUJS (Tripura Upajati Juba Samiti) was also moderate in its policy and whether it had an alignment with the Congress party or not, it stood for integration with the Bengalis. The Communists had now a different approach. Underrating the strength and the depth of the resentment among the tribals and supreme in their belief that they can do no wrong they underestimated the tribal opposition. Trying to play one set of insurgents against another, the CPIM government of Manik Sarkar supported the All Tripura Tiger Force, smaller of the two main outfits, while seeking to oppose the main group of insurgents, the National Liberation Front of Tripura.

In its zeal to butress the ATTF, the Manik Sarkar government went to the extent of appointing a former "reformed" leader of the force, Lalit Dev Burman, Chairman of the Horticulture Corporation. This matter was raised during Home Minister L.K. Advani's visit to Tripura in March 2000. Lalit Dev Burman was even involved in a robbery before his surrender. The robbers of a school, which had withdrawn money for disbursement to teachers, had taken shelter in Lalit's house and while they were arrested he was not. When he finally was arrested he was promptly given bail and allowed to go home. When the question was raised during Advani's visit there was a stony silence.[1]

The Centre supplies paramilitary forces but the complaint is that they are not well used. As many as 25 battalions of these forces are deployed in Tripura for about eight hundred of the insurgents but during the whole of 1999 there were only 23 encounters with the guirellas, not even a full encounter per battalion.[2] Every time the insurgent situation flares up the Chief Minister rushes to Delhi and asks for more of the central paramilitary forces and even troops. In May 2000 there was a bad development and many people were killed; some estimates put the figure at 70.

Arson and abduction are rampant.[1] According to one source, Tripura accounted for 65 per cent of all kidnappings in the North-East of the country. The issue of the training camps in neighbouring Bangladesh was raised during Advani's visit in the March of 2000. According to the Tripura government's information there are some 30 training camps for the insurgents who then come across to India in Tripura. The situation was painted as very grim when several delegations met Advani.[2] A delegation of the Tripura Congress was among those who called on the Home Minister to present their views. Led by Mr. Birjit Sinha, a former minister and Tripura Congress president it pleaded for Central intervention. But when Advani wanted to know what they had to say regarding Central intervention, which under the present circumstance, could only mean imposition of President's rule, the Congress delegation agreed. But when Advani asked them if the Central leadership of the party would support the move the delegation members kept quiet.[3]

Here lies the rub. The government of Manik Sarkar could be dismissed without much ado if the Congress supported the move for imposition of

Central rule. Incidentally, the Nationalist Congress Party (NCP), whose delegation also met the Home Minister, told him that on the average there were two kidnappings every day in Tripura and one murder daily.[4] Even going by official figures, over the last seven years, when insurgency is believed to have begun, 2,087 persons have been kidnapped and some 1,067[4] persons have been killed in Tripura. That is a serious situation considering that Tripura has about three million people in all.

Actually, a high power team from Delhi was sent to Tripura by the Congress president, Sonia Gandhi. The team was led by Congress trouble shooter and senior leader of the party, Pranab Mukherjee and returned to Delhi in the last week of May after the large scale massacre of people by the insurgents. The team included the party general secretary in charge of Tripura, Ambika Soni, and another headquarters functionary. Not only it painted a grim picture of the situation in the state, it also endorsed the Tripura unit's demand for President's rule being imposed in Tripura. The Congressmen in the state were so much agitated that when Mukherjee could not, for the reason that ultimate decision has to be taken by Sonia, give a categorical assurance on President's rule, they shouted slogans against Mukherjee and accused him of not being mindful of their agony.

It is well known that Sonia had gone back on her word when the BJP-led government at the Centre had imposed President's rule in Bihar after she had condemned the Bihar Chief Minister, Rabri Devi, and said in a special statement that Rabri had no moral right to continue as Chief Minister. It was thus easily surmised that the Congress would support the measure when the resolution for President's rule would be tabled in the upper house after its adoption in the lower. That was done as the BJP-led government had the requisite majority in the Lok Sabha but not in the Rajya Sabha. President's rule had to be revoked and Rabri Devi rule, which in effect means Laloo Prasad Yadav rule, continued in Bihar.

That was what the media meant when they reported the visit of the Mukherjee delegation to Tripura and it reported to Sonia and the Mukherjee delegation recommended that President's rule be imposed in Tripura. That the Congress could not hope to come to power if elections were held in Tripura afresh, at most six months after the imposition of President's rule, was obvious to anybody who had even a cursory acquaintance with the situation. In particular, the former Chief Minister of Tripura when the Congress was in power, Samir Ranjan Mazumdar, had joined the Trinamul Congress which had extended its powerful arm to Tripura from its original home in West Bengal. Many others like Mazumdar had also joined the Trinamul which was likely to emerge as a real challenger to the CPIM if the polls were to be held in Tripura—the Trinamul and the new tribal force of Indigenous People's Front of Tripura which had already defeated the CPIM in the Autonomous District Council election. Incidentally the ATC covers an area of 70 per cent of Tripura although in terms of population the area is not that impressive. So far as Congressmen are concerned, those who had not joined the Trinamul were fighting among themselves. The problem which was witnessed in the rest of the country, that is when the Congress party is not in power it indulges in faction-fighting, no matter who is the party President, was also affecting Tripura as conveyed to Sonia by the Mukherjee delegation.[5]

Sonia has so far done a Bihar in Tripura. She is so conscious of her destructive power that she would do anything to keep Rabri in power in Bihar and would do the same in Tripura where her benefactor at the centre, the CPIM, was in power. By now she is so habituated to ignore the feelings of local Congressmen in such crucial matters that the fate of the Congress in Tripura would be the same as in other states like West Bengal, Bihar and elsewhere. What happens to the ordinary people of those states is none of her concern and much less is she worried about the views of the Congressmen from those states.

In June 2000 there was a ghastly massacre in the Aurangabad district of Bihar in which 34 people were killed in an attack on the Miapur village of the district. A nationwide cry went up and there were demands for the dismissal of the Rabri Devi government which, in effect, means Laloo Prasad Yadav regime because the poor semi-literate woman only stands in for Laloo until he hopes to be cleared of all charges against him by the CBI which has filed several cases against him in the special Judge's court in Patna. That is, of course, hoping against hope because it is widely believed that the case against Laloo Prasad is quite solid both in respect of the animal husbandry scam involving corruption of crores of rupees from the accounts or the department when Laloo was Chief Minister and Finance Minister of the state, and also in the case in which both husband and wife duo are charged with Laloo having assets disproportionate to his known sources of income.

In July 1997 Laloo had stepped down and had put his wife in the saddle to the surprise of everyone in the country, but the United Front government of the day at the Centre did nothing against the imposition of an almost totally unducated housewife replacing a seasoned politician. Neither did the political parties supporting the RJD, formed by Laloo after breaking up the Janata Dal of which he was then president but he was going to be ousted from that office in an election. Because he is open-mouthed and effusive in his lying he is the darling of the media which report Laloo's doings but editorially condemn him for his destructive leadership.

The Congress party, under Sonia, had struck up a special relationship with him and sustained his wife in office in the period 1998-99. During the February 2000 Bihar assembly elections, the Congress had severed ties with the RJD but Sonia quickly saw the chance for the party to gain a foothold in the Bihar government because with 125 members out of the 324 seats in the assembly Laloo could not keep his wife in the office of the Chief Minister unless the Congress party gave it support. Under Sonia, the party had managed 23 seats against the 29 seats it had in the dissolved house elected in 1995 but the number was vital to the survival of the Rabri Devi government which had already managed the support of some independent members.

The Congress had cut off all ties with the RJD before the state assembly elections but somersaults in politics are not uncommon. Today's enemies become friends tomorrow and vice versa. In the process of rewarding the Congress party which now joined the Rabri Devi government, the tallest Congress MLA of the 23 MLAs of Sonia was made the Speaker of the Bihar assembly and all the remaining MLAs were made ministers of the government. This is a process made too familiar to bear any elaborate mention. Congressmen know the value of power more than anybody else but it may be said to the credit of some of the Congress ministers that occasionally they show signs of their conscience being pricked and make some noises of protest. Not of course, Sonia and her top advisers who have no place for such mundane things and have to subscribe to the rationalisation of the misdeeds of the Rabri Devi government.

What about the CPIM? As already stated, the party has extremely small stakes in Bihar having just two MLAs and their support is of no consequence to the RJD boss. But he knows the value of the CPIM support to his wife's regime at a time when the other Communists in the state—the CPI, CPI(M-L) and similar locally important parties, oppose Rabri. The CPIM had three states under its bag—West Bengal, Kerala and Tripura and is an important all-India party with a somewhat significant voice in Parliament. The CPIM, on its part, knows the value of Laloo Prasad Yadav whom the media, as we have noted, like for his antics. He has of course, only seven MPs in the Lok Sabha but the leader of the RJD group in the house, Raghuvansh Prasad Singh, makes enough noise for this small group and makes full use of his lung power.

Thus, not only for the RJD's nuisance value, but also because of Laloo's so-called secular image, the CPIM values his friendship. As we have noted this is only a political arrangement between parties which go on changing partners as people who can afford change shirts. The CPIM values the fact that Laloo would be of some use if the party succeeds in its efforts to form a Third Front, outside the BJP and the Congress. The way both the CPIM and the Congress woo Laloo in Bihar this possibility does not appear likely.

The Manik Sarkar government of the CPIM in Tripura has not been able to control the tribal insurgency menace and not afforded protection to the main supporters of party the Bengali Hindus. In a way they constitute the mainstay of the Tripura population and often they swing between the CPIM and the Congress party if there is a manipulator like the former Narasimha Rao minister of state. Although he really belongs to Assam from where he gets elected to the Lok Sabha sometimes he was in charge of the Tripura assembly elections on behalf of the Congress party in 1993 and he did manipulate the destiny of the state in the direction of the Congress which ruled the state for five years but in the next election of the assembly the CPIM turned the tables on the Congress. That was before the CPIM national leaders discovered the virtues of the Italian leader of the Congress and tried their very best without luck to put her on the Delhi throne.

As stated before the Congress is in a bad way in the state of Tripura and many of its leaders having opted for Mamata Banerjee's Trinamul Congress and the remaining fighting among themselves as all Congressmen do when out of power. The CPIM is only slightly better in the state which is bound to suffer in many respects a weak administration which cannot fight the insurgents effectively, the party not able to win the support of the tribals, as evidenced by the recent Autonomous District Council poll, nor hold the confidence of the Bengalis who once constituted the main support base of the party. The Congress the other party which once ruled the state is now in tatters, and in no position to offer any competition to the CPIM. Its plight was in many respects comparable to that of the Congress in the major state West Bengal where the Reds have ruled for the past 23 years.

[8]The tribal insurgents in Tripura brought the Union Home Secretary Kamal Pande to Tripura in June 2000 after the rebels had struck ferociously in May. Pande was to visit the state in May itself but for reasons of pressure on his time had to postpone the trip for a week or so. He was accompanied on this visit by a number of top administrators and police

officials including the Director General of the BSF (Border Security Force deployed in guarding the long border of the state with Bangladesh), E.N. Rammohan, the Director General of the CRPF(Central Reserve Police Force) the Home Ministry's officer concerned with the North East, G.K.. Pillai, and some army top brass. Before Pande arrived in Agartala, the Centre had already sent in ten additional companies of paramilitary forces which included six companies of the CRPF.

There were as many as 25 battalions of the Central paramilitary forces already in Tripura of which the CRPF battalions were ten, four battalions of Assam Rifles, and six of the Tripura State Rifles. The Home Ministry team found the state government strategy unimaginative and could not change its assessment that Tripura lacked the political will to fight the insurgents. The Central forces were being deployed primarily to man picket duties in the affected areas. After a two-day study of the situation and extensive discussions with official colleagues as well as politicians Pande expressed concern over the insurgency in the state. He found that there had been a rise in the abductions and killings of innocent citizens. Pande told the state police and the administration to adopt a more pro-active approach in meeting the insurgency problem. The present situation was that both the non-tribals and the tribals were feeling insecure while the primary duty of the administration was to ensure the security of the people.

In particular, Pande stressed the need for better coordination between the forces fighting the insurgents and for increased accountability for the actions. He also pointed out that there had to be a more effective use of the powers to arrest and detain the trouble makers. The demand of the state government for reassigning the army battalions earlier deployed in Tripura which had been withdrawn when the fighting in Kargil in Kashmir broke out was once again turned down. The Central government had sent more companies of the paramilitary forces to Tripura and it was noted, as stated before, that these forces were not being fully used. Under the rules, the Central forces and even the army companies if these are sent are at the disposal of the state government and the state administration concerned had to deploy them to the best possible advantage. If the political will is lacking and the state is found to be playing politics the insurgents would be able to make inroads into the habited areas and the paramilitary forces would be stranded looking at the scene like idle spectators.[7]

The CPIM government in Tripura suffered a severe setback in the Autonomous District Council (ADC) elections in April-May 2000. As already stated, the CPIM had brought the ADC into existence in 1982 when the veteran Nripen Chakraborty was at the helm. Except on one occasion the party had always won the ADC elections. Despite the extensive insurgency problem the CPIM leadership was confident of giving a good account of themselves in the ADC poll. They had even advanced the elections which were not due until August that year, by full three months perhaps to take advantage of the favourable factors as seen by the leaders of the party and the government. They did not assess the effects of insurgency problems as a real hindrance to their hegemony hopes. They were in fact overconfident that they would win hands down and the National Liberation Front of Tripura (NLFT) guerrillas would not be able to cause much damage to their invincibility.

The facts were completely at variance with the CPIM calculations. Their support base in the tribal areas had declined to a considerable extent while the NLFT had properly organised the Indigenous People's Front of Tripura (IPFT), their political and overboard frontal organisation while the NLFT remains a banned party. On top of it all, there was violence or the fear of violence in many tribal areas, particularly in West Tripura. The NLFT had abducted some of the CPIM or Left Front candidates relatives whom the guerrillas released after the polls were over.

All the same, the elections were held in a comparative peaceful atmosphere. There was no large scale intimidation of the voters, although there was massive retaliation after the elections. In any case, the entire security machinery was at the disposal of the government which was in CPIM hands. As we have seen, the Central paramilitary forces are also under the command of the respective district magistrates who deploy them, of course, under the orders of the government in Agartala headed by Manik Sarkar of the CPIM.

As it turned out, the CPIM and its left allies faced a real defeat in the elections heralding perhaps the CPIM's defeat in the Tripura assembly polls whenever they are held. The party, or its left front allies and itself, got only 10 of the 30 seats in the ADC and what was more the IPFT captured more than the required majority, 18 seats. The two remaining members are nominated by the Governor and there is thus scope for the CPIM to manipulate but the IPFT having already secured a majority there was no fear on that account. The other opposition parties did not have much of a chance. The Congress drew blank again and apart from showing its total eclipse this meant that it had surrendered a lot of ground to the Trinamul Congress of Mamata Banerjee. The Trinamul itself was in a grouping along with the BJP and the TUJS, which once used to have an alliance with the Congress. However, because of the violence caused by the NLFT and some retaliatory attacks by the Bengalis on the tribals when they no longer could endure the suffering caused by the tribal guerrillas and they found the CPIM government powerless to come to their aid there was much bloodshed.

Apart from the signal defeat the CPIM suffered for the first time at the hands of a tribal organisation what followed the elections was an eye-opener to the government. There were large scale riots in the middle and later part of May 2000 after the polls and according to one estimate some seventy persons were killed. There were tribal attacks on the Bengalis and some fellow tribals themselves. Perhaps the insurgents were seeking revenge from the people attacked for not supporting the IPFT candidates in the elections. As already indicated, there were attacks in retaliation and innocent tribals who had nothing to do with the rebels were attacked by the Bengalis. The authorities declared a curfew in the West Tripura area which is difficult to enforce because people live in remote areas and not like those in cities where it is not difficult to lay down the law.

Two large refugee camps were opened and since the media have difficulty in covering the happenings, the government of Manik Sarkar was spared the limelight of bad publicity. Of course the local Bengali press which the people read carried reports and what is more the Congress delegation sent down by Sonia from Delhi, already referred to, saw the plight of the people living in these camps without any facility. The delegation on its return to Delhi highlighted the suffering of the camp dwellers and the report leaked out in the usual manner.

As we have seen the fate of the Manik Sarkar government was hanging in the balance but perhaps Sonia, known for her leanings towards the CPIM in *quid pro quo* relationship, saved the day for poor Sarkar. If only Sonia decides to support the Vajpayee government in its possible decision to impose President's rule in Tripura the decision could be taken and the rule of the party could come to an end in one of three states it rules. West Bengal and Kerala, the other two states under the rule of the CPIM, go to the polls to elect news assemblies in these two states in 2001. There is a strong challenge by Mamata Banerjee's Trinamul Congress party in West Bengal and the Congress-led UDF (United Democratic Front) poses a serious challenge to the CPIM-dominated Left Democratic Front (LDF) in Kerala. Despite Sonia's soft corner for the CPIM, the Kerala Congress and its Muslim and Christian allies are determined to give the CPIM regime a stiff competition in the elections and have a good chance to win the elections.

The CPIM, as we have said more than once, has good people in its fold but what is lacking is good vision. The cadres are often violent in actions and are not distinguishable from the violent in their Naxalite Communists who are quite clear in their intentions and practise violence without any prick of the conscience. Both in West Bengal and Kerala they are violent and indulge in the worst form of criminal action. If the opposition parties are equally violent that is bad enough but when those in power protect their violent cadres they have nowhere to go. Without doubt, battles have been fought in both states in the Panskura area in West Bengal and in Kerala. How is it possible to call this a revolutionary or even a decent party and how can one avoid calling the mask which the CPIM and its fellow organisations are wearing by that name.

The *Hindu* of Madras, now Chennai, had for a long time the reputation of being a balanced paper presenting both sides of a controversy and not offering comments in the correspondent's despatches which seems to be the done thing nowadays. The *Hindu* has been refraining from this practice but after all the paper cannot avoid the prevailing mores. While the editorial comments, in the form of leaders, is the prerogative of the paper where it can offer the views of the paper freely and without caring whether the views would be liked by the powers that be or not the reporters despatches were left free of this encumberance. Of course, the reporter is not expected to carry the propaganda of the political parties and individuals nor is he expected not to add some comments by way of interpretation and explanation and even by backgrounding the story; the phenomenon of free comments which a majority of the papers now indulge in was bound to touch the *Hindu* also.

The paper of June 29, 2000 carried a story—"The Left on an extended vacation"[9] by one of its correspondents, Hasan Suroor. He started by quoting a left leader, whom he does not name, who criticised the Congress party for being in a state of paralysis and not pulling its full weight as the principal opposition party which is not true because the Congress keeps up a running barrage of comments on the NDA government's doings day in and day out. The comment is, however, right to the extent that the party has failed to discharge its duty as the opposition, except that the Leader of the Opposition, Sonia Gandhi, President of the Congress, draws the salary of the office and enjoys all the perks of the post. However, the topic of discussion, as the title of the despatch suggests, is the failure of the Left, meaning the Communists, to discharge their duty as expected by the correspondent.

Suroor called it a state of somnambulantics and said the Left observers among whom one must reckon Suroor himself say that for a political movement which—even in these cynical times—has revolutionary pretensions and whose leaders are forever talking about "mass action" and "mass mobilisation" its current laziness is inexplicable and no less damaging to the opposition cause than the Congress (I)'s inaction. Suroor accused the two major Left (obviously the Communist) parties as being on an extended vacation.

The *Hindu* correspondent, like many journalists of his ilk, committed the mistake of imagining that the Congress was in a state of paralysis and the Left (meaning, of course, the Communists) on an extended vacation rather than the Congress party suffering from a failure of leadership and the CPIM, the main prop of the Congress president, being totally confused as to what its line of action should be. And, above all, the success of Atal Bihari Vajpayee as Prime Minister, against both the Congress and the Communists. But such acknowledgement would hurt Mr Suroor and the paper which are opposed to the BJP, NDA and Prime Minister Vajpayee.

For the rest, the acticle is a lament that the two Communist parties which the writer in turn praises and flays for their alleged "inaction" in the present politicals situation are not playing their part. It went on to recall what the two parties did or did not do in the course of the past few years and concluded:[9] "Nearly two years down the line, however, the party (CPIM) shows no sign of giving up the "soft" electoral route to power. But with organisational strength on the blink, winning election too is becoming difficult and the CPI(M) is in danger of losing its status as a national party".

The CPIM losing the status of an all-India party is a matter of time. But to expect it to give up the electoral route to power is expecting the aged CPIM leaders, Harkishan Singh Surjeet and Jyoti Basu, to perform miracles and the armschair politicians like Yechuri and Karat, to perform even greater miracles and give up their airconditioned comforts in favour of arms. From JNU to the leadership of the CPIM and then on to arms is a forlorn cry, a cry in the wilderness.

It is typical of today's journalism that it expects, the CPIM to perform such miracles and not recognise the basic fact the party wears a mask and is not able to perform any kind of role. If circumstances combine to place it in power in West Bengal for 23 years, where it once had perfected the technique of keeping itself in power for ever, it is incapable of delivering the goods and has in the bargain inculcated a work culture destructive of the real fabric of our society.

Suroor, however, is different from many journalists of today, in that he recognises the many faults of the CPIM and using the tern "alleged" before the CPIM`s brainstorming, its regular reviews of the current situation, grassroots network of cadres and so on. Only some examples of the all-knowing and highly opinionated journalists can be cited here. The *Times of India* rightly prides itself as being one of the leading papers of the world but not everyone in that paper can rate himself as great although they think they find themselves in the seventh heaven. Vidya Subrahmanian (the name spells differently from Subrahmaniam to Subrahmanian) said in a despatch on June 30,[10] 2000 on Kashmir that although there is Kshmiriyat in the state, Muslim boys are recruited for Jehad style militancy. How can Kshmiriyat be reconciled to Jehad only the wise correspondent can explain. Then it is the turn of Asit Jolly of the *Asian Age* who says in the paper of 11 June 30,[11] "Bomb attack on religious meet kills 2 in Jalandhar". There was indeed a bomb blast in Jalandhar in Punjab on June 29 but there was no religious congregation of any kind in sight. There was a congregation a considerable distance away from the site of the blast but it is mere sensational to say that a religious meet was the target. It helps the paper to sell if it can scare away the readers.

REFERENCES

1. "Tripura rapped for 'ultra support'." *The Statesman,* Delhi, April 6, 2000.
2. "A'Grim' situation in Tripura," *Hindu,* Delhi, April 4, 2000. Also, see the *Hindustan Times,* Delhi, April 3, 2000.
3. *Ibid. Hindu.*
4. *Ibid.*
5. "Tripura puts Sonia in a fix," *Pioneer,* Delhi, June 2, 2000.
6. *Hindustan Times,* Delhi, June 18, 2000.
7. *Hindustan Times,* Delhi, May 2, 2000.
8. "Home Secretary in Tripura," *Times of India,* Delhi, June 9, 2000.
9. *Hindu,* Delhi, June 29, 2000, "The left on an extended vacation?"
10. The *Times of India,* Delhi, June 30, 2000.
11. *Asian Age,* Delhi, Calcutta, and other cities, June 30, 2000.

Appendix 1

MADAM'S FAVOURED PETS

T.V.R. SHENOY

There used to be an American television programme called *The $64,000,000 Question*. The Indian Left—perhaps even those from Calcutta, that Mecca of quizzing, might draw away in well-feigned horror if associated with anything so bourgeois as an American quiz-show. Unfortunately, dear Comrades, your conduct reminds me of nothing more than a tacky show.

Let me begin with the name itself. Sixty-four is the precise number of Lok Sabha seats that truly concern the Left Front—42 in West Bengal, 20 in Kerala, and two in Tripura. All pretence to the contrary, the Left is a corpse for all practical purposes outside those three states, "a burden"was Chandrababu Naidu's unkind description after the last General Election.

The Communists were once a force in Bihar and Telengana, in Kanpur and Coimbatore. Once they could win in Faizabad, notable for the fact that it includes Ayodhya. Today, they win seats outside their three strongholds only if another party is willing to be charitable.

I also likened the Left's conduct to a "tacky show". And that too is well merited. American quiz-shows in the early years of television degenerated into a fraudulent farce, which just about sums up the Left Front today. While the Communists claim to be bitter foes of the Congress, that 'enmity'is restricted exclusively to West Bengal, Kerala, and Tripura. Elsewhere, the Left and the Congress have no qualms about sleeping together—as in Tamil Nadu, (Both Marxists and Congressmen are content to play second fiddle to Jayalalitha in Chennai).

All pretence of hostility is given up when the Communists trek to Delhi. Because the sole candidate being put up for Prime Minister by the Left Front is, believe it or not, Sonia Gandhi. On at least two occasions in the past three years, the aged Jyoti Basu was a heartbeat away from becoming the prime minister. Today, nobody is even thinking about such a prospect.

(Strictly speaking, this farce—perhaps 'fraud' is a better word—is more a problem for the voters of Kerala and Tripura than it is for those of West Bengal. For all the sound and fury during elections, it doesn't matter if the citizens of the first two vote for Congressmen or Communists; once in Delhi they sit on the same side. In Bengal, however, there is a real option in the Trinamul Congress-BJP alliance).

I am sure some of the Leftist persuasion shall disagree with my description of their relationship with Sonia Gandhi Inc. as a "fraud". May I remind them of certain events in the history of the Communist movements?

The CPI was an electoral ally of the Congress as far back as the General Election of 1971. (If memory serves me right, the Communists even won Baghpat, Charan Singh's home-turf, thanks to the Indira wave). In fact, this alliance was on the verge of turning into something even more intimate; when the Soviet leader Leonid Brezhnev visited Delhi, he advised the CPI leaders to "strengthen progressive forces" by merging with the Congress. At least S.A. Dange and Mohit Sen took this advice quite seriously.

The CPI went to the extent of enthusiastically supporting the Emergency, a fact bitterly resented by other Comrades. When it sought reentry into the Left Front fold after 1977, a vengeful CPI (M) demanded a public apology, which was duly delivered at Bhatinda. (Someone in the Congress possesses a sense of humour; when the CPI asked the Congress for an electoral arrangement in Punjab in 1998, it was allotted Bhatinda).

Why is the CPI (M) now regurgitating the same arguments that it rejected so violently twenty years ago? I don't know if the Left still uses words like 'progressive' any longer, but substitute 'secular'—an equally meaningless catch-word in today's context—and there is no difference between the Brezhenev of yesterday and the Surjeet of today.

It might be argued that much water has flowed down the Yamuna in the twenty or more years since Brezhnev's visit. Yes, but what about things that happened as recently as three years ago?

The United Front, whose "Chanakya" was Comrade Harkishen Singh Surjeet, repeatedly refused to consider supporting any ministry in which the Congress participated. (Forget about backing a government actually led by the Congress !) It refused to do so after the Uttar Pradesh Assembly polls of 1996. It refused after the fall of Deve Gowda in 1997. It refused after the Congress slid the carpet from under Gujral's feet.

But there was a sudden volte-face in April of this year. After the Vajpayee ministry lost the vote of confidence, the CPIM suddenly began drumming up support for Sonia Gandhi. So much so that Comrade Surjeet angrily questioned Mulayam Singh Yadav's 'secular' credentials when the Samajwadi Party boss wouldn't lick La Gandhi's Guccis.

In other words, the Left Front was amazingly consistent for the past three years about rejecting any explicit partnership with the Congress. What has changed in the brief months since April to force such a u-turn in its policy?

Of course, the Congress is not the only new friend being wooed by the Left. I have already mentioned the alliance with Jayalalitha in Tamil Nadu ; this means Karunanidhi has been given the boot. The Left has also snapped links with Mulayam Singh Yadav—in the hope of snapping up the crumbs from Laloo Prasad Yadav's table. And in Punjab, its bosom buddy is the Akali Dal splinter led by G.S. Tohra—that same Akali Dal denounced as a hotbed of communalism.

I have no idea how long these new arrangements shall last. In fact, the Congress president already seems keen to keep the octogenarian dinosaurs of the Left at bay. Could it be an inherited trait?

Congressmen are strong believers in genetics. Indira Gandhi inherited her talents from Panditji and Priyanka Vadra from Rajiv Gandhi according to the Congress gospel. By that logic, we should look very closely at the late Signor Maino, specifically what he thought about the Communists.

Maino was a Fascist. The Left uses that word loosely, but the Congress boss's father was the genuine article—One of Mussolini's men. Maino named his dog 'Stalin' to demonstrate his contempt for communism. His daughter goes one better—she doesn't hesitate to kick the Marxists, secure in the knowledge that the poodles will creep straight back into the kennels of 10 Janpath.

—*Indian Express,* Delhi, August 14, 1999.

Appendix 2
LEFT IN A MUDDLE

Call it third front, middle path or third way. It has meant many things to many things to many people across the world. Harold Macmillan advocating capitalism with a human face, the Socialist International seeking a way between capitalism and communism, East Europeans propounding socialism with a human face, the German Greens, Swedish Social Democrats, the new Labour in Britain all have reached for such rhetoric hoping to occupy the middle ground between Left and Right. In India, too, the emergence of the Third Front has had the intended objective of providing an alternative to the Congress and the BJP though it has been more opportunistic than ideological.

The Left Front has all along been the backbone of an alternative platform. while the Janata Dal took the help of both the "communal" BJP and the "authoritarian" Congress to sustain it in power even though it sought to maintain a distance from both, it is the Left parties which advocated a symmetrical rejection of both the BJP and Congress. Their policy was one of unambiguous hostility towards the BJP and other Hindutva forces while remaining equivocal towards the Congress.

The very phrase Third Front presupposes an alternative, a choice, a competing political project and a new direction. Today, the ideology has taken a backseat and no one knows whether the Left is Right or Right is Left. The Left and Right division in the world is now certainly less encompassing. As far as the Left politics in India is concerned, it can at best be described as "life politics". After all aren't the Left parties busy finding ways to survive? Haven't they already realised that Marxism Leninism today is a busted faith?

Hegel's dictum that we learn nothing from history is most apt in the case of the Left parties and the Third Front. Each time there are general elections, the interlocutors of the Third Front pump up baloons that are already full of air, unleashing rhetoric about the viability of such a dispensation. The irony is that the Front is hardly ever viewed as a strong contender for power. In fact, it often gets concretised only after elections. The political fortunes of the National Front, the United Front and yet-to-be-officially-floated Third Front tend to wax and wane relative to the Congress and the BJP.

The Left parties too have run out of steam. For far too long they remained bogged down in a terminological morass of competing definitions of who their enemy number one was Congress or the BJP. Now that the "twin danger theory" has been buried, the ideological bankruptcy of the mainstream communist parties has come into sharp focus. The Left ideology, today, seems to have lost the capacity to inspire and political leaders the ability to lead. The Marxists swear by Marxism but play footsie with the market.

Today, the Left parties are on the cusp of a new paradigm. The glib triumphalism of yesteryear about the vibrant Left ideology and the viable Left and democratic alternative is missing. It is not even a one-size-fits-all model of Left unity anymore. If some Left parties and political leaders have forgotten to live by what they had chosen, others live by what they have chosen to forget.

The two communist parties and their strong allies like the Forward Bloc and the Revolutionary Socialist Party are pulling in different directions. The CPI and the CPI-M are fighting both the Congress and the BJP in West Bengal, Tripura and Kerala but in the rest of the country they have aligned formally and informally with the Congress to help the secular forces defeat the BJP. The CPI was keen to align with the Congress in Andhra Pradesh and Sharad Pawar's Nationalist Congress Party in Maharashtra but its alliance has come unstruck. The CPI-M, on the other hand, has forged an alliance with the Deve Gowda faction of the Janata Dal in Karnataka and the rebel Telugu Desam in Andhra Pradesh.

The trajectory of the Left parties has once again changed. Equidistance from the Congress and the BJP is no more a sustainable policy as is evident from their election manifestoes. In the 1998 election, the joint Left manifesto projected the BJP as a "threat to national unity" and the Congress, as a "destabilising" factor in Indian politics. This time the Congress, the CPI-M manifesto says, is "bereft of political and ideological will to rally all secular forces to fight the menace of communalism". And yet, it will "support the Left, democratic and secular forces for a secular government" (read Congress). While the manifesto blames Congress for compromising with communal forces, it finds "its mass base secular".

In a way, the CPI-M has ruled out the possibility of a third alternative, as the Left doesn't have the strength at this stage to put up a third front.

At the same time, the CPI-M manifesto stresses the need for "an alternative" with the intervention of the Left. The CPI's line is hardly any different. The BJP is again the enemy number one and the Congress is secular but has an "anti-people" economic agenda. What is indeed galling is that so long as the CPI and CPI-M maintain equidistance from Congress and the BJP, it is a principled stand, but if the Forward Bloc and the RSP or Mulayam Singh's Samajwadi Party revoke the same principle, it becomes "meaningless".

Compulsion of realpolitik have prompted the Left parties to look for different allies in different States. Ideology and principles have been given a go by. They were at the forefront of a tirade against Laloo Prasad Yadav; once he was tainted by the fodder scam and other scandals. Today, the CPI and CPI-M are hoping to win half a dozen seats in Bihar thanks to Laloo Prasad. As allies of the DMK in Tamil Nadu, they poured venom on Jayalalitha. Today, she is a strong ally of the two Communist parties.

The Forward Bloc and the Revolutionary Socialist Party have stuck to principle and have refused to toe the line of their big brothers. Debabrata Biswas of the Forward Bloc has maintained that the Left parties have no alternative but to fight both the Congress and the BJP, something the CPI-M and the CPI are doing in West Bengal, Kerala and Tripura but not elsewhere. He has been working overtime to build a third front and the Forward Bloc has forged an alliance with the Nationalist Congress Party. Biswas calls both the Congress and the BJP as agents of the capitalist and bourgeois class. While he charges the BJP with being "programmatically communal", the Congress, to him, is an "opportunist communal" party. The Forward Bloc's efforts to forge a Third Front is not for power, it is to create a platform to start a social struggle.

Biswas apparently knows that the Left parties particularly the small ones, have a limited electoral future and hence he talks of a social struggle and a broad coalition where there is place for forces of social justice as also the CPI-ML and some regional parties. The CPI too has reasons to be worried about its shrinking support base and dwindling membership. In 1996, A. B. Bardhan went to the extent of maintaining that the communist parties had paid a heavy price for "bureaucratism, cliquism and careerism within the party organisation". Even CPI-M leader Harkishen Singh Surjeet admitted that "parliamentarism is affecting the party" and that "there is an unhealthy trend among members to try and become MPs or MLA's". The Left parties have paid heavily for running with the hare and hunting with the hound.

—Ash Narain Roy, *Hindustan Times,* Delhi, August 28, 1999.

Appendix 3
WITH ENEMIES LIKE THESE, WHO NEEDS FRIENDS !

On Monday, 5 September 1999, the Home (Police) Minister of West Bengal, Buddhadev Bhattacharyya, designated successor to the chief minister, delivered himself of the observation that Sonia Gandhi was a mere housewife, hugely inexperienced, and thoroughly unsuitable to become Prime Minister. "She has been pulled into the fray because she is from the Nehru family", added the minister putting the issue beyond doubt. A day later Jyoti Basu repeats the contrary view for the umpteenth time, that Sonia is an Indian citizen and can "certainly be the Prime Minister if her party is voted to power". The contrast between boss and deputy cannot be more marked. The question is why? One clear explanation is that Buddhadev does not carry either family or any other baggage. Given the chief minister's age and debility and rapidly reducing powers of concentration, one must look for the explanation extraordinary. His party is 'in a mess, cadres are deserting the CPI-M in droves and Mamata Banerjee has never had it so good. Terror has seized the CPI-M. They do not know whether Congress must be supported or opposed tooth and nail A charitable explanation can be that having secured the economic future of the son and placed him under the constant protection of Advocate-General, N N Gooptu the patriarch is now seeking the political future of the adopted daughter, Sonia Gandhi. Sonia and Chandan are the same age group. Age cannot wither nor custom stale their infinite variety. I have lost count of the number of occasions that Jyoti Basu has begged Sonia to lead the nation, the equal number of occasions on which she has spurned the offer from the two elderly gentlemen, Harkishen Singh Surjeet and Jyoti Basu. But neither will listen although Surjeet has of late fallen silent while Jyoti Basu continues the relentless pursuit of his objective.

It would seem that the CPI(M) leadership are looking for protection should they fall on their face, distinct possibility. That they should be preparing to fall at the feet of the Congress tells its own tale. It needs to be noted that in the last few months there has been a change in the attitude of the two young politburo members, Prakash Karat and Sita Ram Yechuri also. Until recently they boldly stood out against Surjeet and Basu; both now accept Sonia as the next Prime Minister. Corruption has weakened the party and Communism is the god that failed. And Saifuddin Choudhury remains a voice in the wilderness, his loyalty to the party notwithstanding.

Jyoti Basu also joins Sonia in persisting in misunderstanding the truth about objections to her becoming Prime Minister. Thanks to the tenacity of the Hinduja brothers, Prime Minister Atal Behari Vajpayee also chooses to misunderstand. That makes a formidable alliance. They all say that the lady is a foreigner but not a foreign national. The distinction is beyond reason. The objection is not that she does not hold an Indian passport ; she does. Pranab Mukherjee has confirmed that she sent her Italian passport to the Home Ministry and exchanged it for an Indian passport. The requirement was to renounce Italian nationality permanently on affidavit, obtain confirmation that Italy has cancelled her citizenship, send the confirmation to the Home Ministry, apply for Indian citizenship, obtain the necessary citizenship certificate and only on that evidence, apply for an Indian passport. None of this procedure has been followed. No one has asserted the contrary but the formidable trio goes on parroting her Indian citizenship.

Only PN Lekhi, the distinguished lawyer, has proceeded correctly and issued appropriate notices, preparatory to proper legal proceedings. It should not be so easy now to dismiss the application *in limine*, as the Bombay High Court chose to do. The distinction is legal, constitutional and merits a full hearing.

The Hinduja persistence is also evident elsewhere; noticeably in dealing with Quattrocchi's lies. The fact is that the family friend has received over $ 7,000,000 into the account held by him and wife Maria from Bofors. At different times, Quattrocchi's has denied receiving any money from Bofors when this could no longer be denied, he claimed the money was his by right. He even presumes to know what the Congress party spokesman, Kapil Sibal, did not say and what he must be presumed to have said. This is to stand professional relationships on their head. Earlier, his counsel in the Supreme Court, Rajinder Singhvi, asked for and was given time to consult his client as to whether he would agree to come to Delhi and be interrogated for two weeks. If their Lordships protected him from arrest on arrival. Counsel is given a week's time. On instructions Counsel obtains an appropriate order from the Supreme Court. Sonia summons a meeting of the CWC without notice the same day and decides to pull the rug from under Vajpayee. On cue, Quattrocchi issues a statement from Kuala Lumpur repudiating his counsel. On 26 March 1999, the Supreme Court (coram Nanavati and Phukan, JJ) "strongly disapprove the manner in which the petitioner, (Quattrocchi) has conducted himself in proceedings before this court". But Quattrocchi denies he received any money from Bofors and, Quattrocchi is an honourable man! So are the Hinduja brothers, all honourable men! After all they have the distinction of forcing a change in Swiss procedures to prevent such abuses of that country's legal process for the future.

To return to Buddhadev Bhattacharyya, the party will go down with Jyoti Basu just as the Congress, like Indira Gandhi, bids fair to die in Sonia's lap. If the BJP has enemies like the Congress and the CPI-M, who needs friends!

—C. R. Irani, Caveat, *The Statesman,* Delhi and Calcutta, Sept. 8, 1999.

Appendix 4
THE LEFT AND THE CONGRESS

The Marxist Left in India has a historic responsibility at a time when the Soviet Union has collapsed, its truncated successor State, Russia, has opted for the capitalist path, and China has fallen for the market. By the Marxist Left I mean the CPI (M), the CPI, the various strands of the revolutionary Marxist-Leninist organizations, the RSP and the Forward Bloc. The Socialists, deriving their inspiration from Acharya Narendra Deva and/or Dr. Rammanohar Lohia, and now concentrated mainly in the Samata and Samajwadi parties, do not belong to the Marxist tradition as it was evolving in the Soviet Union and China. They, therefore, have no responsibility vis-a-vis it. The Marxist Left, on the other hand, belong precisely to that tradition. Besides, it is a powerful though by no means the dominant political force in India. The Left Front, comprising mainly the CPI (M), the CPI, the RSP and the Forward Bloc, is in power in West Bengal, Kerala and Tripura. The revolutionary Marxist Leninist organizations, generally described by the omnibus word "Naxalites", dominate large areas in Bihar and Andhra Pradesh and have active pockets of influence in Madhya Pradesh, Maharashtra, Orissa, Rajasthan and West Bengal.

All this, of course, assumes that the Marxist-Lenninist-Maoist political tradition has a relevance and a validity that transcends its withering in the Soviet Union and China. Both lie in its humanist essence which needs urgently to be reasserted at a time when man—the measure of all things in Protagorus' classic definition of the philosophy is being turned into a consuming automaton manipulated by advertisements and a trivialized media peddling the consumer culture, the new opium not just of the working class, but all classes. The hackles of many Marxists as well as Humanists will doubtless rise on hearing this. To the latter, the primacy which Marx gave to the collectivity of the class as the embodiment of historical reality, unit of historical analysis and agent of change, and the consequent marginalisation in practice of the individual, militated against the basic philosophical orientation of Humanism based on the principle of the sovereignty of the individual human being. The Marxists, on the other hand, would recall Marx's criticism of Ludwig Feuerbach, the outstanding Humanist philosopher of the 19th century. His attack on Feuerbach and emphasis on the class notwithstanding, Marx's strong humanist orientation will be clear to all readers of his *Economic and Philosophic Manuscripts of 1844* in which he stated that Communism which ended workers'alienation "as fully developed naturalism, equals humanism and, as fully developed humanism, equals naturalism..." Nor does Marxism deny the importance of the individual. Marx and Engels write, in *The German Ideology,* that the Communist society is the only one "in which the genuine and free development of individuals ceases to be a mere phrase."

The Indian Marxist Left has a two-fold responsibility to the Marxist-Leninist-Maoist political tradition as it was sought to be incorporated in the Soviet Union and China into political systems trying to realize its ideals. 'The first is to identify the causes of its collapse. This is the precondition of its further evolution to cope with the cultural, intellectual and political challenge posed by market capitalism. The second is to ensure their own emergence as a major force in Indian politics without which they cannot bring about its global revival.

Emest Mandel shows in *Beyond Perestroika* how the Soviet Union had grown economically and socially since the 1930s and 1940s, and become urbanized and modernized with a highly educated, cultured and conscious work force, and how the entire people of the country, and not just the intelligentsia, wanted reform. They were increasingly unwilling to put up with continued unsatisfactory living conditions, an oppressive and brutal political regime run by a mediocre gerontocracy, and of "structures of domination and control" which were "both ineffective and universally rejected." A similar contradiction between social dynamics and institutional rigidity and authoritarianism was evident in China. Samir Amin admits in *The Future of Maoism,* that "genuine democratic practices have been in short supply" in China. He adds, "This we may attribute to (*a*) the legacy of the workers movement, Leninism, and the Soviet experience, (*b*) a one-sided negative appraisal of bourgeois democracy, and (*c*) an erroneous conception of the state and the party. At certain points, the dangers inherent in foregoing democracy were great indeed."

There is need for a thorough debate on institutional and ownership patterns which can ensure both economic growth and justice and individual freedom in a State seeking to implement Marx's basic goal of creating a society without exploitation and alienation of labour. Equally, there is a need for the Marxist Left to grow and become a dominant force in Indian politics. It is in this context that its attitude towards the Congress becomes critically important. Supporting from outside a Congress-led coalition government or a Congress government—at the Centre with Ms Sonia Gandhi as Prime Minister, would be disastrous. And it is not difficult to see why. No Government at the Centre, whether headed by her or anyone else, can retain its popularity for any length of time given India's intractable and innumerable problems. The failures of a Prime Minister born in India will be attributed to corruption or inefficiency or both. In the case of a Prime Minister born in Europe, like Ms Sonia Gandhi whose physiognomy and manner of speaking clearly proclaim her to be an European, such failures will also be attributed to foreign conspiracy to keep India down, and she would be declared as a foreign plant. Such a charge may be totally unfair but, politics being what it is, it is going to be made. Such an allegation may not be believed today when Ms Sonia Gandhi still retains her sheen as a newcomer; it will be when she becomes unpopular through incumbency. A mass movement to remove her will then follow and it will be given the character of a national liberation struggle against a comprador Government, headed by a person of European origin, supported by qusilings, and installed through a global neo-colonialist conspiracy.

The Communist parties, which have publicly said that Ms Sonia Gandhi's Italian origin is of no consequence and should not prevent her from being Prime Minister, have been accused in the past of being traitors; they will again be so labelled if they are among the props of the Government, and again will they pay dearly. The BJP and its allies, which will lead the national liberation struggle, will return to power with an overwhelming majority and will perhaps continue to rule for years given the severe mauling their opponents would have received at the hustings. Even if Ms Gandhi does not become Prime Minister, the political legitimacy the Communist parties have conferred upon her by endorsing her acceptability as Prime Minister, will cost them heavily. It has helped her to consolidate the Congress under her leadership by demoralizing her opponents who remain in the party even after the departure of Mr. Sharad Pawar, Mr. PA Sangma and Mr. Tariq Anwar.

Given the growing polarization of Indian politics around the Congress and the BJP, the latter's opponents are increasingly gravitating to the former in the hope that, united and reinvigorated, it would be able to pose a better challenge to the BJP than the Third Front parties. The sufferers will not only be parties like the Samajwadi Party and the BSP which will have their vote banks eroded but the Communist parties who will find the political space for their expansion shrinking thanks to a Congress resurrection. This is all the more likely to happen because the need to strengthen secularism is being cited as the rationale for supporting the Congress. This tends to project secularism as the over-riding issue and ideological differences among secular parties as being of secondary importance. Why will then people prefer the Marxist Left parties to the Congress?

Secularism is doubtless of crucial importance but the Marxist left parties have to find a way of strengthening it without withering away in the process and helping the Congress to wax. This is all the more so because the Congress, secular credentials are not terribly convincing.

—Hiranmay Karlekar, *Pioneer,* Delhi and Lucknow, September 24, 1999.

Appendix 5
BACKLESS FRONT

If Indian politics is a circus then the CPM general secretary Harkishan Singh Surjeet is its supreme juggler. He can conjure up things where they don't exist and make his own partymen forget their existential condition. Considering the declining state of the CPM and the Fronts it leads in the two states of Bengal and Kerala, it might have seemed logical for it to concentrate on its own administrative and organisational failings and ideological slideback rather than project an exaggerated national role for itself at the Centre. Yet that has precisely been the CPM's favourite pastime. Were it not for this preoccupation, it would be all too evident to the CPM leadership that the Left Front in Bengal is in disarray; that there is resentment among the smaller constituents such as the Revolutionary Socialist Party and the Forward Bloc at the big brotherly attitude of the Marxists; and that its primacy in these states is under challenge which it is unable to respond to because of its own decrepitude. For a man who prides himself on being "secular" it is indeed surprising that Chief Minister Jyoti Basu should be wooing Muslim votes thought in the last 18 months to have shifted to Ms Mamata Banerjee. Mr Basu and his comrades may be contemptible of the urban electorate but the fact remains that they are losing their appeal for this section, particularly in Calcutta. It is counting on the Congress, its avowed rival in Kerala and Bengal, to divide the votes of the Trinamul Congress and the BJP even while it follows a policy of tailing Mrs Sonia Gandhi's party in other states.

Such tailing is not new to the CPM. But there are new and contradictory dimensions to it which betray its utter lack of direction and opportunism. In Tamil Nadu, for instance, this phenomenon is compounded by a further kow-towing to Ms Jayalalitha of the AIADMK, a formal ally of the Congress. The alliance notwithstanding, Ms Jayalalitha had entered into fresh talks with Mr Surjeet for reviving a 'third front' to meet post-poll exigencies. In return, Mr Surjeet has certified Ms Jayalalitha to be "secular", and the DMK with which it had been sailing till the fall of the Vajpayee coalition as "communal". Although the CPM is an ally of the Congress in several states, it has ditched that party in the state which matters most Uttar Pradesh. After three rounds of polling, the CPM, which had denounced the Samajwadi Party's Mulayam Singh Yadav for not supporting a Sonia-led government only in April this year, has now pitched for him against the Congress. In UP, as in some other states, the Marxists are asking voters to ensure that not a single Congressman is elected even though the party is certified, by no less a person than Mr Surject, as "secular".The dialectical trapeze acts have now swung to take in Mr Sharad Pawar and Mr George Fernandes too, all in the cause of a third front, which Mr Surjeet had pronounced dead some months ago. As in its approach to economic reforms, in its political priorities too the CPM seems determined to keep its growth as well as the country's, in the red.

—The *Times of India,* September 17, 1999.

Appendix 6
CRY FOR HELP

There is no price tag attached to dreams. This is one realm in which human desires and fancies can roam unhindered. Mr Jyoti Basu, the Chief Minister of West Bengal, and Mr Sitaram Yechuri, member of the politburo of the Communist Party of India (Marxist), can therefore be humoured for continuing to dream of a government led by the third front. In Mr Basu's case, the dreams may be fuelled by hopes of becoming prime minister at the twilight of his political career. It does not need any great political foresight to say that dreams of a third front government have no basis in reality. The elections to the 13th Lok Sabha which are now in progress have highlighted the emergence of two big political blocs, one led by the Bharatiya Janata Party and the other by the Congress. It is an irony that there are no major ideological differences between these two electoral rivals. What is clear is that the third front, with all its ideological baggage, has become irrelevant in the field of Indian politics. This plight has aggravated the confusion of the CPI(M), the principal left party and the prime mover now of the third front. At the root of the confusion is the fact that in terms of political influence, the CPI(M) is no more than a regional party: its clout is restricted to West Bengal and Kerala. At the national level, the CPI(M) has spoken of the BJP as the chief enemy and has emphasized the need for strengthening secular forces. In practical terms, this means some kind of an understanding with the Congress. This is not a viable proposition in West Bengal and Kerala where anti-Congressism has been the CPI (M)'s best vote winner. Hence, the fallback of the third front as an electoral device that can be used against both the BJP and the Congress.

By, reviving the rhetoric of the third front, the left is not only beating an antique drum, it is also making itself ridiculous. It is forced into this corner because of its ideological vacuity. Even in its strongholds, the left has very little by way of achievement to show the voters. In West Bengal, trends suggest that in many areas the left is losing support to the Trinamool Congress. Absence of investment and abuse of power are the main reasons for the erosion of the left's popular support in West Bengal's urban areas. The Trinamool Congress leader, Ms Mamata Banerjee, has quite correctly announced that these elections are only the run up to the real test of strength: the assembly polls two years later. The CPI(M) and its allies are caught in a trap. At the national level, it can retain some relevance by being a part of the Congress bloc. But by doing this it runs the risk of losing its bases at the local level in West Bengal and Kerala. The rhetoric of the third front is a cry of despair : The hope of drowning ideology.

—The *Telegraph,* Calcutta, September 14, 1999.

Appendix 6A

ACTION REPLAY OF A FARCE

If an award is instituted for effective use of WWF-type free-style muscle power around the polling booth, it would surely go to the ruling Leftists in West Bengal. Over the years they might have happily dumped the ABC of dialectical materialism in to convenient receptacle of 'bourgeois politics', but surely, when it comes to lifting the 'theory and praxis' of electoral malpractice into a state-of-the-art form, no one can, match the committed vanguard of the CPI(M). Under the benign patronage of their party bosses at Writers' Buildings, they have proved once again that when it comes to the crunch, they care two hoots for the norms of democracy.

Witness the mayhem in which the Marxists indulged on July 2 after a by-poll was ordered at Ward 16 in Salt Lake during the municipal elections in Calcutta. This ward became a life and death question for the 'revolutionaries' because this one seat could tilt the balance in favour of the ruling party. Hence all roads to the polling booths were blocked, legitimate voters were not allowed to exercise their franchise, bogus voters celebrated a free for all, bombs were hurled and an atmosphere of terror prevailed. And this sordid spectacle was unleashed in full public view, even while the State police indulging in their own share of tokenism—fired a few tear gas shells and silently watched the show from the sidelines.

While Mamata Banerjee, as is her style, might be overstating her case by claiming that a virtual 'civil' is on in Bengal all recorded evidence points to the shocking behaviour of the Leftist cadres, sure in the belief that it is they who determine how law and order is maintained in the State. The partisan role of the administration, police and State Election Commissioner has been highlighted in this context. Indeed, a new political culture appears to have developed around the polling booth in Bengal, with the other parties trying to outsmart the Left in its own game. For instance, the Trinamool Congress was accused earlier of using violence and intimidation to win the battle in Panskura. For ordinary citizens, trapped between knife-wielding and bomb-throwing vanguards of this or that party, the Salt Lake episode is nothing but an action replay of a nightmare followed by a farce.

—*Hindustan Times,* Delhi, July 6, 2000.

Appendix 7
IDENTITY POLITICS, OR WHAT'S LEFT OF THE CPI-M

The fundamental dualism of our time is the cosmopolitanism of the elite, living on a daily connection to the world (functionally, socially, culturally), and the tribalism of local communities retrenched in their spaces that they try to control as their last stand against the macro-forces which shape their lives and are out of their reach—Manuel Castells

If there has been anything singularly consistent in the country's Communist "movement", it is the mainstream Communist parties movements away from the extreme Left. First from Left to Centre, beginning with the decision to join electoral politics, and now from Centre to Right, if the move to rename the city and the state is anything to go by.

The shift began in the early Fifties when the undivided Communist Party left behind its Left adventurism as the consensus within the party shifted to the parliamentary line. If the justification for this shift was to mobilise people and spread the scope of the communist movement, the party was fairly successful in the venture, emerging the second largest party in Parliament in its electoral debut. However, the mutual suspicion between the party and the national bourgeoisie persisted, as Nehru's sacking of Kerala's communist government clearly demonstrated.

Over the years, this anti-bourgeoisie undercurrent of the Communist Party ebbed considerably to the extent that post-split, the CPI openly took a more accommodating line towards the Indian state, as manifested in Mohan Kumarmangalam's joining the Indira Gandhi Cabinet. The CPI even went on to support the Emergency. The CPI-M on the other hand, still maintained a stronger Left rhetoric. Just the rhetoric, however, as compulsion of electoral politics were already beginning to show.

The CPI-M' riding to power in West Bengal and Kerala in the 1977 elections was largely based on this distinct Left rhetoric. This time, sans the shadow of distrust of the national bourgeoisie. Clearly, the CPI-M, like its estranged other half, had managed to negotiate a cosier relationship with the Indian state.

Over 20 years in power in West Bengal and in out of power in Kerala since then, the CPI-M at the turn of the century does not inspire vision of a revolution even to its stupidest die-hard. Its leaders speak against liberalization, but nobody really believes that the party's stand over the issue is any different vis-a-vis the economic concensus that the other mainstream parties seem to have struck. The CPI-M's distance from the Centre, if any, has not been any shorter.

For those who thought from the party's "movement" would stop in its centrist abode, the culture-cum-police minister's "decision" to rename the city and the state came as a pointer that the right-wards shift as far from over. If anything, the time it may be wandering dangerously towards the far Right. One wonders if Buddhadev Bhattacharya himself realises this import of this latest misadventure.

A report compiled by the CMDA this year shows Calcutta, over the years, has grown more cosmopolitan. A demographic study in 1951 showed that the Bengali population stood as 65.6 per cent in Calcutta. A later study undertaken in 1954-1958 by Professor S N Sen of Calcutta University showed the Bengali population had dwindled to 61 per cent. A similar study by the Indian Statistical Institute in 1976 showed Bengalis at 58.7 per cent, whereas the latest study by CMDA shows them at 57.5 per cent.

Nothing unusual, as cosmopolitanism no matter how intensely Bhattacharya and his "intellectual" friends hate it, is an inextricable component of urbanization. This is also evident in the state's demographic profile compiled by the CMDA. Whereas in rural Bengal, the Bengali population stands at 97 per cent, in the non-municipal urban area, it is 79.2 and in CMC are, it is 61.2 per cent. In other words, the more the urbanisation, the less the Bengali population.

By ordaining that the city will be given a name that is closer to the identity of the 57.5 per cent of its residents (let us assume it is, though this argument itself is based on very shifty grounds), Bhattacharya, and by extension his party, has obviously decided what and for whom the city stands. The 57.5 per cent. The rest be damned. Between the unity of the modern world and the partiality of ethnicity, the party has chosen to side with the latter.

Unmistakably, the honourable minister is into identity politics. Identity politics of the majority, which is a stone's throw from fascism. Not very different from the "barbaric" BJP or the Shiv Sena, as Bhattacharya and his chief minister seldom fail to apprise the Bengali audience.

To many, the name change proposal would appear to be plain sub-national assertion. For others, it could be spectacle of a communist regime trying desperately to distil the character of a complex society in to a mere name. Actually, it is a reaction to a more complex phenomenon the gradual expulsion of the Bengali to the economic periphery.

Superficially, ethnicity is associated with a sense of identity arising from shared customs, languages and culture, physical characteristic, and so on. But there is a firm casual link between the consciousness of ethnic identity and the material organization of social life.

A sense of identity can be derived from the material reality of belonging within a shared mode of production despite ethnic divides. This explains why, though slowly, ethnicities disappear or become politically irrelevant.

Vandals and Goths were replaced by German ethnicity. Normans and Saxons were replaced by English ethnicity. And this is the reason why Protestants and Catholics in England and Germany are not at each other's throats in emulation of their brothers in Belfast.

The CPI-M's attempt to assert a Bengali linguistic and cultural identity is not far from ethnic assertion, an ethnicity which does not recognise this ethnic dynamics.

A common mode of production and shared material intercourse instill a sense of kinship. Again, advanced capitalism integrates the world system and universalises material intercourse between different peoples.

There is thus hardly any chance of an ethnicity manifesting as the embodiment of identity of a separate conciousness arising from the stamp of an isolated mode of production.

The fact is, despite being in the majority, the Bengali today does not in his own state command the capitalist economy, or the mode of production, the way he did at the dawn of Independence, and is actually a junior partner in economic enterprises—more often the employee than the employer.

The question of a kinship over the shared material space thus does not arise. Bhattacharya, in proposing a "Bengali" name has just articulated this frustration. Only, this frustration when it comes from the majority race runs the risk of slipping into a Fascist pit. The example is far too well known to be cited.

Actually, the CPI-M is a seasoned player of this politics of disappointment. Squarely responsible for Bengal's dwarfed economic stature, the party itself has long played on the Bengali's injured pride by carefully instilling in them a false notion of cultural superiority, predicated on the supposed pre-eminence of the Bengali language, to compensate for his sense of loss in the economic arena.

We do not make industries, so what? Did not our forefathers engineer the nation's cultural renaissance? Is not our city the cultural capital of India? Are not we the only *bhadralok* around? What's money for us?

If this is not venomous xenophobia coated with sugary respectability, what is? If this is not civilization myth to perpetuate a sense of racial supremacy, what is?

The CPI-M's notion of *apasanskriti* has been an important tool in the construction of this Bengali exclusives vis-a-vis the Marwari (which has become a generic term for any non-Bengali speaker who is minting money, for whom the enraged *Babu* in all probability has to work or take orders from).

Having perched itself on the high ground of Bengali upper-crust culture, the party has reserved for itself the right to arbitrate "culture". Thus western songs are *apasanskriti.* So are the Hindi ones. Sari is "culture", salwar-kameez not and jeans for woman taboo in most SFI-run institutions. It just does not fit the party's perception of Bengali womanhood.

To give the devil its due, despite the cultural bond the party has so laboriously forged with the Bengali by disparaging all other forms of culture, the CPI-M has done remarkably well in co-opting the support of the non-Bengali business class (the "non-Bengali" part is probably redundant here) when it comes to campaign finance. Unlike the Bengali, the self-appointed champion of his culture has managed to share the material space with the non-Bengali on equal terms. On what terms, though, is not quite clear.

Finally, one would like to remind the honourable minister that a Marxist analysis of culture essentially accepts that culture must be produced continuously and unlike a house or a field, it is not inherited.

Hell-bent to change Calcutta to Kolkata, which in his scheme of things amounts to establishing the "true" identity of the city and its "culture", he would do well to note that Marxist theory accepts the fact that there exists a wide range of socially organized institutions which produce culture. Not just the ethnic majority, as Bhattacharya would like us to believe. Not even if it forms the backbone of the "communist movement".

As for "movement", there must be a considerable amount of it for poor Marx in his grave.

(The author is on the staff of The Debasish Roy Choudhury *Statesman*, Calcutta).

The Statesman, Delhi and Calcutta, September 14, 1999.

Appendix 8
THIRD FRONT A MEDIA CREATION, SAYS CHANDRA SHEKHAR

While the efforts of the four former prime ministers have failed to garner much support in reviving the Third Front the most important man from the ex-PM's club Mr. Chandra Shekhar says that the entire plot was a media creation.

"The issue of revival of the Third Front has never been discussed. At least not with me. What's Third Front? Which are the first and the second?" Says the man from Ballia non-challantly.

Mr. Chandra Shekhar is seen as a vital catalyst in the proccess of the political realignment that could have revived the Third'Front. But his blunt denial has ended the speculation about the motives of former Prime Ministers including Mr. I.K Gujral, Mr. H.D. Deve Gowda and Mr. V.P. Singh.

Mr. Chandra Shekhar said the former prime ministers had the opinion that the country was passing through a difficult phase and they must express their concern from a common platform. "We just wanted to tell people how dangerous was the mindless process of economic liberalisation, and hence came together. "he said Reacting to a query. Mr. Shekhar said :" It all started with an incident involving a minor injury in my leg. They had all come to meet me and inquire about my health. It was discussed that we should sit together to talk about the prevailing political and economic situation in the country. At no point did the concept Third Front crop up during discussions. Nor was it ever discussed in our subsequent meetings,"

Recalling his Calcutta visit. Mr. Chandra Shekhar related how he along with Deve Gowda and V.P. Singh had gone to Calcutta on .. routine visit. They were invited by Chief Minister Mr. Jyoti Basu for lunch at his residence."The issue of the revival of Third Front was not discussed at all at our luncheon meeting. But the next morning, newspapers were screaming about it. And on return to Delhi from Calcutta. I came to know through the media that Jyoti Basu has been named as the leader of the Third Front, a responsibility that he was to take up after his retirement from chief ministership." said Chandra Shekhar.

Mr. Shekhar also does not agree with Mr. V.P. Singh's role in his new avatar as "champion of jhuggi dwellers". He feels that rehabilitation of slum dwellers is an issue which can be discussed with the government, a comprehensive national policy needs to be evolved on the subject." One must also understand another important concern related to the issue. There is already an exodus from the rural areas to the metropolises. If we give shelter everyone migrating from the villages. rural society and economy will be ruined in the long run.The thrust should be on providing employment opportunities for people in the rural areas said Mr. Shekhar.

Mr. Shekhar sounded cynical about an alternative force emerging in the near future because in his view most of the parties nurtured similar views on economic liberalization. "This is dangerous trend and I can't support it. My supporters want me to compromise on vital issues I cannot let them compromise and grab power. That has never been my wont," said Mr. Shekhar.

—*Pioneer*, Delhi, June 16, 2000.

INDEX